British Multiculturalism and the Politics of Representation

D1610644

For Aitana and Carmina, master negotiators of identity and inclusion

British Multiculturalism and the Politics of Representation

Lasse Thomassen

EDINBURGH
University Press

Edinburgh University Press is one of the leading university presses in
the UK. We publish academic books and journals in our selected subject
areas across the humanities and social sciences, combining cutting-edge
scholarship with high editorial and production values to produce academic
works of lasting importance. For more information visit our website:
edinburghuniversitypress.com

© Lasse Thomassen, 2017
Edinburgh University Press Ltd
The Tun – Holyrood Road,
12(2f) Jackson's Entry,
Edinburgh EH8 8PJ

Typeset in 11/13 Sabon by
IDSUK (Dataconnection) Ltd,
and printed and bound in Great Britain by
CPI Group (UK) Ltd, Croydon CR0 4YY

A CIP record for this book is available from the British Library

ISBN 978 1 4744 2265 9 (hardback)
ISBN 978 1 4744 2266 6 (paperback)
ISBN 978 1 4744 2267 3 (webready PDF)
ISBN 978 1 4744 2268 0 (epub)

The right of Lasse Thomassen to be identified as the author of this work has
been asserted in accordance with the Copyright, Designs and Patents Act 1988,
and the Copyright and Related Rights Regulations 2003 (SI No. 2498).

Contents

Acknowledgements   vi

Introduction: Identity, Inclusion and Representation   1

1. Hegemony, Representation and Britishness   12

2. Subjects of Equality   45

3. (Not) Just a Piece of Cloth: Recognition and
    Representation   90

4. Tolerance: Circles of Inclusion and Exclusion   132

5. Hospitality beyond Good and Bad   184

Conclusion: Multiculturalism, Britishness and
Muscular Liberalism   220

References   227
Index   243

Acknowledgements

This book was written across several years, countries and institutions. I started working on it during a research fellowship at Centro de Estudios Políticos y Constitucionales in Madrid, and I finished writing it when I had returned to the School of Politics and International Relations at Queen Mary, University of London. A lot of the book was also written at Universidad de la Rioja. I am most grateful to all three institutions and, especially, my colleagues there for providing an inspiring and productive working environment. In the School of Politics and International Relations, I am fortunate to be part of the TheoryLab, a welcoming and open environment for thinking about the world through theory. The School funded a workshop on a draft manuscript for the book; I am very grateful to J. F. Drolet, Eric Heinze, Kim Hutchings, Mike Kenny, Margarita Palacios and Mark Wenman for taking time to read and comment on the draft. At Universidad de la Rioja, I thank Raúl Susín Betrán, Head of the Department of Law, and José María Aguirre Oraá for their hospitality, and David San Martín Segura and Sergio López González for sharing their office, intellectual conversations and coffee breaks with me. In addition, I would like to thank the following people for reading and commenting on what eventually became book chapters: Peter Bloom, Clayton Chin, Lincoln Dahlberg, Sam Dallyn, Mary Dietz, Elena García Guitián, Ghufran Khir Allah, Beatriz Martínez Férnandez, Sean Phelan, Marina Prentoulis, Ángel Rivero, Yannis Stavrakakis and Lars Tønder. I would also like to thank Miri Davidson for applying her excellent copy-editing skills to the manuscript. I dedicate this book to Aitana and Carmina, two small master negotiators of identity and inclusion and exclusion.

An earlier and shorter version of Chapter 4 was published as Lasse Thomassen, '(Not) just a piece of cloth: *Begum*, recognition and the politics of representation', *Political Theory* 39: 3 (2011), pp. 325–51. I thank Sage for permission to reuse this material here.

Introduction: Identity, Inclusion and Representation

Identity, inclusion and representation

In a much-cited speech at a security conference in Munich in February 2011, then British Prime Minister David Cameron identified the roots of extremism and terrorism as 'a question of identity' (Cameron 2011a).[1] The identity in question was that of 'young men who follow a completely perverse, warped interpretation of Islam'. In the background lurked another identity: that of Britishness. The solution to the identity confusion of the young male extremists was, Cameron argued, to be found in Britishness, in 'a clear sense of shared national identity that is open to everyone'.

In the course of his speech, and in other speeches on Britishness and immigration, Cameron introduces a number of distinctions (see Cameron 2011b; Cameron 2011c; Cameron 2011d, Cameron 2014; Cameron 2015).[2] There is a distinction between Islam as a religion and Islamist extremism as a political ideology; a distinction between Muslims and extremists who use Islam as a justification for terrorism. There is an implicit distinction between whites and the others.[3] There is a distinction between us – and 'our way of life' – and those others who share our political values, but are nonetheless different from us. 'We' are positioned as at home, opening the door to others who are marked as different when they are welcomed to share in our identity. They are included, but in a way that establishes a hierarchy, positioning some at the centre and some at the margins of the inclusive identity of Britishness.

And there is a distinction between the old answers to multiculturalism and Cameron's 'muscular liberalism'. Among the old
answers, 'the hard right' as well as 'the soft left' treat all Muslims
as the same, the hard right by associating all Muslims with the
violence of political extremism, and the soft left by blaming terrorism on the discrimination of some Muslims. Cameron associates
multiculturalism with a 'weakening of our collective identity': 'the
doctrine of state multiculturalism' has left cultures and communities to lead 'separate lives, apart from each other and apart from
the mainstream'. Cameron's alternative is 'a much more active,
muscular liberalism', one that is articulated around certain values that it actively promotes: democracy, freedom of speech and
worship, equality and the rule of law. In Cameron's words, 'this
is what defines us as a society: to belong here is to believe in
these things'.

In Cameron's speech, identity and inclusion are closely connected, and this book sets out to examine how we think about
identity and inclusion and the relationship between them. The
book intervenes on the scene I will call 'British multiculturalism'.
I will have more to say about this scene below; suffice it to say
for now that the key questions on this scene – as also evidenced
in Cameron's speech – are questions regarding the meaning and
future of Britishness, liberalism, the politics of race, ethnicity,
culture and religion, and, of course, multiculturalism. The concept
of identity looms large here, and I will argue that identities are
constituted in the terrain of representation. As a result, we need to
pay particular attention to two questions: *which* representations
of an identity are dominant? And *whose* representations are they?
For instance, to say that representation is constitutive is to say that
there are no 'real' Muslims out there independently of representations of Muslims. Identities are representational in this sense. Consequently, we need to examine which and whose representations
become dominant in any given historical place and time, and to
trace the evolvement of those representations. For instance, how
Muslims have been and are represented, both by agents identifying
as Muslims and by agents who do not identify as such.

The other concept, apart from identity, that looms large on the
scene of British multiculturalism is that of inclusion. There has

2

been a lot of talk about inclusion over the last couple of decades, and inclusion has its own history, often linked to 'community' and often in juxtaposition to equality and solidarity. In Cameron's speech – and more generally, I shall argue – inclusion and identity are intrinsically linked. Consider for instance the way Cameron represents British identity, and how he wants to include some and exclude others from that identity. British identity is made possible through the exclusion of extremists. But identity and division are more than a division between us and them. While Cameron divides a space in two between those who are included and those who are excluded, the space of the included is graded. Cameron says: 'let us give voice to those followers of Islam in our own countries – the vast, often unheard majority – who despise the extremists and their worldview. Let us engage groups that share our aspirations.' The 'followers of Islam' are at once included, part of us and yet cast as different and in the role of 'them' who can share 'our' values. Cameron only manages to include Muslims by branding them as different, and different from 'us', thus also identifying 'us' as non-Muslim. Inclusion of someone is only possible by identifying – that is, differentiating – them (Minow 1991).

There is no identity without exclusion, but inclusion and exclusion are not just matters of either/or. Inclusion is inclusion into a particular identity; and exclusion is exclusion of particular others. Identity and inclusion are closely connected then, and, since identities are representational, this complicates how we think about identity, inclusion and exclusion, and how we think about critique. For instance, we might oppose Cameron's more muscular than liberal, more exclusive than inclusive, British identity with a more inclusive identity, one more open and less insistent on the differentiation between us whites and them Muslims. But, if there is no inclusion without exclusion and the representation of identities, then we must also analyse how, in each case, inclusion, exclusion and identity are articulated together. And if exclusion is constitutive of inclusion, then we cannot oppose exclusion in the name of universal inclusion, not even only as a critical ideal. The task is then to examine how the relationships between inclusion and exclusion, and between inclusion, exclusion and identity are negotiated or, with a term I shall use in the following, articulated.

The scene of British multiculturalism

This is a book about how we conceptualise identity and inclusion and the relationship between them. There is no identity or inclusion in the abstract, and so I examine them in the context of what I will call the scene of British multiculturalism. By 'scene' I mean context, but I use the term scene because I want to stress how this scene – like any context – is one that is staged (see Ulbricht 2015: 1–4). The characteristics and limits of the scene are by no means given or self-evident. They are the result of decisions by the researcher.[4] In the theoretical terms I will use later in the book, British multiculturalism is a representational space, or a discursive terrain, but it is a space that is not easily individuated. For instance, when does British multiculturalism begin? If it has changed, is the British multiculturalism we recognise under that name the same as the one people recognised as such in the 1970s? And, with all the talk of the end of multiculturalism, do we still live under something we can call multiculturalism in Britain today? Even if British multiculturalism could be distinguished in time and space, the next problem would be to identify which articulation of it to use as representative of British multiculturalism as a whole. Multiculturalism is not a coherent representational space. Within this space there exist a number of competing articulations of the ideas and practices said to define British multiculturalism. Those articulations compete with each other on a common ground taken as given: the already sedimented representational space of British multiculturalism. But they also try to articulate that space in their own particular way and to hegemonise it. This is why we cannot simply take that space as given: any analysis or interpretation of multiculturalism invariably takes sides in the hegemonic struggle over the meaning of multiculturalism. The task of the researcher is double: to identify British multiculturalism as an object that can be analysed *and* to pay attention to the ways in which the characteristics and limits of that object are constantly put into question.

Earlier I wrote that I take representation to be constitutive of identities. In Chapter 1, I shall develop this idea, but it also applies to the attempt to characterise and delimit multiculturalism. To say that representation is constitutive of identities means that representation does not simply reflect a non-representational reality. Rather, representation performatively constructs identities. There are identities – they are real, they exist – and, when represented, these identities are at once reflected in and constituted by the representations of them (see Derrida 1997; Derrida 1982; Laclau 2014: ch. 6; Thomassen 2007a). Similarly with multiculturalism. When Cameron says that state multiculturalism has failed, we should treat this as a representation of something (state multiculturalism) that refers to, and reflects, already existing representations of multiculturalism. What (state) multiculturalism *is* consists of those representations, where representations are not restricted to talk and writing and images, but also include practices, institutions and structures. Multiculturalism is real enough, but not extra-representational. We then have different representations of British multiculturalism, but no extra-representational British multiculturalism to compare them with. *Any* representation of the scene or representational space of British multiculturalism will be a particular representation of it, vying for legitimacy among other representations within and on the edges of that representational space. The representational space of British multiculturalism consists of many different scenes, all of them part of that space, but also particular prisms through which British multiculturalism takes on a certain shape. Often, the more you look at and research a representational space, the more it appears riddled with tensions and the less it appears as one space.

British multiculturalism is, to use the words of Davina Cooper (2004: 35; see also 5, 15) from a slightly different context, 'not a single, unified perspective but a discursive terrain organised around particular questions, premises and concerns'. I will start from a working definition of British multiculturalism as a representational space that emerged from the late 1960s in the UK, but especially in England, and spans different partly overlapping sectors of society: law, public policy, ideology, everyday social interactions, some social and economic structures, the arts, and so on. Within this representational space the dominant view is that culture matters and should matter, and that the UK is a society consisting of different cultures, where the content of 'culture' varies (race, ethnicity, culture, religion, nationality, language, among others).

I will use the following working definition of multiculturalism from Bhikhu Parekh: multiculturalism refers to the fact that there is a multiplicity of cultures within society and to the normative non-assimilationist response to this fact (Parekh 2006).

Overview of the book

This book takes British multiculturalism as its object in order to examine the concepts of identity and inclusion and the relation-ship between them. I draw on post-structuralist theory broadly conceived. In particular, I draw on the works of Ernesto Laclau and Jacques Derrida. From Derrida, I take a deconstructive way of reading texts. Although there is no deconstructive or Derridean 'method' as such, there are nonetheless a number of themes and quasi-concepts – for instance, 'iterability' and 'hospitality' – that lend themselves to the analyses in the following. I do not claim to apply deconstruction as an already established method, understood as a technique or set of tools and concepts; instead I take some of Derrida's readings as well as others' deconstructive analyses as examples and exemplary of deconstruction (see Derrida 1997: 157–64; Derrida 1988; Derrida 1992a; Thomassen 2010a). From Laclau, I take his theory of hegemony as articulation as well as his ideas of contingency and discourse (representation) (see Laclau and Mouffe 1985; Laclau 1990; Laclau 1996a; Laclau 2005; Thomassen 2005). I develop the post-structuralist approach, and Laclau's theory of hegemony in particular, in Chapter 1.

Drawing on post-structuralism, I start from three theses. The first thesis is that there is no inclusion without exclusion. Among post-structuralists, broadly conceived, it is a long-established truth that there is no inclusion without exclusion: any inclusive procedure, space or identity will be constituted through certain exclusions. This does not mean that there cannot be more or less inclusive institutions or spaces, but it does mean that there is always some exclusion. It is then a matter of analysing the ways in which particular institutions and spaces of inclusion rest on explicit or implicit exclusions. While we may agree that exclusion is unavoidable, we do not have to accept any particular exclusion.

With another phrase from post-structuralist theory, particular exclusions are contingent.

The second thesis is that inclusion and exclusion are intrinsically linked to identity. This works both ways. From a post-structuralist perspective, identities are constituted through relations of difference. Identities are relational, and they are contingent; there is nothing essential about them, and they are open to rearticulation, even if they may appear sedimented and fixed. Britishness, for instance, is constituted through relations of difference with other identities: English, Scottish, French, Muslim, and so on. Because identities are constituted through relations of difference with other identities, any identity is constituted through some element of exclusion, even if this does not necessarily take the form of antagonism. To take the example of Britishness: this identity is articulated in many competing ways at any one point in time. Sometimes it is articulated as different, sometimes as excluding another identity, and sometimes as both different from and overlapping with, and including, other identities. So, no identity without exclusion.

Inclusion always takes place through a particular identity. Difference is included in something: an identity, whether a national identity, a religious community, a class, or whatever. The space of inclusion is represented in a particular way and as different from what is outside it; it is shaped by images of home and belonging, by laws and institutions determining the status of those who can be part of it, and by social and economic structures making the inclusion of others more or less likely. So, inclusion and exclusion are made possible by particular articulations of identities, of the including party and of the included and the excluded. The upshot of the second thesis is that we must examine inclusion and exclusion through the ways in which identities are articulated, and that we must examine identities through the relations of inclusion and exclusion they establish.

The third thesis is that, because identities are constituted in the terrain of representation, we need to analyse identity and inclusion as what I will call the politics of representation. That means, among other things, that we must always ask *which* and *whose* representations are hegemonic. In short, identity and inclusion should be studied as the results of hegemonic struggles over representations.

The task is then to examine the ways in which practices of inclusion rely on particular representations – explicitly or implicitly – of the kind of subject that can be included. For example, discourses on equality may be based on an explicit reference to the human and on implicit images of what it means to be a human being. To be clear: saying that representation is constitutive does not mean that representations are not real, let alone not material; rather, it means that reality is itself constituted on the terrain of representation, and therefore that politics must be analysed at this level. There really is only one level (representation) and not two (reality and representation).

Saying that representation is constitutive also means that representation is not taken as a distortion of a non-representational reality. There is no non-representational beyond on which to base critique of, and resistance to, representations. Although we do not have to take any particular representation as given – they are contingent after all – all we are left with are attempts to posit one representation against another and to challenge them in this way. We may – and I will – criticise the ways in which identities are represented. However, those representations cannot be opposed as misrepresentations to a non-representational reality, for instance a more complex reality that has been reduced and, thereby, misrepresented. Representation is constitutive, and representations cannot be opposed as false or wrong on the basis of a reference to some non-representational reality. Put differently, representations cannot be reduced to ideology understood as the distortion of reality (intended or not). Representation frames what can be seen as true and false, and the framing always excludes something, but there is no extra-representational way of assessing the truth of the frame itself. The question is then how inclusion, exclusion and identities are negotiated through this political struggle over representations.

Although a book about identity and inclusion, this book contains no analyses of identity and inclusion as such. What it does contain are analyses of the ways in which identity and inclusion have been articulated. Taking the representational space of British multiculturalism as my object, I structure the book around four concepts and practices of inclusion: equality, recognition, tolerance and hospitality. Scholars identify important differences among these concepts and practices, but, as I will try to show, they also share important structural similarities. Equality, recognition and tolerance are all concepts that have been widely debated in conjunction with British multiculturalism. Most often they have been taken as concepts and practices of inclusion, even if multicultural inclusion is sometimes seen as at odds with equality, and I return to this in Chapter 2 when discussing the liberal egalitarianism of Brian Barry. Looking at hospitality allows me to examine another important part of the scene of British multiculturalism, namely liberalism. In each case, I examine particular, but representative, representations and discourses of equality, recognition, tolerance and hospitality.

The first chapter lays out Laclau's theory of hegemony as the theoretical framework that, together with Derrida's deconstruction, guides the analyses of the cases studied in this book. To help illustrate the implications of this framework, I use Gordon Brown's discourse of Britishness.

Chapter 2 then turns to equality. I begin with the legal case *Mandla* from the late 1970s and early 1980s. The decision in that case played a pivotal role in rearticulating the meaning of Sikhism, race and ethnicity, and, as such, it plays an important role in British race relations legislation because it redefined the meaning of 'race'. The discussion of the case takes me to a discussion of the debate between the liberal multiculturalist Bhikhu Parekh and the liberal egalitarian Brian Barry. The discussion of *Mandla* and of the Parekh–Barry debate both show that equality is articulated through identity, which is to say that we need to pay attention to the way identities and categories are represented: 'Sikh', 'race', 'human', and so on. Equality is always connected to particular images – representations – of what it means to be, for instance, a Sikh or a human being. The politics of equality is a politics of representation.

Chapter 3 turns to the concept and practice of recognition so often associated with identity politics and multiculturalism. I show how recognition and representation are mutually implied. Representations must be recognised and taken up in order to have force; and recognition is always recognition of particular representations. I develop this through a detailed discussion of *Begum*, a legal case from the mid-2000s. The case is particularly useful because, while it concerns recognition and the limits of multiculturalism, the parties to the case all subscribe to the importance of recognition and multiculturalism.

In Chapter 4 on tolerance, I also make use of *Begum*, but this time together with three other cases from the same period: *X v Y*, *Playfoot* and *Watkins-Singh*. Here I analyse the debates about the cases in two broadsheets: *The Guardian* and *The Telegraph*. The cases all concerned the rights of schoolgirls in state schools to wear particular kinds of religious clothing and symbols: two different versions of the hijab, a Christian purity ring and a Sikh bangle. Examining the way tolerance and difference and identity are articulated across the debates about the four cases, I show how lines of inclusion and exclusion are articulated, existing side by side and competing within the same representational space.

The final chapter on hospitality stands out from the others in several ways while also cutting across them. It breaks with the chronology of the other chapters by going back to the time around the millennium and the first years of the New Labour government. It is also different in that I take a novel – Nick Hornby's *How to Be Good* – as my object of analysis. The chapter also stands out by being more about 'us' (white, liberal middle-class, and so on) than about those marked as exotic others, those whom multiculturalism is usually taken to be about. Through an analysis of the novel's treatment of hospitality and charity, I show how a certain liberal subjectivity is central to the scene of British multiculturalism. As with equality, recognition and tolerance, I show how hospitality is always caught in a tension between unconditionality and conditionality, between openness and closure.

Together the analyses and discussions of these chapters serve to show that there is no inclusion without exclusion, that inclusion and exclusion are intrinsically linked to identity, and that, since identities are constituted at the level of representation, we need to analyse identity and inclusion in terms of the politics of representation. What we must examine when examining identity and inclusion is, then, which and whose representations come to dominate, and how identity and lines of inclusion and exclusion are articulated.

Notes

1. Unless otherwise stated, quotes are from this text.
2. I return to these other texts in the Conclusion.
3. On the racialist and racist aspects of Cameron's speech, see Gilroy 2012.
4. Here I am following Derrida on context, see Derrida 1988.

1 Hegemony, Representation and Britishness

Introduction: identity, contingency and hegemony

Identity politics is as important today as it ever was, and not just the identity politics of 'exotic' others, but also the identity politics of conservatives and liberals. The likes of David Cameron and Gordon Brown are no less engaged in identity politics than is Shabina Begum, and Brian Barry no less so than Bhikhu Parekh. Identity politics is not something only 'they' do, while 'we' are concerned with the higher causes of justice, equality and liberty. Identity politics is more than particularistic identities articulated in terms of their difference from other identities; there is also an identity politics of identities that aspire to include through universal principles. Universal claims rely on particular representations of the kind of being who can be the carrier of human rights, and identity politics usually draws on discourses of *equal* recognition, tolerance, and so on. This challenges the perceived opposition between particularism and universalism (Laclau 1996a: ch. 2). It also challenges the perceived opposition between the politics of recognition and the politics of redistribution, as if particularity is unambiguously on the side of the former and universality on the side of the latter (Fraser and Honneth 2003).

Identity persists as a site of inclusion and exclusion; the latter are negotiated through claims to, and about, particular identities. Often this happens in an explicit way, as in the case of Gordon Brown's Britishness discourse when Brown represents Britishness as an open and inclusive identity. It also happens in legal cases involving school uniforms and religious attire – cases such as those that I will discuss in chapters to come. But the negotiation of inclusion and exclusion through identity politics need not be explicit; sometimes it is implied, as when David Cameron makes implicit assumptions about the relationship between the identities of 'Muslim' and 'British'.

This book is about identity and inclusion and the relationship between them. I examine how inclusion and exclusion are negotiated through representations of identities; and how identities are articulated and negotiated through relations of inclusion and exclusion. Cameron's (2011a) speech on security, Islam and Britishness was a good example of both: of the way in which identity is a site for the negotiation of inclusion and exclusion, and of the centrality of inclusion and exclusion for the construction of identity.

This chapter develops the theoretical framework for the analysis of the cases in the subsequent chapters. The framework is a post-structuralist one, and it draws on the works of two thinkers in particular: Jacques Derrida and Ernesto Laclau. From Derrida, I take a deconstructive way of reading as well as a number of quasi-concepts such as iterability and hospitality. More generally, from Derrida and Laclau, I take the view that identities are constituted through relations of difference, and that exclusion and representation are constitutive.

In order to make the deconstructivist and post-structuralist framework more amenable to political analysis, I turn to Laclau and his theory of hegemony and discourse developed together with Chantal Mouffe (Laclau and Mouffe 1985; Laclau 1990; Laclau 1996a; Laclau 2005). Laclau explicitly draws on Derrida and other post-structuralist thinkers while articulating a theory of politics. For my purposes, what is particularly useful is the way in which Laclau and Mouffe challenge the way we think about identity and difference, and universality and particularity. For them, identity is contingent; identities are constituted through relations of difference and through exclusion. There is no inclusion without exclusion, which is another way of saying that the universal is always articulated through the particular. From the theory of hegemony, I get a number of conceptual categories – equivalence and difference, the empty signifier, antagonism, and so on – and below

I will explain how they can be used for the analysis of identity and inclusion.

A central starting point for Laclau's post-structuralist political theory is that identities – and the social much more broadly – are contingent. This is why they are open to negotiation and rearticulation. There is nothing natural, necessary or essential about identities; they are not the result of human nature, cultural essences or underlying structures of capitalism just waiting for us to discover them. They are contingent.

It is important to be clear about the exact meaning of contingency, however. Contingency, in the way I use the term, does not mean chance or accident, nor does it mean the simple absence of structures. Contingency is not diametrically opposed to necessity, and we are not dealing with a continuum from full contingency to full necessity where it is a matter of the relative plasticity of identities. As such, contingency also escapes the opposition between structure and agency. It is no doubt important to analyse the ways in which, for instance, structure and agency interact in particular circumstances, but contingency refers to something else here, namely to a general condition of any agency and any structure, and of any identity and any practice.

There are different ways of conceptualising this contingency. Derrida thought of it in terms of undecidability (Derrida 1992a; Norval 2004), Lacan in terms of the real (Stavrakakis 1999). Drawing on Derrida and Lacan among others, Ernesto Laclau and Chantal Mouffe argued for a conception of what they called 'radical contingency' (Laclau and Mouffe 1985: 114, 128; Laclau 1990: 26–31). They named this contingency 'radical' to signal that this kind of contingency cannot simply be opposed to necessity. As Laclau wrote: 'We are dealing not with a *head-on negation* of necessity (which as such would leave it conceptually unchanged), but with its *subversion*' (Laclau 1990: 26–7). No identity can be fully constituted because it is marked by this radical contingency, and this is so whether we think of identity in terms of agency or in terms of structure. The sovereignty of an agent is only possible through others' recognition of it, thus decentring the agent's sovereignty into a web of recognition and signification over which the agent cannot be sovereign. And a structure, as a system of difference, can only stabilise itself in a way that simultaneously subverts its differential logic, its structuricity; there is always something radically contingent about the structures.

This radical contingency makes it possible to analyse identity politics in terms of hegemony. The 'necessity' and relative stability of identities and practices are the result of contingent articulations, or what Laclau calls hegemony. Starting from the view that identities and practices are contingent, we must analyse how they came to be, and to be perceived, the way they are. If there is nothing natural, necessary or essential about Britishness, why is it that certain discourses of Britishness have become dominant? If there is nothing necessary about the kinds of things we take race, ethnicity and religion to be, why is it that particular meanings of race, ethnicity and religion have come to shape legislation and practice in the ways that they have? And so on and so forth.

There are different ways of pursuing such an analysis, but Laclau's theory of hegemony has a number of advantages. It takes identities as contingent and takes articulation, or hegemony, as primary. This is useful if we want to think of identity and inclusion as sites of hegemonic struggle and rearticulation. In his work, Laclau has sought to rethink the question of identity and difference, which bears directly on the relation between identity and inclusion and exclusion. Finally, contingency and hegemony go hand in hand with power and exclusion, which makes the theory well suited to address the relationships between inclusion and exclusion and between identity formation and inclusion and exclusion.

When I make use of the theory of hegemony in the following, I do not mean to simply apply it to a set of cases. Indeed, it could be argued that it is impossible to simply apply a theory, and that the application of a theory is always also a rearticulation of it. In Wittgenstein's terms, a rule cannot be defined in a definite way prior to its application, and so the application of a rule also contributes to its definition (Wittgenstein 1958; Thomassen 2010a). In more Laclauian terms, if meaning is contextual and relational, the categories of the theory of hegemony are rearticulated when transposed from one site to another. Although Laclau presents his theory of hegemony as a general theory of politics, it was articulated in response to specific historical phenomena and events – above all

Latin American populism and the crisis of the Left in the 1970s and 1980s – and I will put the theory to use in a different context: in relation to contemporary British discourses of identity and inclusion. The aim is not to be true to an authentic Laclauian theory of hegemony, but to show how it can be useful for the purposes of my own problematic. Therefore, what follows is not a simple exposition of Laclau's theory of hegemony.

This book examines the concepts of identity and inclusion and the relationship between them. It does so in the context of British multiculturalism. The present chapter uses Laclau's theory of hegemony to set out a theoretical framework for analysing identity and inclusion. Here the key concepts are those of contingency, hegemony and articulation, and representation. It does so while illustrating the concepts with the help of an analysis of one of the important discourses of identity from the last decades of British multiculturalism: Gordon Brown's Britishness discourse. That discourse resonates with many of the debates I will be looking at in subsequent chapters; and there are important continuities and discontinuities between Brown and Cameron on Britishness (I return to Cameron in the Conclusion). I will attempt to show how the theory of hegemony can account for some of the tensions in Brown's Britishness discourse. For the purposes of the problematic of this book, these tensions concern, above all, the relationships between identity and difference and between inclusion and exclusion, and the way in which Brown's Britishness discourse rests on a dual claim to represent an already existing British identity and for the need to create this identity.

Identity and difference, inclusion and exclusion

Laclau's theory of hegemony was first articulated in its full form in 1985 in the book *Hegemony and Socialist Strategy: Towards a Radical Democratic Politics*, written together with Chantal Mouffe. The book is a deconstructive genealogy of the concept of hegemony in Marxism, but the concept of hegemony is rearticulated by Laclau and Mouffe as a more general theory of politics. Although it was a response to debates among Marxist theoreticians and practitioners about the strategy to be pursued by the Left at the time, I am more interested in some of the key categories of the theory. My aim is then to transpose the theory of hegemony and some of its key categories from their articulation by Laclau to the scene of the politics of identity and inclusion in contemporary Britain, what I have also called the discursive terrain of British multiculturalism. To some extent this has already been done by Laclau himself when engaging with identity politics and multiculturalism (Laclau 1996a: ch. 2; see also Mouffe 1992; Mouffe 1994), and I build on this work here.

For Laclau, identities are contingent. There is nothing essential, natural and necessary about them, and they do not simply reflect a position within a structure. Identities are relational, constituted through relations of difference; in this, Laclau follows the post-structuralist appropriation of the linguistic structuralism of Saussure, which holds that meaning is relational and therefore that identity is constituted through relations of difference. No identity without difference. An identity is always constituted through a relation to something other: something different, something that it is not, and so on. Take Britishness as an example: taking the view that identities are differential rather than reflecting some underlying essence or structure, Britishness is constituted through relations of difference vis-à-vis other identities, both those said to be outside it (say, 'terrorist') and those said to be partly overlapping with it (say, 'Scottish'). If difference is constitutive of identity, then Britishness must be exclusive in order to be something rather than just anything and nothing.

While identities are constituted at the level of differences, those differences do not make up a structure of fixed positions; this marks the post-structuralist departure from structuralism. That is not to say that there are no structures and no fixity, only that these are the result of relatively sedimented articulations of difference. Identity can be thought in terms of identification rather than identity. Since all identity is marked by contingency and therefore 'fails', all we have are identifications and the more or less stable identities as outcomes of those identifications.

Identities are contingent, and they are discursive. 'The structured totality resulting from the articulatory practice, we will call *discourse*', Laclau and Mouffe write (1985: 105). Discourses are not reflections of anything extra-discursive. Rather, discourse is the terrain in which meaning and objectivity are constituted, and so there is nothing meaningful or objective outside of discourses. As already mentioned in the Introduction, and as I will argue throughout the text, representation is constitutive, and here representation corresponds more or less to what Laclau and Mouffe call discourse. Given contingency, articulation – or hegemony – becomes central: 'we will call *articulation* any practice establishing a relation among elements such that their identity is modified as a result of the articulatory practice' (1985: 105). While Laclau and Mouffe talk of discourses as totalities, they are never completely fixed and closed totalities. The point is that identities are the result of articulations of differences into discourses, for instance Britishness. The articulations are contingent, and it is always possible to rearticulate the identities in new ways, even if some identities, or discourses, will be more sedimented than others. Identities are then articulated at the level of discourse (representation), and their articulation is contingent, which does not mean that it is accidental or that identities are completely plastic. They are articulated – or: re-articulated – in an already partly sedimented discursive terrain, and rearticulation is limited by existing relations of power. Moreover, discourse is material; a discourse can be any meaningful totality, and this includes not just speech, but also institutions, practices, law, clothing, and so on.

The question is then how particular identities have become articulated, but before looking more closely at the category of articulation, I want to introduce Gordon Brown's Britishness discourse as a contemporary example of identity politics. I will do so in some detail, both because it provides a useful illustration of key aspects of the theory of hegemony, and because his discourse relates to the period of British politics from which I draw my cases in the chapters that follow. I draw on speeches and writings from his time as Chancellor and Prime Minister and in opposition, and will also examine some of the legislation and materials related to changes in naturalisation for British citizenship, which Brown connected to the creation of a British identity.[1] I use Brown's representation of Britishness here more as an illustration and less to critically engage with it.

Gordon Brown's Britishness discourse is just one among other competing discourses. Here I shall not go into much detail about these competing discourses, although, in the Introduction, I addressed one of them: Cameron's representation of Britishness, which is in turn different from earlier Tory representations of Britishness, multiculturalism and race. Brown himself wants to position his version of Britishness as an alternative to several competing discourses, some of them of Britishness, some not: the discourse of the Scottish National Party (SNP) and discourses of Englishness that articulate Scotland and England as different nations with interests so different that they call for the break-up of the Union (see especially Brown 2014); discourses of, and about, multiculturalism that articulate certain cultural, ethnic and religious identities as contrary to, and therefore unable to coexist with, a sense of belonging to the UK (Norman Tebbit's 'cricket test' is an example); more exclusive discourses of Britishness that articulate British identity in terms of race or ethnicity (at the time when Brown was writing, the British National Party (BNP) was an example of this); political discourses that were divisive, for instance Old Labour discourse based on a class analysis of British society, or Thatcherite discourse that singled out particular groups for particular scorn; and those who argue that, in a modern globalised world, there is neither room nor need for national identities. Brown's Britishness is articulated as an alternative to all of these other representations of Britishness.

Brown's Britishness discourse aims to articulate a collective identity where that identity is lacking or at least seen as insufficient for integrating an increasingly diverse society in an age of globalisation. In this, Britishness discourse can also be seen as a response to academic debates about universalism and particularism, and about the thinness and thickness of a collective identity required to integrate a diverse society. These debates – between liberals and communitarians, between liberals and republicans, and among different liberals, for instance liberal nationalists (Mason 2010; Joppke 2008; Laclau 1996a: ch. 2) – also concern how inclusive and exclusive a collective identity such as Britishness can and should be.

In Gordon Brown's case, Britishness is a response to three specific developments. The first is devolution and the rise of Scottish

nationalism, even more important today after the 2014 independence referendum and the 2016 Brexit referendum. Brown's
Britishness is an attempt to convince the Scottish that British does
not equal English, and an attempt to convince the English that they
are not first and foremost English but British (Brown and Alexander 1999: 7; Brown 2014; Lee 2007: ch. 5). The second development is multiculturalism and, especially the Muslim question. Here
again, the aim is for diverse groups to identify with the same collective identity. Brown also relates Britishness to a third development.
Britishness is part of the 'new Britain', a post-ideological Britain
beyond the 'old' politics of Left and Right, and a Britain where we
are all in the same boat (Lee 2007: chs 1–2). In this new Britain,
there is already a consensus on basic values and goals, and so the
only differences that need to be included are not ideological, but
national and cultural, ethnic and religious differences. The shared
purpose and the shared British values make it easier 'to make the
hard choices on priorities that will determine our success' (Brown
2006a: 6). If successful in establishing a shared identity and shared
goals, 'hard choices' are no longer so hard because they are reduced
to technical choices about how to tinker with the market, and are
not choices about which goals to pursue. This is the Britain of New
Labour where New Labour tried to disarticulate itself from its
former class basis and rearticulate itself as a broader post-class
discourse. In this new Britain, the legal status of citizenship was
the medium of inclusion and exclusion, not solidarity for example,
and it is the new Britain that forms the background for the cases
I analyse in Chapters 3, 4 and 5.

In all three cases – devolution, multiculturalism and the post-
ideological discourse of New Labour – the discourse of Britishness does not only consist of representations in the narrow sense
of speech, writing and symbols. Brown's Britishness discourse is
material and includes practices (flag flying), institutions (citizenship and citizenship tests), constitutional structures, and policies
(immigration and industrial policy). Together these discursive
elements make up a particular discourse – articulation, representation – of Britishness. The latter serves as a point of identification
for groups otherwise recognised as, or recognising themselves as,
different. With Laclau, we can say that the discourse creates an

equivalence among these differences, and one of the differences (Brown's Britishness) takes the role of quilting the differences together.

The relationship between identity and difference is important for the discussion of identity and inclusion in this book. For Laclau, identity is constituted through relations of difference, and we are always facing an unstable tension between identity and difference. Consider Brown's Britishness as a hegemonic project to create a collective identity that will include different particular identities by making the latter identify with, and prioritise, the common identity.

The first thing to consider is the relationship between Britishness and the particular identities included within it. We are starting from the existence of a plurality of different identities: workers, British, English, Scottish, British-Pakistanis, Londoners, and so forth. These identities are to a greater or lesser extent sedimented, but they are contingent, and it is therefore possible to rearticulate them in new ways. One of the identities becomes a point of identification for all of them: Londoners, British-Pakistanis, Scottish, and so on, all come to identify as British. Or, to be more precise, they come to identify as *also* British, because the identification with their particular identities does not necessarily disappear, even if it may change. The particular identities remain different, but they are also rearticulated: the differences are not seen as antithetical to their all being (also) British. Of course, this is contested. Not only do different identities vie for the role of common identity, but there will also be disputes as to whether it is possible to identify as, say, both Pakistani and British.

Inclusion takes place through the creation of an identity that can be shared by different groups (and recall that the identity consists of images, practices, laws, institutions, and so on). In Laclau's terms, the shared identity is articulated through the creation of a chain of equivalence among the different particular identities. One of the particular identities – here: Britishness – comes to represent the chain as a whole, thereby being able to stand in for the others. This happens through the emptying of its particular content. Although this emptying is never complete, it facilitates the inclusion of other identities into this shared identity.[2]

In Laclau's terms, Britishness functions as an empty signifier. Different things can function as empty signifiers: a leader (Perón is one of Laclau's favourite examples), a symbol (such as the symbols of Solidarność), a word, and so on.[3] The empty signifier works as a point of identification for the other elements of the chain of equivalence; it quilts them together. The notion of the empty signifier is first introduced by Laclau in the 1990s (Laclau 1996a: ch. 3). In *Hegemony and Socialist Strategy*, Laclau and Mouffe use the notion of a nodal point to express something similar: nodal points are 'the privileged discursive points of [the] partial fixation' of meaning within a discourse (Laclau and Mouffe 1985: 112). I shall return to this in Chapter 4, but the two notions – the empty signifier and the nodal point – suggest different images of the representative space of something like Britishness. If Britishness is taken as an empty signifier, it is taken to be connected to the creation of a chain of equivalence and an antagonistic frontier. If Britishness is taken as a nodal point, it suggests that Britishness is organised around a centre towards which other identities orientate themselves. In the first case, inclusion and exclusion tend to be matters of either/or (although I shall qualify this in a moment); in the second case, inclusion and exclusion tend to be matters of more or less.

There is, however, a further qualification to be made about the empty signifier: it is never empty, only tendentially empty. If it were completely empty, it would be empty of meaning; and Brown's Britishness, for instance, does have some content, and it is one conception of Britishness among others. This has implications for the relationship between Britishness and the other identities, for the relationship between the empty signifier and the other parts of the chain of equivalence, and for the question of inclusion.

Inclusion is mediated by identity, and identity is constituted through relations of difference. Although inclusive, the shared identity – the equivalence, in Laclau's terms – is interrupted by the differences that remain among the particular identities included in the chain of equivalence. Those identities are precisely equivalent and not identical. This includes the differences that remain between the shared identity (which is only tendentially empty) and the other identities included within it. Even when articulated as an identity shared by Londoners, Scottish, British-Pakistanis, and so on, Britishness remains different vis-à-vis those other identities. The universal is articulated through the particular, and the inclusive space of Britishness is contaminated, and limited, by the particularity of Brown's Britishness.

Some identities will be more different from Britishness than others, not essentially but because they are articulated as such. They may not be totally at odds with Britishness, but they will be relatively marginalised, as when hyphenated identities are marked as different through both parts of their identity: the person identified as 'British-Pakistani' is differentiated from those who are just 'British' and from those for whom it goes without saying that they are 'British'. It is important to stress that Britishness will always retain some particularity and will always be a particular articulation of Britishness. As a result, it will stand in particular relations of difference vis-à-vis the other identities in the chain of equivalence; it will at once represent the chain as a whole and be one particular difference in the chain. This is important: inclusion is possible through the articulation of an 'inclusive' identity, but identity is constituted through relations of difference. There is then a close relationship between identity/difference and inclusion/exclusion.

It therefore matters which, and whose, identity comes to represent the chain as a whole: it matters whether it is Britishness or Englishness, just as it matters which, and whose, representation of Britishness we are dealing with. Depending on which identity comes to represent the shared identity, other identities will be included to a greater or lesser extent. Inclusion and exclusion become matters of more or less, not either/or. This is so whether we think of the construction of Britishness in terms of the creation of a chain of equivalence represented by an empty signifier or in terms of concentric circles around a nodal point.

Britishness is also articulated through a negation of what it is not. Here we are dealing with a particular kind of difference, with what, following Laclau, we might call an antagonistic relation. In Brown's articulation of Britishness, for instance, Britishness is opposed to terrorism, slavery and sometimes to the 'old society' of ideological cleavages in such a way that Britishness and, for instance, terrorism are mutually exclusive. One cannot be both British and a terrorist, and the terrorist is not a candidate for inclusion into the chain of equivalence of Brown's Britishness. In its original formulation in *Hegemony and Socialist Strategy*, antagonism was the limit of objectivity and the way that radical contingency manifested itself. Later, Laclau rightly noted that antagonism is just one discursive articulation among others, and that it is a relation of difference that supports and helps define the two identities (Thomassen 2005), as when Brown argues that the struggle against slavery is a sign of the fairness of Britishness.

Britishness is articulated around a common point of identification, it is differentiated from what it is not, and we can think of the differences within this collective identity as concentric circles around a core identity. Brown articulates Britishness around three political values: liberty, responsibility and fairness. The three core values are spelled out in more concrete institutions and values such as the voluntary sector and 'a uniquely British settlement' of the relationship between state and market (Brown 2006b: 217). Brown also makes historical references to things said to represent a unique British articulation of the three core values: Magna Carta, Adam Smith, the struggle to abolish the slave trade and John Stuart Mill. Because it rests on political values, Britishness is inclusive; it is 'a strong sense of shared patriotism' that does not rest on a 'cricket test' (Brown 2009: 27; Brown 2006a: 6–7). Brown writes:

> This is not jingoism, but practical, rational and purposeful – and therefore, I would argue, an essentially British form of patriotism.
>
> Patriotism . . . defines a nation not by race or ethnicity, but by seeing us all as part of a collective project from which we all gain and to which we all contribute. Society is – as the great thinkers have long told us – a contract, even a covenant, in which we recognise that our destinies are interlinked. (Brown 2008)

It is possible to have dual or multiple identities: for instance, British and Scottish are not 'exclusive identities' (Brown 2006a: 6). Brown (2009: 32) also refers to this as 'Britishness-plus'. This notion of Britishness makes it possible to have a shared identity while retaining our differences. The diversity within the shared political identity is positive, according to Brown (Brown and Alexander 1999: 30–1), but note that the diversity is cultural, ethnic, religious and national. Britishness should be able to include cultural, ethnic, religious and national differences because these differences are important to people, but at the same time they must be relativised vis-à-vis the shared political identity. And this works only insofar as the two levels – political and cultural – can be clearly distinguished. Only if Britishness is unambiguously political (as opposed to cultural), can it include cultural differences equally. However, as pointed out above, the empty signifier (here: Britishness) is always contaminated by particularity, whether political or cultural. Brown tries to get around this via the distinction between political and cultural, but this ignores how the universal (Britishness in this case) is always articulated through the particular.

Britishness is the sum of the mutual articulation of the three values of liberty, responsibility and fairness, and this mutual articulation is the result of a particular British experience. This is Brown's response to those who, quite rightly, ask why these three values are particularly British, and how they can distinguish Britishness from what it is not. This touches upon a more general issue. Britishness must be both inclusive and exclusive. It is meant to include differences, yet must also be exclusive in order not to mean just anything and nothing. We could also say that the question is how thin Britishness needs to be in order to be inclusive, and how thick it has to be in order to function as a shared point of identification.

The introduction of a particular British historical experience may help distinguish Britishness from, say, Frenchness. However, it does not take into account that there is no single British historical experience because Britain and Britishness are the results of hegemonic struggles among different discourses, among which Brown's Britishness is only one. This is evident when considering Brown's historical examples of Britishness. For instance, as an example of the core value of liberty, Brown cites the abolition of the slave trade and, later, of slavery. 'When Charles Darwin challenged Britain on slavery, it was precisely because slavery was an affront to national values which championed liberty' (Brown 2006c: 33–4). Yet the very need to 'challenge' Britain suggests that the liberty of slaves was not part of a universally shared consensus; quite the contrary. The British nation was divided over slavery as well as the meaning of liberty. Brown also appropriates the American War of

Independence for 'the British idea of liberty': 'perhaps ironically – the American War of Independence was fought by both sides "in the name of British liberty"' (2006c: 33). If both sides fought in the same name, the name ('British liberty') does not help us distinguish British from what is not British. Instead we have a hegemonic struggle over different articulations of 'British liberty'.

Brown pays plenty of attention to the differences included within Britishness – his representation of Britishness is a response to those differences. What he does not pay attention to is the way in which those differences are at once differences *within* and *over* Britishness. Britishness is articulated by Brown as a representational space within which different identities (Scots, British-Pakistanis, Londoners, and so on) can be inscribed – that is, Britishness is something with which these identities can all identify, despite their differences. But the representational space of Britishness is not a fixed identity with fixed borders. It is a space marked by difference and tensions; Britishness is marked by what Laclau and Mouffe call radical contingency. The point is not to dismiss Brown's history as a partial interpretation – of course it is! – but to show how his discourse of Britishness is caught, and necessarily so, in a tension between identity and difference. Inclusion is asserted through an identity (Britishness) that is also different vis-à-vis what it includes; and its inclusive character is articulated around values claimed to be both universal and particular. To put it in Laclau's terms, Britishness is articulated through the creation of a chain of equivalence where there is an irreducible tension between identity and difference, and between universality and particularity.

The creation of an inclusive identity is disrupted by the tensions between identity and difference, and between universality and particularity. An inclusive identity is always also marked by some element of exclusion, which may take different forms: difference, negation or antagonism, and so forth. This is so because identity is constituted through difference. The tension between identity and difference means that the lines of inclusion and exclusion are never clear-cut. The tension between identity and difference, and the unstable relationship between inclusion and exclusion, undermines the ability of any discourse, hegemonic or not, to differentiate itself in a clear-cut manner *and* to include and exclude differences in an unambiguous way. Britishness is a good example of that.

Hegemony as articulation and representation

A further aspect of Brown's Britishness discourse helps shed light on the process of articulation: in Brown's case, he articulates Britishness around references to events, symbols, institutions and practices already taken to be British, if not by everybody then at least by some. They include the struggles for the abolition of the slave trade and slavery, the Union Jack, the National Health Service (NHS), and many more. From a Laclauian perspective there is nothing inherently British about these events and institutions; their Britishness is a result of their articulation (representation) as British. Here articulation refers to 'any practice establishing a relation among elements such that their identity is modified as a result of the articulatory practice' (Laclau and Mouffe 1985: 105). Different elements – events, institutions, and so on – are articulated together into a discourse. Since meaning is relational, this changes the meaning of those elements because they are now related to other elements in new ways. For example, the Union Jack may be disarticulated from an imperialist discourse and rearticulated within Brown's Britishness discourse as a symbol of liberty and decency because it now becomes associated with the struggle against slavery and institutions such as the NHS (Brown 2006d; Brown and Straw 2007: 58). For Laclau, hegemony must be understood as articulation, where articulation is constitutive of the meaning of what is articulated.

Properly understood, articulation and representation can then be seen as interchangeable. Hegemony can then be understood as a relation of representation, but where representation has a clear performative aspect to it: representation does not simply reflect what is already there, but constitutes it. Although Laclau emphasises the performative aspect of representation, this is never the whole story. The practice of representation proceeds in a manner both performative and constative (Derrida 1997; Derrida 1982; Laclau 2005: ch. 6; Thomassen 2007a). The representative claim is a claim to re-present some pre-existing identity (for example, 'Britain'); this reference to something already there, which, it is claimed, is merely reflected in the representation, is essential for the legitimacy of the representative claim. At the same time, the representation must create that identity, otherwise there would be no need to represent it in the first place – the act of representation must contribute something new.

This dual constative and performative aspect of representation is evident in Brown's Britishness discourse. Britishness is a normative project, an attempt to articulate a collective identity that is missing or at least seen as lacking in some respect. Take, for instance, the following quote: 'beyond the battleground on individual issues some common ground does exist; it is the recognition of the importance of and the need to celebrate and entrench a Britishness defined by shared values' (Brown 2006a: 11; similarly in Brown and Straw 2007: 53–9). Britishness exists to be reflected and celebrated in official discourse and policy, but it also needs to be celebrated in order to bolster it. For example, as part of its Britishness discourse, New Labour introduced a citizenship test and a ceremony for recently naturalised citizens. The test and the ceremony were supposed to signify the significance – the importance and the meaning – of citizenship and naturalisation (Brown 2008; Home Office 2003: 8; Home Office 2008: 3; Home Office 2009b: 3). They were meant to *reflect* this significance, but they were also meant to *make* citizenship and naturalisation significant. The need to entrench Britishness suggests that it is lacking, whether partly or wholly, in which case it cannot simply be reflected as a fact. Brown's Britishness discourse claims to reproduce a Britishness already there to be (re)discovered, *and* it is an attempt to create an identity of Britishness as something to be collectively aspired to. The former is its constative aspect, the latter its performative aspect.

The performative articulation of Britishness through representations of Britishness happens through the representation of existing events, institutions and identities in new ways. Articulation is a combination of disarticulation and rearticulation. Articulation, or representation, takes place in an already partly sedimented terrain, where discourses have to a larger or lesser extent, but never completely, been able to fix the meaning of, for instance, British-ness or the Union Jack. These meanings must be disarticulated from their current articulation in order to be rearticulated in new ways. A rearticulation, or representation, is itself an attempt to fix meaning in a new way, as for instance when Brown writes that 'we should assert that the union flag is, by definition, a flag for tolerance and inclusion' (Brown 2006d: 262). A hegemonic representation is one that has been successful in defining, for instance, Britishness in a way that is recognised by others as legitimate or self-evident. As I shall argue in Chapter 3, representation depends on recognition: representations depend for their 'force' on being taken up by others, on being recognised as representative.

Representation – or the process of dis- and rearticulation – cannot be reduced to a matter of true or false. Take Brown's example of the struggle for the abolition of the slave trade. For Brown, this is an example of British values at work. He writes:

> let us remember what we can achieve together. Two hundred years ago this year it was the British people who came together and with the biggest mass petition that had ever been mounted in the history of our country brought the slave trade to an end. (Brown 2007a; compare Brown 2006c: 33–4; Brown 2007b: 65, 125)

Historians may agree or disagree with Brown's description, but the important point is that the representation of a historical event is not just a description, but a rearticulation that places Brown's Britishness as the continuation of certain historical struggles. At the same time, Brown conveniently neglects to play up the fact that we are precisely dealing with struggles over the future of Britain and the meaning of Britishness: 'the British people . . . came together', but they came together against other British people who also struggled in the name of 'Britain'. The bottom line is that there is no extra-representational fact here to support Brown's Britishness discourse; there are only facts that have already been articulated as facts within a particular discourse. The question of meaning is prior to that of truth/falsity. The legitimacy and success of a representation depends on these 'facts' being taken as facts; that is, the success of Brown's representation of British history depends on its being taken by others, not as a normative and performative claim, but as a reflection of historical facts. The performative aspect of representation must disappear behind its constative aspect in order for the representation to have force.

If there is no extra-representational truth, then critique cannot proceed simply by comparing representations to an extra-representational reality. Instead it must proceed first of all by articulating alternative representations, which is to say counter-hegemony. Take, for instance, Simon Lee's claim that Brown's Britishness discourse amounts to 'misquotation and misrepresentation':

> The most intriguing element of and flaw in Brown's British Way is the extent to which it can only be sustained by drawing on examples of English history or writings specifically about England and the English and reinventing them as if they were about Britain and the British. (Lee 2007: 147, 145; see also 154–5; Crick 2008: 77).

Lee (2007: 146) correctly observes that 'The British Way is . . . dependent on reinventing literary Englands as if they were about Britain and Britishness'.[4] Brown does indeed reinvent his examples when articulating them as examples of Britishness rather than Englishness. However, we have no extra-representational truth with which to oppose this representation. Representation proceeds in the mode of 'as if', and hegemony consists in making others see, for instance, 'English' literary references *as if* they are 'British'.

In the final analysis, Lee himself implicitly acknowledges the performative character of Britishness and Englishness when, at the end of his critique of Brown, he writes:

> It would be possible to construct an alternative politics and inclusive concept of citizenship based on Brown's 'golden thread of liberty', [Jack] Straw's 'core democratic values of freedom, fairness, tolerance and plurality' and the historical lineage and literary quotations that have been advanced to substantiate the British Way. However, that particular history and literature have given concrete expression to the possibility of an 'English Way'. (Lee 2007: 155)

It is possible to 'construct' Englishness out of the same elements that Brown uses to construct Britishness because those elements are not essentially English or British, and because there is nothing essential about Englishness and Britishness.

In this book, I take representation as a general category of analysis, and, with Derrida and Laclau, I take representation to proceed in a manner at once constative and performative (Derrida 1997; Derrida 1982; Laclau 2005: ch. 6; Thomassen 2007a). I prefer representation to hegemony because the theory of hegemony is associated, by adherents and detractors alike, with populism and the creation of chains of equivalence, empty signifiers and antagonistic frontiers. My wager is that these are only some of the ways in which meaning and identity are constituted; although useful, these concepts are not sufficient for analysing identity politics. Although the theory of hegemony may well be able to account for other forms of identity formation,[5] representation is a more general category. We can think of representation as the terrain in which identities are constituted; identities are 'representational' in this sense, which does not mean that there is no reality, only that there is no non-representational reality. And representations are material: there is nothing non-representational about citizenship tests, the cloth of a hijab, laws regulating religious symbols and clothing in schools, and so on.

The question then becomes which, and what kinds of, representations become hegemonic, and whose representations they are. This is what I refer to as the politics of representation. This is the lens through which I approach identity and inclusion because identities are representational, and because inclusion is intrinsically linked to the representation of identities.

To illustrate how I use the notion of representation, consider how it differs from a typical progressive discourse such as that found in two recent books dealing with 'the Muslim question': Peter Morey and Amina Yaqin's *Framing Muslims* (2011) and Anne Norton's *On the Muslim Question* (2013). Both books are close to my position on contemporary representations of Muslims, but work with a different conception of representation. It is no coincidence that a lot of contemporary critical work on inclusion, identity and representation centres on Muslims, and several of my own cases also concern images of Muslims. Having said that, the argument about representation is applicable beyond the contemporary preoccupation with 'the Muslim question'.

In *Framing Muslims*, Morey and Yaqin argue that the way in which Muslims are represented in the West is revealing of how we conceive of ourselves. The identities of 'Muslims' and of 'the West' are constituted in a mutual relationship, through exclusion of the other part, and sometimes through forms of inclusion that also exclude. In *On the Muslim Question*, Norton too is interested in the ways in which Muslims are represented, and in the ways in which the representations of Muslims constitute the identity of Muslims and of Islam as well as the identity of 'the West'. This is what she refers to as 'the Muslim Question': the ways in which 'the West' is constituted through discourses about Muslims. 'Our' identity is constituted in a relationship of difference and exclusion with 'their' identity, and 'our' representations of 'them' say as much about us as about them. My analyses in the chapters that follow confirm Morey and Yaqin's and Norton's conclusions, but they also diverge from them.

Examining contemporary representations of Muslims, Morey and Yaqin take the view that there is no meaning and communication without stereotyping. They refer to this as 'necessary' stereotyping (Morey and Yaqin 2011: 30): it is part of making sense of, and acting in, the world to impose categories – that is, stereotypes – onto social complexity. This is 'the social utility of stereotyping' (2011: 31). It is stereotyping because it simplifies what is otherwise more complex; as such, stereotypes are also misrepresentations of the world. Stereotypes distort reality, but they also help people manage an otherwise complex world and stabilise their identities.[6] Like Morey and Yaqin, Norton argues that Muslims are not as bad and different as we think, and that we in the West are not as good and homogenous as we think. If we look closely, the distinction between us and them, the West and Muslims, is blurred. The image of a clash of civilisations 'is not true' (Norton 2013: 195). In response to stereotypes about Muslims, Norton uncovers complexity.

For Morey and Yaqin (2011: 1), the reality of Muslim lives and identities is 'varied' in a way that is not captured by the representations of Muslims. Their book 'seeks to trace the restricted, limited ways that Muslims are stereotyped and "framed" within the political, cultural, and media discourses of the West' (2011: 2).

32

'The framing of Muslims', they continue, 'amounts to a refraction, not a reflection of reality' (2011: 3–4). Like Norton, Morey and Yaqin (2011: 13) are interested in the effect of misrepresentations on the lives of real Muslims: 'Turning the spotlight on stereotypes and repeated imagery does not mean that we are unconcerned with the very real human problems in which such representations are rooted and of which they offer a distorted yet telling echo.' While Norton and Morey and Yaqin have their eyes on representations of Muslims, Muslim reality serves as a check on those representations.

For Morey and Yaqin, there is no way to avoid some misrepresentation of the world, but they rely on a distinction between representation and what is represented: their 'book is about the gap that exists between representation and reality' (2011: 1), and that reality is not itself constituted at the level of representation. While, for Morey and Yaqin and for Norton, representations are important, they are so to the extent that they represent or misrepresent the social world; representation is not constitutive of that world. This has consequences for the kind of critique they pursue.

To the (mis)representations of Muslims, Morey and Yaqin oppose 'a space beyond the frame'. They go on to explain:

> Perhaps that space lies in the everyday, lived experience of low-level, peaceful, and communal (in the best sense) interaction that the mediated picture habitually ignores. This is not a call for a return to some premediated state of face-to-face relations. Rather it is a suggestion that such relationships already exist, 'out there' in the space beyond the camera, and should be admitted back into the mediascape, into law, into political discourse. (Morey and Yaqin 2011: 214)

There is a space outside the representations, in everyday life. This space can be used as a critical yardstick with which to assess representations of Muslims, and it can be used as a starting point for better – more just: fairer and more precise – representations of Muslims.

Likewise, Norton refers to the complexity of the ordinary, as opposed to government and media discourses. It is the ordinary lives of Muslims and non-Muslims in places of ordinary interaction: in the street, in the local neighbourhood, in the grocery store, in the impersonal relations of the market society – in short, 'ordinary people, going about their ordinary lives' (Norton 2013: 214). Those ordinary lives 'are not without conflict', but people get on with their intersecting lives – referred to as 'conviviality' (2013: 195, 220). There is a sort of 'practical wisdom' in the ordinary lives of people who just get on with it (2013: 226), and this is the starting point for criticising negative representations of Muslims.

Morey and Yaqin and Norton assume that stereotypes and misrepresentations do not reach the space of the everyday and the ordinary where the inclusion of Muslims is possible. It is a space of complexity that cannot be captured by the simplicity and distortion of dominant representations of Muslims. I would not want to argue that there is no simplicity in government and media discourses, or that there is no complexity on the ground. However, this complexity is not limited to the everyday and the ordinary – it is everywhere, also in media and politics. We cannot simply oppose the simplicity of representations to the complexity of real life. The simplicity of representations of Muslims is everywhere too, and those representations are also part of how people act on the street and in the supermarket. There is nowhere to turn to avoid the simplistic and negative representations of Muslims; they are not located in only one part of society. More generally, there is no reality that is not always already representational.[7]

If representation is constitutive, then there is no beyond representation, no space outside the frame. It is of course possible to criticise particular representations and frames, but not from an extra-representational, unframed or non-stereotyped perspective. There is an outside to particular representations and frames, but that outside is made up of other representations and frames. Any critique of representations will be based on other representations, positing one representation against another. In fact, that is what Morey and Yaqin and Norton are doing: they are presenting us with alternative images, stories and stereotypes about Muslims. My point is that those representations are not more (or less) true in relation to some non-representational reality; they are only true or false in relation to other representations. There is no '"out there"' (quotation marks or not), no 'as they are' (Morey and Yaqin 2011:

214, 216), that can be opposed to and compared to particular representations of Muslims.

This also applies to self-representations. Morey and Yaqin argue that a way to counter misrepresentations of Muslims is to make the voice of (more) Muslims heard:

> A greater diversity of voices must be brought to the table, allowed to speak *and be seriously listened to*, before any progress can be made to unpick stereotypes and allow Muslims as they are to walk out of the frame and into the political life of the twenty-first century. (Morey and Yaqin 2011: 216)

This is a familiar argument from both government and critics of government policy. In order to be properly represented 'as they are', Muslims must speak for themselves, and not through others or their self-declared representatives. However, self-representations are also representations. Self-representations cannot be completely distinguished from other-representations, because both kinds of representations draw on existing representations – which is to say others' representations – in order to be meaningful and have an effect. There is no voice of an ordinary Muslim that is not already caught up in this web of representations, no voice that is entirely his or her own.

What we have are representations and representations, and then more representations. This is so whether we are dealing with government discourse, with representations in the media or with the self-representations of Muslims in their 'everyday, lived experience'. Muslims can be represented 'as they are', but what 'they are' is not something distinct from representations of them. The problem is not that there is a layer of representations that we cannot break through, in order to gain access to Muslims 'as they are'. Their 'everyday, lived experience' is itself representational, even if the representations constituting it may be more or less complex, and more or less in tune with media representations of 'the Muslim'.

We must analyse identities as constituted in the terrain of representation. The relevant questions are, then: how do agents talk about identities, whether their own or those of others? How do they live and practise those identities and the relations to other identities? What representations are dominant: how do particular

35

practices (re)produce particular identities and constellations of in/exclusion?

The category of hegemony still has a role to play, but it is not connected to a particular kind of articulation or representation. The representations may take many forms: difference, exclusion, antagonism, metaphorical substitution, analogies through contiguity, and so on.[8] Identity politics must be analysed as a politics of representation, as a hegemonic struggle with and over representations, or, in Laclau's terms, a hegemonic struggle between discourses.

Given that, as we have seen in the discussion of Brown's Britishness, there is no identity without difference, and no inclusion without exclusion, we can examine identity/difference and inclusion/exclusion as two sites of this politics of representation. Moreover, because identity and inclusion and exclusion are intrinsically linked, we can examine the politics of identity as a site where inclusion and exclusion are negotiated, and the politics of inclusion and exclusion as a site where identities are negotiated.

What is Britishness?

The politics of representation is transformative. Identities are rearticulated, lines of inclusion and exclusion are redrawn, and the two things are closely connected. This book is first and foremost a discussion of how we think about identity and inclusion and the relationship between them. It is first of all analytical, but there is no analysis that is not also normative. To argue that questions of identity, inclusion and exclusion are important, that Laclau's theory of hegemony is useful for analysing these questions, and that British multiculturalism is a suitable case through which to study them – these are not neutral decisions. Although more analytical than normative, this book therefore also takes sides; it is partisan. This is difficult water to navigate. Post-structuralists and deconstructivists tend to emphasise contingency and openness and to recoil from the calls of normative – both analytic and critical – theorists to come up with an alternative. I will not come up with a full-blown alternative here, but I will make some suggestions about how we can think about identity and inclusion.

There are a number of things to take into consideration here. The first is that there is no going back on radical contingency. It is there, and we cannot do away with it. But recall also that radical contingency in no way means that everything is open, or that identities are completely plastic. We are always dealing with a partly sedimented representational space, for instance that of British multiculturalism. Representations draw on and come up against this reality (which is not an extra-representational reality, but one that is constituted at the level of representation). Some representations are more sedimented than others, and some identities are represented as fixed – for instance, as natural – when in fact they are not. The task is then to intervene analytically and politically to 'undo' this fixity and show how things may be otherwise. But this intervention is necessarily limited by existing representations and by the structures of power in the space of representation in question. Radical contingency is the starting point, and it is then a question of how to negotiate this.

The second thing to keep in mind is that post-structuralists often do talk explicitly in normative terms. This is certainly the case with Derrida, Laclau and Mouffe as it is with Judith Butler, Joan Scott, Christoph Menke, Jacques Rancière and others that I draw on in this book. However, there are two reasons why post-structuralists are not often seen, even by their own kind, to be engaged in normative political theorising. First, the language and the concepts post-structuralists use are different from the ones that dominate analytic political theory and critical theory (see Chin and Thomassen 2016). Second, post-structuralists never engage in the construction of a full-blown normative theory à la Rawls's *A Theory of Justice* (1971). That is not because justice is not important to them, but because, from their perspective, justice cannot be analysed in the way that Rawls and others do, but only as discourses or representations of justice. Representations of justice and of primary goods and so on can be analysed and criticised, but only by showing the tensions and exclusionary effects of those representations. And they can be opposed only from the perspective of other representations. Again we could say that radical contingency is what distinguishes the post-structuralist approach.

To give an indication of how we might think about identity, inclusion and the relationship between them, I turn to Britishness again. The question is how we can think of identity and inclusion in the context of Britishness and in a way that accepts radical contingency. There is going to be some closure and some exclusion. Britishness may be radically contingent, but it is going to mean something rather than nothing and anything. Above I have argued that we need to think of identity and inclusion in terms of the politics of representation – that is, as struggles over the way Britishness is represented. The question 'what is Britishness?' is then really a matter of 'how is Britishness represented?' and 'how should it be represented?' There are going to be different and competing answers to those questions, but I will argue for a position where the question 'what is Britishness?' is part of the definition and representation of Britishness. One could argue that, since Britishness is radically contingent, this question will invariably be part of Britishness, even if suppressed. That is true, but my argument is that we should make it an explicit part of the Britishness we strive for.

Lest it be misunderstood, this is not a call for greater vagueness or for a more abstract notion of Britishness in order to make it more inclusive. Nor am I claiming that the question 'what is Britishness?' expresses the essence of Britishness; at most it is a sort of strategic essence (Fuss 1989). Nor is it a neutral definition of Britishness, a definition that is open to any other definition of it, or a meta-level from which to debate different definitions of Britishness. In the final analysis, what distinguishes this representation of Britishness, and what integrates the differences within it, is only the question 'what is Britishness?', but that does make a difference. Any representation of Britishness – also one that makes the question 'what is Britishness?' as central to it – already assumes some answer to that question, something taken as given, however provisionally: there is a claim that '*this* is Britishness'. Making 'what is Britishness?' part of a Britishness to be strived for is a particular representation of Britishness – one partisan definition among others. There is a tension then: closure coexists with differences within Britishness, differences that are also differences over how Britishness should be represented.

To show that this is not only a matter of public debates where agents discuss the answer to the question 'what is Britishness?', consider citizenship education and citizenship tests.[9] These were part of New Labour's broader discourse on Britishness, and they are explicitly linked to the creation of a British identity in Brown's speeches and writings. For instance, in a 'Speech on managed migration and earned citizenship', Brown (2008) stated that, together with policies to deal with illegal immigration, the policies of managed migration 'amount to a fundamental statement about what we expect of those who aspire to British citizenship and how we intend to strengthen the idea of what it means to be British'.[10] Similarly in the reports and the materials accompanying the test, for instance in *The Path to Citizenship*: 'Across Government we are introducing reform to strengthen our shared values and citizenship. The purpose of this paper is to set out how reform of a newcomer's path to citizenship or permanent residence can contribute to this agenda' (Home Office 2009c: 6).[11] The legal institution of citizenship is part of the push for a British identity. The new legislation was meant to represent the significance of belonging to the United Kingdom: to reflect this *and* to make it significant.

The new policies encouraged immigrants to apply for citizenship and, in this way, to become British. Compared with other countries, the process is relatively simple and citizenship relatively easy to obtain – it is relatively inclusive, we might say. At the same time, the new policies increase the difference (in rights) between citizens and non-citizens, and so between British and non-British.[12] Everybody can become a British citizen and take part in Britishness, but citizenship (and the test and the ceremony) is also meant to clearly distinguish who is British from who is not. The naturalisation rules and the citizenship test are meant to make citizenship both more inclusive (because relatively straightforward) and more exclusive (because widening the differences between citizens and non-citizens).

The citizenship test provides us with a hard case because a test is supposed to test who is, and who is not, British – who belongs to a collective and legally instituted identity and who does not, who is included and who is excluded. When introduced, the test consisted of twenty-four unseen multiple-choice questions, and it was accompanied by two small guide books for applicants to prepare for the test. In addition, there was an English language requirement as well as requirements related to residency and criminal record.[13] The test was meant to demonstrate whether the applicant had 'sufficient knowledge' about life in the United Kingdom to become a British citizen (Home Office 2003: 3). A test, and particularly a multiple-choice one like the British citizenship test, assumes that you can answer correctly or wrongly, leaving no room for the applicant to question its content.

The citizenship rules and the test have undergone changes over the years, and immigration rules have been tightened. In the laws and materials, we find two views of citizenship.[14] One is a civic republican conception of citizenship with the emphasis on active participation in communities. This conception of citizenship emphasises disagreements and the imperfect character of British institutions; this is the view associated with Bernard Crick and the 1998 'Crick Report' on citizenship education in schools (Qualifications and Curriculum Authority 1998: ch. 2; Crick 2002; critically, see Pykett 2007). The view is reflected in the writing of some of the materials accompanying the citizenship tests. For instance, in the introduction to the first chapter of *Life in the United Kingdom*: 'Any account of British history is . . . an interpretation. No one person would agree with another what to put in, what to leave out, and how to say it' (Home Office 2004: 17; see also Home Office 2007: 7). The other view of citizenship is of the citizen as a well-behaved, but passive subject who respects the law of the land and goes about his or her own business. This is a liberal view of citizenship as instrumental for both the individual and the state, and it is found in the 2007 edition of *Life in the United Kingdom*, that is after the 2005 bombings in London.[15] Looking at the materials over time, the first view of citizenship gradually makes way for the second view. Two different views of citizenship, two different view of Britishness.

Any notion of citizenship, legally instituted or not, will have to distinguish between who is and who is not a citizen – in short, it will have to negotiate a line between inclusion and exclusion. That line may be expressed in the form of a citizenship test, which will in turn have to rely on some distinction between correct and wrong answers where some agent is able to decide how and where that distinction should be drawn. This is even more so in the case of a multiple-choice test like the British one where there is no room for registering disagreement over what Britishness is, and what it means to be British. At most, disagreement can feed into the making of the test in the form of active, direct or indirect participation in the making of the laws, although this will be restricted to persons who are already citizens, and it assumes a particular conception of citizenship.

In response to these shortcomings of the citizenship tests, Patricia White (2008: 229) has suggested that, instead of the current citizenship test, immigrants applying for citizenship should go through a teaching programme similar to that of citizenship education for school pupils where there is more emphasis on participation, values and critical engagement. What might be the content of a citizenship course like this, with or without a test at the end? Consider the Crick Report, which formed the basis for the introduction of citizenship education in schools. The report articulates the need for citizenship studies as a response to 'worrying levels of apathy, ignorance and cynicism about public life' (Qualifications and Curriculum Authority 1998: 8). In effect, this is a response to the kind of view of citizenship and democracy that one finds reflected in the 2007 edition of *Life in the United Kingdom*. Although the report does not mention Britishness explicitly, it refers to the need 'to find or restore a sense of common citizenship, including a national identity that is secure enough to find a place for the plurality of nations, cultures, ethnic identities and religions long found in the United Kingdom' (1998: 8, 17). Teaching citizenship should not only be the teaching of knowledge, but should teach the pupils the skills to become active and critical citizens in a society characterised by difference and disagreement, according to the report (1998: 7–8, 13, 37, 56–9).[16] These are exactly the kind of skills needed for a conception of Britishness centred on the question 'what is Britishness?'

This view of citizenship is further expressed in the *Diversity & Citizenship* report that reviewed citizenship education in 2007. The report proposes a new strand of citizenship education focused on diversity and identity, and it takes identities as representational rather than essential or natural. As a consequence, pupils must 'develop critical literacy . . . which allows them to reflect on their own cultural traditions and those of others' (Department for Education and Skills 2007: 24). This applies not just to minority identities, but also to 'Britishness': 'The term "British" means different things to different people' (2007: 8), and the report emphasises that the dominant identities and norms must also be subject to critical reflection. That critical reflection is supposed to help pupils question their inherited identities while also developing a new sense of shared belonging. This is reflected in the question the report makes central to the teaching of identity and diversity: 'who do we think we are?' (2007: 13, 98–100). 'Who do we think we are?', or 'what does it mean to be British?': although there is a reference to a 'we', that 'we' remains in question all the same. Here we have an example of how the question 'what is Britishness?' might be institutionalised as part of a discourse on Britishness that would take a different approach to citizenship, citizenship tests and education.

Including the question 'what is Britishness?' in our representation of Britishness can be a way of bringing out the contingent and representational character of Britishness – in short, the transformative character of the politics of Britishness. We do not escape the problem of having to take as given some idea of what British and Britishness mean, at least not if we want to judge who can, and who cannot, become a British citizen. More generally, there is no Britishness if it is not distinguished from what it is not, however abstract and minimal is our definition of Britishness. There will inevitably be exclusion. This is no less so if we make the question 'what is Britishness?' central to our definition of Britishness. While in question, this definition of Britishness also involves an assertion of what Britishness is, and that it is this rather than that. Although a paradoxical undertaking, this should not keep us from trying to institutionalise the contingent and representational character of Britishness. The point can be generalised: including the question 'what is . . .?' in the representation of an identity is a way to put into motion a certain self-deconstruction of that representation and that identity (Derrida 2006a; Thomassen 2007b: 123–32). Bringing radical contingency to the fore helps open up the space for hegemonic struggles over Britishness or any other identity as struggles over representations, and thereby it opens the space for rethinking inclusion and exclusion.

Britishness is just one example of identity and inclusion and how they interact. It is an important one for the representational space of British multiculturalism and the cases examined in the chapters that follow. Here I have presented the general theoretical framework that informs the analysis and discussion of those cases. Drawing on Derrida and, in particular, Laclau, I have argued for the starting point that there is no inclusion without exclusion, that inclusion and exclusion are intrinsically linked to identity, and that, since identities are constituted at the level of representation, we need to analyse identity and inclusion in terms of the politics of representation. The key terms here are inclusion and exclusion, identity, representation and hegemony. The aim of the chapters that follow is to show the contingency of identities and how inclusion and exclusion is negotiated through the representation of identities. This will serve to show the contingency of identities and representations – among them, Britishness – and of the discursive terrain within which representations vie for hegemony. And that in turn makes it possible to think of identity and inclusion in terms of a politics of representation.

Notes

1. Brown's representation of Britishness is part of a long history of representations of Britain and Britishness; see Ward 2004. For critical assessments of Britishness and Brown, see Lee 2007; Sales 2012.
2. On this and what follows, see Laclau and Mouffe 1985: ch. 3; Laclau 1996a: ch. 3; Laclau 2000: 281–307; Laclau 2005: ch. 4.
3. I would add that, in any given discourse, there is usually more than one signifier working as an empty signifier and organising the structure of the discourse. For instance, one could think of Brown's Britishness discourse as organised around several more or less empty signifiers such as 'Britishness', 'liberty', 'fairness', and so on. Rather than finding *the* signifier functioning as the empty signifier within a discourse, it is then a matter of analysing the relative emptiness (or nodal-ness) of different signifiers within a discourse. I try to do this in Chapter 4.

4. With its constative and performative dimensions, the concept of (re) invention would be another way to think about rearticulation and representation (Derrida 2008a: 6, 39, 45–6).
5. I will address this in Chapter 4. See also Norval 2004; Thomassen 2005.
6. For a different – deconstructive – view of stereotypes, see Rosello 1998.
7. On the danger of essentialising representation as some 'always already', or truth, see Fuss 1989: 15–18.
8. Many of these are discussed in Laclau's later works, for instance Laclau 2014.
9. For full details of the different routes to naturalisation, see Nationality, Immigration and Asylum Act 2002 (Part 1); and Borders, Citizenship and Immigration Act 2009 (Part 2). For a critical assessment of the citizenship test, see Brooks 2012.
10. Brown 2008 adds in the same place that the managed migration policy 'reflects the value we place on British citizenship and the urgent need to be clear about our collective national identity and common purpose'.
11. For similar statements, see Home Office 2002: ch. 2; Brown and Straw 2007: Foreword, ch. 4; Goldsmith 2008: 9–12, 115–21; UK Ministry of Justice 2009: Foreword, ch. 1, pp. 52–4.
12. This was also the view of the government, see Goldsmith 2008: 77–9.
13. Various materials accompany the test: Home Office 2004; Home Office 2008; Home Office 2009a; Home Office 2009b. The most important, and interesting of these is the first: *Life in the United Kingdom*. A second edition was published in 2007 and a third edition in 2014. As my focus is on Britishness under New Labour, I focus on the first two editions. The third edition does contain some significant revisions, but nothing that changes the conclusions reached here.
14. See White 2008. The differences are most notable in chapters 1–4 in the 2004 and 2007 editions of *Life in the United Kingdom*.
15. Another difference between the two editions of *Life in the United Kingdom* is that the emphasis on tolerance disappears from the 2007 edition.
16. This is not to neglect the problematic aspects of the report, including the lack of attention to institutional racism.

2   Subjects of Equality

Mandla, race and equality

In July 1978, Gurinder Singh Mandla's father wanted to enrol him
in Park Grove School, a private school in Birmingham. According
to the school uniform policy boys must wear a cap, and they had
to cut their hair so that it did not touch the collar. As 'an orthodox
Sikh . . . who therefore wore long hair under a turban' (*Mandla*
HL 1983; for an introduction, see Poulter 1998: 301–5), Gurinder
Singh Mandla was told by the headmaster, A. G. Dowell Lee, that
he could not attend the school. Was Mandla subject to discrimination and unequal treatment when the school of his choice refused to
accept him because he had long hair and wore a turban? This was
the issue in *Mandla v Dowell Lee* decided by the House of Lords in
1983. There was no question of direct discrimination: the school did
not have a rule stating that Sikhs were not allowed to attend. What
was alleged was indirect discrimination because the school's policy
was such that it would make it impossible for (orthodox) Sikhs to
comply with the school uniform policy and attend the school.

I begin the examination of equality and inclusion in 1978 and
with the *Mandla* case. There is nothing necessary about this starting point, but nor is it a coincidence. The *Mandla* decision is,
in many ways, representative of developments in the 1970s and
1980s, and I use it as a privileged discursive site through which to
explore equality and inclusion by looking at British race relations
legislation. This chapter examines what I will call a discursive
terrain that could be characterised in different ways according
to which discursive sites within it are emphasised: British race
relations legislation, British multiculturalism, liberalism, and so

on. The discursive terrain is characterised by these different discursive sites where different discourses compete over the meaning of key signifiers, such as 'British', 'liberalism', 'race' and 'multiculturalism'. The discourses compete on the discursive terrain, taking the latter as their ground, and the discursive terrain works as a horizon for the ways in which it seems possible to think and act.[1] However, the individual discourses also shape the nature of that terrain when successful. There is no self-evident discursive terrain of, for instance, multiculturalism; the terrain is itself being constantly rearticulated, sometimes to a lesser degree, sometimes to a greater degree; and the distinction between discursive terrain and discourse is never absolute. With a term from Laclau and Mouffe, we can say that the discursive terrain is also a field of discursivity in the sense that no discourse – and no discursive terrain – is ever completely fixed. Any discourse, and any discursive terrain, is always open to the possibility of rearticulation, even if this possibility may be more or less limited in any particular circumstances (Laclau and Mouffe 1985: 111).

The identification and individuation of discursive terrains and discourses is by no means straightforward. Terrains and discourses are identified through their differentiation from other terrains and discourses, but this is only possible through a decision by the researcher to delimit a terrain or a discourse in one way rather than another. Although terrains and discourses are always defined by their limits too, these limits are defined in a field of discursivity that continues to undermine any discursive closure. As Jacques Derrida (1988: 131) writes on how to delimit the context of a text: 'the determination, or even the redetermination, the simply recalling of a context is never a gesture that is neutral, innocent, transparent, disinterested'. My examination of equality as a concept and practice of inclusion thus inscribes itself upon a particular discursive terrain and set of discourses. That could not be otherwise, as discourses are all we have got, but this does not absolve us from reflecting critically on the decisions – because that is what they are – we make as researchers. In this book, I am interested in questions of inclusion and exclusion and identity politics, and I bring these questions to bear on a discursive terrain that could be characterised as British, liberal multiculturalism.

The discursive terrain that I will examine is one that emerges gradually from the late 1960s, where race, ethnicity and, finally, religion become key signifiers, and where multiculturalism is both taken as a discourse in its own right and part of the discursive terrain at once presupposed and called into question. It is a discursive terrain that has evolved over the years, where some discourses and signifiers have retreated (for example, 'race') and others have come to dominate (for example, 'religion' and 'Islam'). It is also a discursive terrain characterised by the ways in which, through legislation, equality was displaced into domains of employment, schooling, traffic rules, and so on. Cases often involved Sikhs, prior to *Mandla* for instance in the context of motorcycle helmets and hard hats for construction workers. *Mandla* is then one more case in a line of cases that became emblematic of the emergence of multiculturalism as an institutional discourse, and where Sikhs were considered to be good multicultural subjects unlike the unrulier subjects of Caribbeans, Rastafarians and, later, Muslims. This case law and these representations of different subjects form key parts of British multiculturalism.

At key sites such as law, courts and official politics, British multiculturalism is characterised by a conception of equality as equal opportunities that can best be described as liberal. My aim is not to challenge this particular liberal conception of equality and substitute it with another, although I start doing so in Chapter 5 in the context of charity and hospitality. But taking this conception of equality as my starting point and focus is not meant as an endorsement. All it does is to point to the fact that this conception of equality became progressively dominant and became enshrined in law, and, as we have already seen in the Introduction and shall see in subsequent chapters, it forms the background for later cases and debates. In this regard, it is also significant that, in *Mandla*, we are dealing with a middle-class family and a private school. Although not my focus here, this is not trivial, and it was part of what made it possible for Mandla to get support from the Commission for Racial Equality who used the case as a test case. It also means that the case was well placed to become paradigmatic of a conception of equality as equal opportunity so important to British multiculturalism in its liberal and institutional variant.

While some of the multicultural critique of legislation and policy, and of British culture and society, challenged specifically liberal norms and, so, liberal conceptions of equality, much of the debate between liberals and multiculturalists also took a broadly liberal conception of equality as given. This will become evident when, later in this chapter, I turn to the debate between Brian Barry and Bhikhu Parekh. This chapter then focuses on debates about and around liberal British multiculturalism.

Mandla is particularly useful for my purposes. It concerns a demand for inclusion through the assertion of equality: Gurinder Singh Mandla wants to go to Park Grove School, and he is making a claim for his Sikhness to be treated as equal to racial identities as stipulated by the recently introduced Race Relations Act 1976. His demand for inclusion is facilitated by equal opportunities legislation. Moreover, we are dealing with a struggle over identities – over what it means to be a Sikh, and over what categories such as race and ethnicity mean.

Gurinder Singh Mandla and his father had chosen this particular school. At the same time, the father 'wished his son to grow up as an orthodox Sikh' (Lord Fraser in *Mandla* HL 1983). The latter meant not cutting his hair and wearing a turban 'because the turban is regarded by Sikhs as a sign of their communal identity' (ibid.). Without the turban, you would not be a Sikh. In Sikhism, outward signs of belonging to this community are particularly important, and the five Ks (*kara*, *kesh*, *kanga*, *kirpan* and *kaccha*) are what make the Sikhs 'a separate community' (ibid.). The turban identifies and differentiates Sikhs, and we therefore have to consider their equality in the context of the tensions between identity and difference and between universality and particularity. The particularity appears to get in the way of universal equality before the law. The question is whether the particularity, or difference, is one that should be ignored or not, that is, whether equality is achieved through blindness to this difference, or whether this difference should be taken into consideration when treating like alike and different differently. As well as in many other academic and political debates, this is also the key issue in the Barry–Parekh debate.

When the school made clear that they could not accept Gurinder Singh Mandla as long as he was wearing a turban, his father sued the school for racial discrimination. The case was supported by the Commission for Racial Equality who used the case to test the limits of racial discrimination, in particular the definition of race in the Race Relations Act 1976. The school won in the County and Appeals Courts, but lost in the House of Lords. The House of Lords decision is important, above all because *Mandla* was the first time that Sikhs were considered a race and, as such, protected by the Act. The *Mandla* case not only concerns the limits of multiculturalism and the relationship between multiculturalism and liberalism. It also concerns the character of the 'cultures' (races, ethnicities, religions, and so on) whose multiplicity challenged the self-representations of liberal Britain.

The case essentially boiled down to two questions: what is 'race'? and, do Sikhs constitute a race? This is how the case connects the questions of inclusion and identity. As Lord Fraser states, writing for the majority:

> the main question in this appeal is whether Sikhs are a 'racial group' for the purposes of the Race Relations Act 1976. For reasons that will appear, the answer to this question depends on whether they are a group defined by reference to 'ethnic origins'. (Lord Fraser in *Mandla* HL 1983)

The issue is what practices and symbols are racial – for instance, the Sikh turban – and therefore protected under the anti-racial discrimination legislation. The judges in the County and Appeals Courts held that Sikhs are not a racial group and that, therefore, there could have been no racial discrimination. For instance, in the Court of Appeal, Justice Kerr concludes:

> Sikhs and Sikhism do not as such fall within the Race Relations Act 1976 at all, any more than members of the Church of England, Catholics, Muslims, Quakers, or Jehovah Witnesses, or any other groups which are only distinctive because they adhere to distinct religious, political or social beliefs or customs. (Justice Kerr quoted in Herman 2011: 144)

From the perspective of the lower courts, Mandla was treated equally; he was as free as anyone else to attend the school and comply with the school uniform policy. However, the Law Lords held that Sikhs do constitute a racial group, and they did so because they introduced a different understanding of race.

The Race Relations Act 1976 defines racial discrimination in the following way in Section 1, Part 1:

> A person discriminates against another in any circumstances relevant for the purposes of any provision of this Act if (a) on racial grounds he treats that other less favourably than he treats or would treat other persons or (b) he applies to that other a requirement or condition which he applies or would apply equally to persons not of the same racial group as that other but (i) which is such that the proportion of persons of the same racial group as that other who can comply with it is considerably smaller than the proportion of persons not of that racial group who can comply with it and (ii) which he cannot show to be justifiable irrespective of the colour, race, nationality or ethnic or national origins of the person to whom it is applied and (iii) which is to the detriment of that other because he cannot comply with it. (Race Relations Act 1976, as quoted by Lord Fraser in *Mandla* HL 1983)

What is important for the *Mandla* case is Part (b) on indirect discrimination, and the first matter of importance is the meaning of race. The latter is defined here as 'colour, race, nationality or ethnic or national origins', and Section 3, Part 1 specifies that '"racial group" means a group of persons defined by reference to colour, race, nationality or ethnic or national origins, and references to a person's racial group refer to any racial group into which he falls'.

The Law Lords assume that Sikhs are not a distinct race on the basis of 'colour, race, nationality or . . . national origins'. What remains is the category of 'ethnic origins', and whether Sikhs are a race or not therefore comes to depend on the definition of 'ethnic'. Lord Fraser takes ethnic not 'in a strict racial or biological sense'. He proposes a different kind of definition of ethnicity and race, namely the ways in which these terms are commonly used. The question therefore becomes whether a group see themselves, and are seen by others, as a racial or ethnic group – in short, whether the group is recognised and represented as a racial or an ethnic group. This is how Lord Fraser expresses the view that it is the recognition and representation of a group as ethnic that makes it an ethnic group: 'For a group to constitute an ethnic group in the sense of the 1976 Act, it must, in my opinion, regard itself, and be regarded by others, as a distinct community by virtue of certain characteristics' (Lord Fraser in *Mandla* HL 1983).[2] The meaning of equality is mediated by representations of identities and of categories such as 'race', and agents' recognition of those representations, and as a result, we must analyse equality through these discourses and representations.

Equality is representational in two senses. First, equality is constituted at the level of representation, or discourse. We only have discourses of equality, not equality as such. Later in this chapter, I shall propose that Laclau's theory of hegemony offers a way to think of how equality is articulated. Second, and more important for my present purposes, equality is articulated through particular representations of categories and identities. In the case of *Mandla*, the important categories are those of race and ethnicity and the important identity is that of Sikh. We therefore have to ask 'which equality?' and 'whose equality?' We must ask who gets to articulate and define, for instance, 'race' and 'Sikh'. Put differently, we must examine equality as a result of struggles over representations – in short, as a politics of representation.

This is what I propose to do in this chapter: to analyse the arguments of judges over what equality means in a concrete legal case, and to analyse a debate between two political theorists – Brian Barry and Bhikhu Parekh – over equality and identity politics. Treating equality as representational opens up possibilities for showing the contingency of particular images of the subject of equality.

The difficulty in *Mandla* was to identify those 'characteristics' that make a set of persons 'a distinct community'. As Lord Templeman notes in his concurring opinion, 'it is common ground that some definitions constitute the Sikhs [as] a relevant group of ethnic origin whereas other definitions would exclude them. The true construction of "ethnic origins" must be deducted from the 1976 Act' (Lord Templeman in *Mandla* HL 1983). This is what Lord Fraser does when he goes on to list two essential characteristics ('a long shared history' and 'a cultural tradition of its own') as well as additional relevant characteristics, such as a common geographical origin. Defining 'ethnic' in this way means defining it 'relatively widely' and giving the category 'a broad, cultural/historic sense'.

In *Mandla*, Lord Fraser concludes 'that Sikhs are a group defined by a reference to ethnic origins for the purpose of the 1976 Act, even though they are not biologically distinguishable from the other peoples living in the Punjab' (Lord Fraser in *Mandla* HL 1983). The rearticulation of ethnicity – and, thereby, of race – makes the categories of the ethnic and the racial more inclusive. It broadens the basis for claims about racial discrimination, and it means that more differences must be taken into account when deciding how to treat everybody equally. If non-discrimination and equal treatment mean treating like alike and different differently, and if Sikhs are different in a relevant way, then their equal treatment may depend on treating them differently, for instance through exemptions from part of the school uniform policy.

Equality is mediated by representational categories such as 'race' and 'Sikh', and, as a result, when 'race' is redefined, so is equality. The rearticulation of race is also important for another legal aspect of the Race Relations Act, namely the meaning of 'can' in 'can comply with'. This is important because we are dealing with the liberal conception of equality as equal opportunity, so here we are dealing with what it means to have an opportunity, but also with implicit images of the kind of subjects facing opportunities. Everybody should have the same – equal – opportunity to take advantage of a given set of opportunities, for instance when choosing a school. According to the law, individuals should not be disadvantaged from enjoying opportunities just because, as members of a particular racial group, they cannot comply with the norms of an institution. This was the issue in *Mandla*: did Mandla have the same opportunity to go to the school of his choice as non-Sikhs had? Racial identity should not get in the way of equality; what should decide if we are treated equally should be our status as human beings, citizens, residents, and so on. This does not exclude unequal treatment: it is legitimate to treat people differently on the basis of the choices they make (to be poor rather than rich, to be a vegetarian, and so on), as long as those choices are choices and are made from a set of opportunities that is identical for everyone. For instance, someone who insists on wearing a Star Trek costume may rightfully be turned away from a school whose school uniform policy does not allow for that kind of dress. This is assuming, of course, that Star Trek cannot be categorised as a race, ethnicity, religion, and so on, and the issue in *Mandla* was precisely whether Sikhism could be categorised as an ethnicity and, hence, as a race.

The problem is the indirect discrimination taking place when certain options are unavailable to a racial group because of its race. If race – including ethnicity – is 'inherited or unalterable', this appears straightforward. If your race is not something chosen, but given to you, and therefore not a matter of free choice, then 'can' may mean 'can physically', and compliance may then be said to be physically impossible (Lord Fraser in *Mandla* HL 1983). If race were understood in this way, Gurinder Singh Mandla could comply with the school uniform policy by cutting his hair and removing his turban. Growing one's hair and wearing a turban could be construed as a choice, the costs of which should be borne by the boy himself.

Lord Fraser and the majority of the Law Lords redefined race from 'a strict racial or biological sense' to what are commonly recognised as racial differences. Simplifying, we might say that he redefined race from biology to convention, and from nature to culture. Consequently, 'can' is redefined from '"can physically"' to '"can in practice" or "can consistently with the customs and cultural conditions of the racial group"'. Understood in this way, it no longer matters that growing one's hair and wearing a turban are possibilities physically and theoretically open to Sikhs in the same way as they are to everybody else. They are no longer seen as choices whose costs should be carried by a chooser. We can take Sikh ethnicity as a given, and it is possible to argue that a Sikh cannot comply with the school uniform policy *given that he is a Sikh*. This sort of practical necessity is reflected in the statement of Mandla's father that Mandla was 'an orthodox Sikh . . . who *therefore* wore long hair under a turban' ('Headnote' in

Mandla HL 1983, my emphasis). The case boiled down to the nature of this 'therefore'. If we take Sikh ethnicity as a given, then opportunities are relative to identity, here ethnic and racial identity, and equality *qua* equal opportunity is mediated by those identities, or representations of them, in which case we must ask 'what is a Sikh?' and 'what is ethnicity and race?' And those are just the kind of questions that open onto a political struggle of which and whose representations become the basis for law and public policy.

In this chapter, I will argue that equality is representational in the sense that it rests on representations – images, categories; both explicit and implicit – of the subject of equality. Equality will always be limited by exclusions and inequalities that simultaneously constitute it in one way or another. This is so because equality rests on representations of the kind of subject that can be counted as equal, yet the meaning of equality is inherently open to rearticulation. Indeed, we must analyse what judges, political theorists and others do with equality as a form of politics where they rearticulate the categories of equality and, thereby, what equality is. We can therefore think of the politics of equality as a politics of identity and representation along the lines of Ernesto Laclau's theory of hegemony.

Liberal egalitarianism and multiculturalism: Barry vs Parekh

A brief look at *Mandla* has suggested that, to appreciate the politics of equality, we must think of equality and the categories of, for instance, race as representational. I shall return to *Mandla* below, but I now want to show how treating equality as representational helps us make sense of a debate over multiculturalism between Brian Barry and Bhikhu Parekh (Barry 2001a; Barry 2001b; Barry 2002; Parekh 2002; Parekh 2006; Uberoi and Modood 2015). The aim is to show how equality rests on particular representations of the subject of equality; this is seen in the ways in which the authors think about the opportunities facing subjects. That was precisely the issue in *Mandla*: the question of what constitutes an opportunity was key to the definition of equality, and it was inherently connected to the rearticulation of the categories of race and ethnicity and of Sikh identity.

Debates around multiculturalism often pit liberals against multiculturalists. Often these debates are considered to be debates between universalism and particularism with multiculturalists arguing that the alleged universalism of liberalism is a false one, and that liberalism actually rests on a particular liberal, and cultural, image of what it means to be a person. Conversely, liberals believe that we must abstract from the particularities of culture to focus on equal respect for every person as a person, and not as carrier of this or that identity. This is what makes the debate between Barry and Parekh, as representatives of liberalism and multiculturalism, useful for my purposes: multiculturalists such as Parekh believe that the liberal self is just a particular representation of what it means to be a person, but both liberals and multiculturalists rely on some representation of the subject of equality.

The debate between liberals and multiculturalists can obviously not be reduced to the debate between Barry and Parekh, but there are good reasons for using their debate as exemplary of how equality was approached in debates between liberals and multiculturalists: Barry represents the kind of (early) Rawlsian egalitarian liberalism that has been, and remains, popular, and Parekh represents a sophisticated and practically oriented form of multiculturalism. Parekh is also arguably the most politically influential British multiculturalist, for instance through the Parekh Report, even if it was too radical for the then New Labour government (Commission on the Future of Multi-Ethnic Britain 2000). While liberalism and multiculturalism cannot be reduced to Barry's and Parekh's respective positions, the debate between them is representative of how the question of equality was approached within dominant discourses of, and on, multiculturalism, for instance around *Mandla*. Note, however, that we are dealing with a debate which is at once a debate between liberalism and multiculturalism and a debate within liberalism, more specifically British liberalism.

As we shall see, Barry (and other liberals) does not dismiss the importance of identities altogether, only when it comes to justice. Conversely, although mainstream liberals such as Barry saw Parekh's defence of multiculturalism as radical at the time, Parekh (and most multiculturalists) connects a case for the importance of particular identities with a case for universal equality. It is because we are culturally different that we must be treated differently in order to be treated as equals.

Moreover, in the case of Barry and Parekh we have a liberal egalitarian and a liberal egalitarian multiculturalist who both think about equality as equal opportunity. In this context, the central point of dispute is what it means to have an opportunity, and this is where their different conceptions of the person enter into the picture. They rely on different, and more or less explicit, representations of the subject of equality; in particular they differ over the role of culture in constituting the person and in defining opportunities. Thus I wish to extend the argument about *Mandla* to show that the debate over equality between liberalism and multiculturalism can be analysed as a clash between different representations of the categories on which their respective definitions of equality rest.

Although the discussion about opportunities may at first appear technical to those coming to debates in liberal political theory from a post-structuralist perspective, it will quickly become clear that the discussion goes to the heart of more typical post-structuralist concerns about identities and subjectivity. Conversely, bringing a post-structuralist perspective to bear on liberal analytic theory is a way to show how the latter relies on assumptions that may usefully be examined through a post-structuralist lens.

For Brian Barry, opportunities are objective. 'The critical distinction is between limits on the range of opportunities open to people and limits on the choices that they make from within a certain range of opportunities' (Barry 2001a: 37).[3] For two persons to have equal opportunities means that they face an identical set of choices, and justice requires that everybody face identical choice sets, whereas the choices that individuals make within that choice set are not a matter of justice. Importantly, for Barry, when it comes to justice, culture is irrelevant as culture; there is no place for culture in claims for justice and equality.

Barry uses the metaphor of a harbour to illustrate his view of opportunity. When the wind and the tide are favourable, sailors have the opportunity to enter and leave the harbour. This opportunity exists irrespective of whether they choose to take advantage of it or not; it is 'an objective state of affairs' (Barry 2001a: 37). The opportunity does not depend on the culture or religion of the sailors, for instance if their religion does not allow them to set sail after the fall of darkness on a Friday. The opportunity is not subject-dependent because it does not depend on the identity and preferences of the individual sailor; only their choice to take advantage, or not, of the opportunity depends on that. There is only one way in which the opportunities are subject-dependent and therefore not identical to all sailors, because the ability to take advantage of the opportunity to enter or leave the harbour 'might depend on [the] build and . . . rigging' of the ship (2001a: 37). That is, physical differences among ships may mean that some sailors do not in fact face the same set of choices as other sailors, just as physical disabilities and material inequalities may mean that some people do not have the same opportunities as others.

Culture is not in itself the basis for 'limits on the range of opportunities open to people' for Barry (2001a: 37). The opportunities faced by individuals – for instance, the sailors – are the same irrespective of cultural differences, hence why the opportunities are objective. Culture may put 'limits on the choices that they make from within a certain range of opportunities' (2001a: 37), but that is different from the limits that may exist on the opportunities that people face. The range of opportunities cannot be limited by culture, only the choices you make can be limited by your culture, and that is not a matter of justice.

For Barry, the costs of taking advantage of opportunities should be taken into consideration. For instance, the income distribution in a society may be such that only some sailors can afford to go in and out of the harbour at all times, while others must take work on land in order to make ends meet, and therefore cannot choose when to go sailing in search of opportunities. This inequality unjustly limits the opportunities of the latter group of sailors. A similar argument may be made about private schools. If we assume that private schools are better than state schools, then those who are forced to choose between sending their children to private school and feeding them properly have their opportunity sets unjustly limited. The sailors and parents with lesser means may theoretically face the same opportunities as others, but the costs they face in realising those opportunities must be factored in – the opportunities are cost-dependent. Importantly, however, for Barry (2002: 217), the costs that must be factored in are not 'culturally derived costs'. If the choice of a particular school comes at the price of compromising on one's culture, that cost is irrelevant for justice and for equal opportunities.

In the language of *Mandla*, we might say that, for Barry, opportunities must be more than physical or theoretical opportunities, they must be practically available. The objectivity of opportunities need not refer to something physical, but may simply refer to the objectivity of the social order as a brute fact. However, while the objectivity of opportunities is socially constituted in this way, it is not shaped by *culture*. We might ask, though, how costs are to be calculated if opportunities are cost-dependent. In order to decide that, we would need to know what costs a normal and reasonable person would bear, and so the subject of equality must conform to an image of a normal and reasonable person (Miller 2002: 51–2). To identify objective opportunities, we need an image of the person – a subject of equality.

It is important to stress that Barry is not saying that differences among individuals are irrelevant. Some differences matter, others do not. The challenge is to identify those differences that matter to *opportunities* and to distinguish them from those differences that matter only to the *choices* you make among the opportunities you face. Barry writes that ideally,

> the rules define a choice set, which is the same for everybody; within that choice set people pick a particular course of action by deciding what is best calculated to satisfy their underlying preferences for outcomes . . . If uniform rules create identical choice sets, then opportunities are equal. (Barry 2001a: 32)

You cannot blame culture for (perceived) limits on opportunities; you may blame culture for the choices you make, but that has no bearing on justice. Barry writes:

> If two people with the same opportunities make different choices, then as between them different outcomes are fair. . . . the main determinant of different opportunities is that people start out with different resources (personal and material) for which they are not responsible. (Barry 2002: 221)

The disadvantages that you 'start out with' are not the responsibility of the individual, and responsibility passes over to society to make sure that, irrespective of those disadvantages, people will face identical sets of opportunities. Those disadvantages are the kind of disadvantages resulting from the different make-ups of the ships in the harbour metaphor or from the socio-economic structure of society. The individual is responsible for his or her choices, but not for objective limitations to them. Everything comes down to establishing the distinction between what is objective and what is subjective.

Note that Barry is not saying that you can abstract individuals from their culture; what he does say is that you can abstract justice from culture. He is not saying that culture, as opposed to, for instance, disability, is a matter of choice and free will. As he writes:

> I explicitly reject the notion that either beliefs or preferences are in general a matter of choice. We can in many circumstances be held responsible for the choices we make from the available options, but choice does not go 'all the way down'. There's no such thing as free will. (Barry 2002: 215)[4]

Culture is not simply a matter of choice.

This is, then, Barry's image of the subject of equality: it is someone who is shaped by his or her culture and society in ways that are beyond his or her will. In this sense the subject of equality is not an atomistic and abstract individual. But, at the same time, there is an image of an individual rational chooser who, faced with a set of objective opportunities, makes a choice and is able to take responsibility for that choice. Barry (2001a: 32) does not want to make justice and equality relative to cultural identities, and justice requires the image of an individual who can make choices and be held responsible for them. Barry's position may be more complex than his critics admit, and more ambiguous than he himself would admit.

I labour Barry's take on equality because it is important to see the exact image of the subject of justice and equality behind it. This subject is not simply the atomistic and asocial individual that liberalism's communitarian and multiculturalist critics often allege. Liberalism's communitarian and multiculturalist critics hold that liberals subscribe to an unencumbered self (see Sandel 1998; Taylor 1994). The real issue may be less whether the individual is defined by his or her culture in ways beyond his or her choosing, and more whether this should matter for justice, that is, whether the existence of a multiplicity of cultures should matter for how we organise the basic institutions of society. At the same time, it is important to note that there is a particular image, or representation, of the subject of equality at the centre of Barry's theory of justice, and this image defines what equality (and justice) means.

In relation to *Mandla*, Barry is equivocal about the status of Mandla's identity (Barry 2001a: 61–2). Like Parekh, Barry concludes that the House of Lords decision was correct, even if he does not share Parekh's reasons for arriving at this conclusion. What interests me here is the rationalities that frame their conclusions. Whereas Parekh conceives of Mandla's identity as cultural and *therefore* relevant for justice, Barry's treatment of Sikhs in other places shows that he is keen to make certain exemptions for them, just not on the basis of their *cultural* difference. However, Barry adds another consideration, namely a notion of universal objective interests that are the same for all human beings. It is such a notion of objective interests that is doing the work here, making Barry able to argue that an exemption for Mandla would make him able to flourish as a person in a way that he would not in a lesser school (Mendus 2002: 40–1; Barry 2001a: 262–3, 285).[5] What really matters to Barry is social and economic equality.

There are at least two representations of the person in Barry: the rational chooser (whose choices may be partly defined by his or her culture, even if that culture is irrelevant for his or her opportunities) and the person as a bearer of universal objective interests. The two representations may be combined, but what matters here is that, when Barry thinks about equality, he has in mind a particular image of what it means to be a person. His theory of equality rests on a particular image of the subject of equality, and the particularity becomes more visible when compared with the image of the subject of equality in Parekh's work. What I suggest is that both Barry's universalist liberalism and Parekh's multiculturalist liberalism – both the universalist politics of redistribution and the multiculturalist politics of recognition (see Taylor 1994; Fraser and Honneth 2003; Tully 2000; Parekh 2004) – are based on particular representations of the subject of equality. The debate between them over what equality means can be understood as a dispute over what image of the person should underlie an egalitarian society. Their images of the subject of equality differ, and this leads to different views of what equality and justice demand.

For Bhikhu Parekh, opportunities are subject-dependent:

> Opportunity is a subject-dependent concept in the sense that a facility, a resource, or a course of action is only a mute and passive possibility and not an opportunity for an individual if she lacks the capacity, the cultural disposition or the necessary cultural knowledge to take advantage of it. A Sikh is in principle free to send his son to a school that bans turbans, but for all practical purposes it is closed to him. (Parekh 2006: 241)

Parekh's position is in line with Lord Fraser's opinion in *Mandla* in its move from theoretical ('mute and passive') to practical ability to take advantage of an opportunity. Opportunities are opportunities for an individual subject, not for an abstract human being, and the individual subject is a culturally defined subject.

Drawing on Oakeshott, Parekh thinks of cultures as traditions and takes these as his starting point, but not as fixed. For him, culture is important in a way that other differences are not. As human beings, we are also – always and already – cultural beings, and since culture is constitutive of who we are, so culture must be taken into account when making policy and law. 'Since human beings are culturally embedded, such concepts as equal respect for persons, equal opportunity and equality before the law need to be interpreted in a culturally sensitive manner' (Parekh 1997: 150). This is so in two ways.

First of all, as cultural beings, our culture defines who we are. Therefore equality involves both universalist policies of redistribution, where everybody is treated the same irrespective of their cultural identity, and a politics of recognition of cultural identities. The latter is needed because equal treatment means treating like alike and different differently: 'Equality involves not just rejection of irrelevant differences as is commonly agreed, but also full recognition of legitimate and relevant ones' (Parekh 2006: 240). If, as is the case in the UK, we live in a multicultural society, then policy and law must take notice of cultural differences; only then will culturally different people be treated equally and face equal opportunities.

In a case like *Mandla*, Parekh believes that the decision in the House of Lords was correct because we are dealing with someone who cannot comply with the school uniform policy because of his culture. Culture is a relevant difference that must be taken into account in order to treat people equally, and so Mandla can be given an exemption in the name of equality (Parekh 2006: 241, 347–8, 354–5).

Equality means 'equal treatment of those judged to be equal in relevant respects' (Parekh 2006: 242). However, the fact of multiculturalism means that there is a lack of agreement over what those 'relevant respects' are, and this is what Barry overlooks, according to Parekh. As Parekh writes, identifying relevant respects

> presupposes a broad agreement on what respects are relevant in a given context, what kind of response is appropriate to them, who are equal in respect to them, and what treatment counts as equal. The agreement is not easy to obtain even in a culturally homogeneous society; in multicultural societies it is exceedingly difficult. (Parekh 1997: 123)

The fact that we live in a multicultural society means that we must take cultural differences into account, which then raises the problem of identifying the relevant cultural differences – which is in turn particularly difficult to agree on given those very same differences. The differences amount to different images of what it means to be a person; only with a particular image of what it means to be a person is it possible to identify those differences that are relevant for equality. This is the second way in which culture must be taken into account.

Note that Parekh believes that our conceptions of what it means to be a person are culturally framed, that is, representational in the terms I have used here. This is unlike Barry. However, like Barry, and as I will show, Parekh also works with a particular image of the subject of equality and reifies this image.

What, then, is the nature of cultural differences for Parekh? Although opportunities can be individualised, opportunities are not, strictly speaking, relative to *individual* subjects. What makes opportunities different to different individuals is the fact that they are members of different cultural *groups*. It is their culture – as in their belonging to a cultural group – that limits their opportunities. We are thrown into culture(s), which are constitutive of who we are and not down to choice or preferences. Culture is constitutive of choices and preferences, and we can view culture as a matter of chance or luck. For Parekh, cultural differences are like physical differences, and he likens cultural differences to physical disability and a medical condition, which are down to chance as opposed to choice (Parekh 1997: 151, 135). For Barry, cultures are something that individuals have; for Parekh, cultures are something larger that individuals are part of.

Cultures are hybrid and change over time, and you can be a member of more than one culture at any one time. Still, for Parekh, cultures have an objectivity to them. There must be something to which I can point and say: 'I am bound by my culture, it's my culture that made me do it.' For me to make a claim that my culture limits my opportunities, and that I am not treated equally as a result of my cultural difference, my culture must be represented as a culture by myself and others, and it must be recognisable and recognised as a culture, and not just a preference for, say, Star Trek. And my culture must be taken as a given by myself and others and with certain norms about how to act and with limits that distinguish it from other cultures.

The difficulty is visible in *Mandla* where Sikhism must first be recognised as a race (in the House of Lords decision) or, beyond that, as a religion or culture (in Parekh's view). It must then be possible to identify norms and limits that define what it means to be a Sikh and what opportunities are open to a Sikh *as a Sikh*. Only then does it become possible to argue that, as a Sikh, one *therefore* has to wear a turban. It is the representation and recognition of a culture as a culture and with particular norms that establishes the connection between identity, practices and opportunities.

The distinction between objective and subjective opportunities is important for both Barry and Parekh. Opportunities are objective insofar as they do not depend on who you are, on your identity; in that case, everybody is treated equally when they are treated the same. For instance, if culture is irrelevant for equality and justice, then a school uniform policy will treat different cultural groups equally when the policy is the same for everyone irrespective of their cultural differences. Opportunities are subjective if they depend on who you are, on your capacities, cultural disposition and cultural knowledge, to use Parekh's terms. In that case, a uniform school uniform policy treats pupils unequally because only some of the pupils can take advantage of the opportunity, while others cannot do so, *given who they are*, that is, given their cultural identity. Exemptions and special rights are then ways of treating people differently in order to treat them equally.

Barry and Parekh disagree over how to draw the distinction between objective and subjective opportunities, not over the possibility of drawing it. Yet, we must ask how objective opportunities are established as objective, that is, how the distinction between objective and subjective is established. The distinction is drawn hand in hand with a particular image of the subject of equality; in Parekh's case, that is an image of the person as a bearer of a culture. For Parekh, opportunities are subjective or subject-dependent, but it is important to note two things. First, as argued above, opportunities are only relative to individual subjects as bearers of cultures. Opportunities are subject-dependent only to the extent that we take cultures as subjects writ large; they are strictly speaking culture-dependent, where cultures should be seen as objective states of affairs that are not, in this sense at least, to be distinguished from bodily or physical differences.

Second, Parekh makes a distinction between cultural practices and lifestyle choices. While culture is constitutive of who we are and not subject to individual choice, lifestyle choices should be seen as voluntaristic and so the costs of them must be borne by the individual. Culture defines opportunities and subjects; in the case of lifestyle choices there is an individual chooser prior to the choice (Kelly 2003: 99). For Parekh, persons are culturally saturated, and the subjects of equality must be viewed as bearers of recognisable cultures. However, this raises the problems – evident in *Mandla* in relation to Sikhism – of how cultures are individuated, and how culture is distinguished from what is not culture but, for instance, lifestyle.

Barry and Parekh disagree over where to draw the distinction between objective and subjective opportunities. For Barry, culture (as culture) is not relevant for thinking about equal opportunity; for Parekh, even if cultures are different, subjects are always defined by their culture, and equality is therefore mediated by culture. Although the dispute over objective and subjective opportunities may, to outsiders to the liberal analytic tradition, appear as a technical issue, it is highly political because it reflects different views of what kind of subjectivities can be considered relevant from the perspective of equality. Put differently, one can only be a subject of equality in relation to these identities and categories; inclusion through equality is only possible for subjects already subjectified as particular kinds of subjects. The politics of inclusion, equality, identity and representation are inherently entangled.

Both Barry and Parekh take something as given, namely a particular image of the person, and this is what defines what equality means. James Tully (2002) criticises Barry on this point. Barry, he says, takes rights and equality as given and as things that have to be discovered. A different way of looking at equality is to treat it as contingent and as the result of an open-ended process of articulation and rearticulation. Looked at in these terms, the House of Lords decision in *Mandla* is a new articulation of equality and of the subject of equality; from *Mandla* onwards, equal opportunity is mediated by the category of ethnicity in a way that it was not before. Likewise, we can think of the debate between Barry and Parekh, and more generally between liberals and multiculturalists, as attempts to rearticulate who can be counted as an equal, and establish a particular image of the person as hegemonic.

Looking at equality in this way is a way of putting the freedom of equality as equal opportunity to work in the concept of equality itself (Derrida 2005: 48–9). If equality means equal opportunity understood as the equal (negative and positive) freedom to take advantage of opportunities, and if we take those opportunities to be representational in the sense argued here, then we can think of equality as itself subject to freedom. That freedom is the contingency of the concept of equality and the freedom – however limited in particular situations – for agents to rearticulate the meaning of equality. We might want to rearticulate equality to make it more inclusive, or to include in a different way, whether including different constituencies at the expense of others or letting inclusion take a different form, if that is possible. Of course, others may seek to rearticulate equality in ways that will be more exclusionary.

In the remaining part of this chapter, I will unfold an approach to equality that can account for the ways in which equality is representational, and always entangled in inequality, and how equality is rearticulated. I draw on post-structuralist theory and on the work of Ernesto Laclau in particular. His theory of hegemony treats equality as discursive or representational and, therefore, contingent. It is also able to account for how any articulation of equality at once includes and excludes, and more generally it can account for how equality is rearticulated through hegemonic struggles over its meaning. What I shall put forward is not simply a different conception or theory of equality, but a way to account for differences between conceptions and theories of equality, for instance those between Barry and Parekh.

The subject of equality

The rest of this chapter unfolds an account of equality. This is not another theory of equality, of what it means to be an equal, but an account of how discourses of equality work, including those discourses we call theories of equality such as those of Barry and Parekh. For this account, I draw on Laclau and Mouffe's theory of hegemony whereby equality can be understood as the articulation of differences into a chain of equivalence. The theory of hegemony has three advantages. First, it can account for the representative character of equality so that we can understand the politics of equality as a struggle over representations of particular identities and a struggle over how to represent the subject of equality. This in turn makes it possible to connect equality and identity formation. Second, the theory of hegemony can make sense of the way in which the extension of equality is not only emancipatory but also binds the subjects of equality to particular representations and categories, as when, for instance, Sikhs become ethnic and racial subjects. Third, from the perspective of the theory of hegemony, the relationship between equality and freedom is not simply an external relationship of competition, but one marked by mutual imbrication as well as subversion. In order to arrive at the account of equality, I start, in this section, by identifying a central problem of equality, namely the way in which the subject of equality is bound by the representations of it, and how, as a consequence, equality is always bound up with inequality.

Consider *Mandla*: a Sikh claims that the Race Relations Act 1976 protects his son against discrimination on the basis of his ethnicity, thereby claiming that the ethnicity can be recognised and counted as a relevant difference by the law. Mandla and his father make their claim with a foot squarely inside existing discourses (including the law) and as those who are counted as equals in other respects. The result is that they can be counted as equals in a new way: now their Sikh ethnicity is relevant for their equal treatment by the school. We are dealing with neither a complete break with, nor a simple extension of, a norm; rather, the norm of equality is being rearticulated because race, ethnicity and Sikhism take on new meanings. In addition, Mandla and his father and other Sikhs may come to represent their identity in a new way as they draw upon this possibility given to them by the law to speak as ethnic and racial subjects. The claim for equality starts from existing representations – of Sikhism, of race, of equality, and so on – but the claims are not confined to these existing representations, and there are usually competing representations circulating at the same time and within the same discursive terrain.

Consider another example, that of the French revolutionary Olympe de Gouges (Scott 1996: ch. 2). De Gouges assumed herself to be equal with men. She made the claim in two ways. First, she made an analogy: if she 'has the right to mount the scaffold; she must equally have the right to mount the rostrum' (de Gouges quoted in Rancière 2006: 60; see also Rancière 2010: 57). If she can be held responsible for her actions, she must be counted as a responsible person – also when it comes to political rights. Second, she grafted her claim to equality on to an existing rights discourse circulating at the time, including the Declaration of the Rights of Man and Citizen. For instance, she took an existing conception of what it meant to be a responsible and rational person and used this in order to make her analogy between the scaffold and the rostrum, between criminal law and political rights. De Gouges speaks from a subject position – as a reasonable and responsible person – with which she could not previously be identified. The result is to disrupt the dominant norm of equality including its identification of 'human' as 'man'. We get a different idea of what it means to be human, and of what it means to be a rational and responsible person, a more abstract and, therefore, inclusive image of who can be counted as an equal human being. As in the case of *Mandla*, the categories on which equality rests – Sikhism, race, ethnicity; woman, man, human – are rearticulated through analogies and redescriptions.

De Gouges is faced with a version of Wollstonecraft's dilemma (Pateman 1990). If she represents herself through existing categories, her struggle for equality will be limited by those categories and by the hierarchical relationships between them. Her claim to equality can be recognised – she can be seen and heard – but only if she speaks and acts in accordance with those categories, for instance in accordance with the expectations of a rational person. If, on the contrary, she represents herself in a way that breaks with existing representations, the chances are that her claim will not be taken seriously and will not be recognised as a serious claim made by a rational person. Either way, her claim to equality is only possible in a way that simultaneously reproduces existing representations and hierarchies, for instance between 'man' and 'woman'.[6]

There is no equality without subjectivation, without a subject of equality. In order to be counted as a subject of equality, one must first be subjectivated as one. There are different ways of expressing this. Jacques Rancière writes of how a norm of equality is constituted on the basis of a particular representation of the subject of equality. The norm defines who can, and who cannot, be counted as an equal (Rancière 1995; Rancière 1999). You can only be counted as an equal if you are first represented and recognised as the kind of subject that fits the image of the subject of equality, as for instance when the law stipulates a definition of 'race' according to which discrimination can be identified. With a phrase from Christoph Menke (2006: 14), equality is 'description-relative', by which he means that any claim about equality contains an explicit or implicit description of those who are said to be equal and of the circumstances in which they are equal: 'the claim to consider everybody equally is always accompanied, not only in its realization but already in its formulation, by a determination and description of its addressees' (2006: 19).

This is precisely what we have seen in the discussion of the *Mandla* case and the Barry–Parekh debate: whether in law or in political theory, equality is articulated through particular images, or representations, of the subject of equality. Those images make certain claims possible (or easier) and other claims impossible (or more difficult). As there is no natural equality, it must be articulated, but the articulation of equality can only happen in a way that simultaneously limits equality. The representation of equality – above all the image of the subject of equality – opens up a space of equality *and* closes it off, and the former is not possible without the latter. As I shall argue in the following, the condition of possibility of equality is simultaneously its limit; put differently, equality is only possible as always already limited. There is no equality without exclusion. Equality is conditional, and those who are included as equals become bound by equality or, more precisely, bound to an identity, for instance when Sikhs had to cast their claims in terms of race and ethnicity rather than, say, culture and religion. Agents become bound to representations (of 'Sikh', for instance) that are recognisable by others and by the law.

Equality is constituted through a norm that defines who can be counted as an equal. Drawing on Todd May's reading of Rancière, it could be argued that equality creates a hierarchy between the state and passive subjects of equality. Passive equality, May (2008: 3) suggests, is 'the creation, preservation, or protection of equality by governmental institutions'.[7] The problem with passive equality is that it positions some subjects as passive recipients of equality. While I would add that passive equality does not necessarily emanate from the state, it is expressed in a norm that is taken as given and in relation to which subjects are then placed in order to be treated equally. This is what distributive justice does: 'distributive theories of justice seek some form of equality that is to be recognised, and on the basis of this argue for a redistribution of goods that will create, preserve, or protect that equality' (2008: 5).[8] With legislation against racial discrimination, for instance, subjects are empowered to make claims about equality and discrimination, but those are claims made to the state and on the basis of the law. Whether recognised or not, the claims assume a hierarchical relation between the subject and the state and law. Both liberal and multicultural discourses of rights and equality place the subjects counted as equals in a bind with the state.

I would like to add an important proviso to this, however. Different groups are differently positioned within society and vis-à-vis the state – think, for instance, of Sikhs and travellers and their very different legal, social and economic positions. Some groups are also considered more 'other' than others. This influences the control that groups, and group members, have over how they are represented, above all the extent to which they can control the ways in which their self-representations and their claims to equality are recognised and reproduced by others. This applies to those to whom equality is denied as well as those to whom it is extended. The former may, for instance, be a group unable to have its self-representation as 'racial' recognised by the legal system and by wider society. The latter may be a group, such as the Sikhs, that is included but on the condition that they represent themselves as a racial or ethnic group as opposed to, say, a religious group. This suggests that exclusion is not only a matter of either/or (as it is for some groups), but also a matter of more or less, of the relative marginalisation of some included subjects because of their difference from the norm of equality.[9]

This is the dilemma facing de Gouges and Wollstonecraft and many others: they can speak like a man (and be heard, but as a man), or speak like a woman (and risk not being heard, or being heard only as a woman, which may in the end amount to the same thing). In both cases, their claim to be counted as an equal reproduces existing normative hierarchies between the identities of 'man' and 'woman' (Minow 1991).

Barry's response to this dilemma is to articulate an abstract subject of equality: human beings who are endowed with the potential for freedom and rationality. The solution becomes to evacuate the law of those categories and determinations that result in equality being at odds with freedom. Parekh's response is to add culture and membership of a cultural community as a consideration because we are cultural beings as much as we are human beings. It is not that culture does not bind – it does – but, for Parekh, multiculturalism makes possible the combination of equality and freedom, and equality and difference, in such a way that one does not encroach upon the other. In another common contemporary response, Jürgen Habermas (1998) argues that there is no right balance between equality and freedom, and between equality and difference, except for one that is the outcome of the free, equal and rational deliberations of those who are subject to the law. Law binds, as do the categories underlying the law, but it need not colonise the freedom of the subjects as long as the law is the result of rational deliberations.[10] But, as is evident from Habermas's treatment of religion and the conditions he puts on religious discourse in politics, the deliberations are biased in favour of a particular image of the rational and secular citizen (Thomassen 2006).

Articulating equality: equivalence, difference and inequality

Mandla and de Gouges make claims to be treated as equals. Their claims are grafted on to and repeat existing norms of equality, but also alter those norms, or in de Gouges's case seek to alter them. The rearticulation involves both repetition and alteration.[11] Their claims are also claims that are simultaneously descriptive and normative. They claim that something is the case ('we are equals!'), a fact simply waiting to be recognised, but they also claim that something ought to be the case ('you ought to recognise us as equals!'). Thus, their claims combine a constative and a performative dimension. The process of rearticulation has an irreducible performative dimension to it; it is (also) an act of naming someone as an equal and naming the norm of equality (Laclau 2005: 101–3, 230–1; Butler and Laclau 2004). To say that the claim is an act of naming is to say that it does not simply reflect an already existing fact of equality, but also constitutes what it names. Thus, the performative claim to equality constitutes two things at once: a norm of equality according to which someone counts as equal, and the identity of those who are said to be equal.

It is not a pure performative of naming though, and this is so for two reasons. First of all, the performative act does not take place in a vacuum, but in a context where signifiers are already invested with particular meanings, and where some signifiers carry more force than others.[12] Second, and related to this, in order for a claim to equality to have any force, it must be taken up by others. The claim must be recognised as a meaningful claim uttered by a more or less rational being. Some claims are more likely to be recognised than others, depending on their content and form and on who is making them. When de Gouges wrote her *Declaration of the Rights of Women and the Citizen* she most certainly had another and already widely recognised *Declaration* in mind, as did her audience. Likewise, when British Sikhs argued for a motorcycle crash helmet exemption, they drew upon existing images of Sikhs fighting for the UK in World War II. And once an exemption had been given in one area, it was easy to make analogies to other areas, for instance schools (Poulter 1998: ch. 8). The performative claim does not create equality out of the blue, but draws on existing meanings and identities – hence *re*articulation. For instance, *Mandla* could be read as the result of gradual rearticulations of 'race', 'ethnicity' and 'Sikhism' in legislation, case law and in the public sphere, where the dominant view of these categories gradually shifted.

These analogies are ways of making the performative appear like a constative, making the normative claim appear like a simple description of an obvious, if previously unrecognised, fact. Indeed, it is the confusion of the performative as a constative that gives it its force. From the perspective of the earlier use of signifiers such as 'equality' and 'person', their reappropriation may appear as a misappropriation. De Gouges's claim to equality no doubt seemed like a misappropriation of the rights of men. There is nothing 'proper' about equality because there is no essential meaning to equality, nothing inherent to equality, only inherited articulations of it. Consequently, there can be no essential limit to the reappropriation or rearticulation of equality (Butler 1995: 128). As a reappropriation that is also a rearticulation, any appropriation of a signifier is also a misappropriation if we by that mean that it changes the inherited meaning of the signifier. The fact that some rearticulations are more likely to succeed than others is a different matter, and the long and still unfinished history of women's struggles for equality show that rearticulations are not necessarily felicitous. De Gouges, for one, was sent to the guillotine. And equality is open to progressive as well as non-progressive articulations, for instance when conservative communities claim equality between their conservative community and the surrounding liberal society.

Laclau and Mouffe's theory of hegemony can account for the articulation of equality because it takes equality as performative, and therefore inherently open-ended, while at the same time also being able to account for the ways in which equality binds singular subjects to particular categories and subject positions. There is nothing natural about equality (or inequality), inclusion (or exclusion), difference or identities. They are all constituted at

the level of representation, or discourse, understood as a 'structured totality resulting from [an] articulatory practice' (Laclau
and Mouffe 1985: 105). What we need to do, then, is to analyse
the discursive constitution of equality and of inclusion and identities. The key terms here are hegemony, articulation, chain of
equivalence and empty signifier.

The first key term is that of articulation: 'we will call *articulation* any practice establishing a relation among elements such
that their identity is modified as a result of the articulatory
practice' (Laclau and Mouffe 1985: 105). This is how Laclau
and Mouffe conceived of hegemony: as articulation. As we saw
in Chapter 1, articulation refers to the dis- and rearticulation
of meaning in a discursive terrain where meanings – including
 the meaning of equality – are already partly sedimented. The
articulation is performative in that it is constitutive of what is
articulated. To understand equality as the result of articulations,
and to understand hegemony in terms of articulation, is therefore to understand equality in terms of hegemony.

The second key term is that of chain of equivalence, because
this is how we can understand the way in which equality is articulated. The background for Laclau and Mouffe's development of
the theory of hegemony in *Hegemony and Socialist Strategy* is
a view of modernity as, among other things, the emergence and
gradual extension of what they call the egalitarian imaginary
where the value of equality is progressively unleashed in different
areas of society (Laclau and Mouffe 1985: 152–9). New and old
differences are no longer taken as natural or as mere differences,
but are articulated as relations of subordination and oppression
and, importantly, as contingent and open to change. This happens in areas such as political rights, civil law, gender, class and
race. For instance, in the case of multiculturalism in the UK, new
and old differences (for example, race, ethnicity, religion) became
articulated as sites of inequality and discrimination through the
displacement of an egalitarian rights discourse. Those differences
are, then, no longer taken to be natural or trivial, depending on
the case in question, but are articulated as relations of subordination and oppression and as relations that are contingent and,

therefore, open to change.[13] Put differently, the logic of equivalence is extended to new areas and new relations. Those relations are politicised inasmuch as they are articulated as contingent, as changeable, and this is how the egalitarian imaginary is displaced to new fields. While the extension of equality through the logic of equivalence may appear unequivocally progressive, there is nothing necessary about its extension or about its progressive effects. It may well be used by conservatives to argue the equal status of different communities against the imposition of egalitarian measures by the state (1985: 168–9).

In an egalitarian discourse, the equivalence is represented through the so-called empty signifier (Laclau 1996a: ch. 3).[14] This signifier – for instance, 'man' or 'human' – can stand in for all the parts in the chain, so that the latter can see themselves as part of, for instance, 'British', 'man' or 'human'. In short, the parts in the chain can be seen, and can see themselves, as represented by the empty signifier. There is nothing natural or necessary about the ability of particular signifiers to function as empty signifiers or about their inclusive or exclusive character. 'Human' may act as an empty signifier for a chain including men and women, blacks and whites, but, in order to do so, it must be articulated in a particular way, as must 'man' and 'woman', 'black' and 'white'.[15] The chain of equivalence does not reflect a non-discursive equality, but establishes the egalitarian space within which particular subject positions can be represented as equal. In other words, the norm of equality and the subjects counted as equals are constituted at the level of representation, specifically through the chain of equivalence.

The parts of the chain of equivalence are split between an equivalential content (the way in which they are the same) and a differential content (differences that remain despite their similarities):

> Hence the ambiguity penetrating every relation of equivalence: two terms, to be equivalent, must be different – otherwise, there would be a simple identity. On the other hand, the equivalence exits only through the act of subverting the differential character of those terms. (Laclau and Mouffe 1985: 128)

The articulation of identities into a chain of equivalence does not erase all the differences among those identities: 'total equivalence never exists; every equivalence is penetrated by a constitutive precariousness' (Laclau and Mouffe 1985: 184). This is important to keep in mind in the context of equality because equality is a discourse meant to deal with differences, but not by simply erasing them. Any norm of equality is marked by both identity and difference. This is so when stressing identity or equivalence because the equality (*qua* equivalence) never turns into pure and simple identity; and it is so in discourses stressing difference because the differences are said to be equal in their differences. The upshot is that the particular relationship between equivalence and difference is a contingent one, and therefore everything comes down to the way it is articulated.

The empty signifier is also split between an equivalential and a differential content, and it is therefore always only tendentially empty. This has important implications for how the space of equality and inclusion – which is constituted through the representation of the equivalence – is also always limited. This can take different forms.

Consider first discourses that establish equality through an antagonistic frontier dividing those who are equal from a common enemy. The first may be 'the people' and the second the political and economic elite, and common to this kind of populist discourse is that it establishes equality through the drawing of a clear line of exclusion. This kind of discourse has been the subject of plenty of attention in Laclau's and Mouffe's works (see, especially, Laclau 2005), but it is less relevant for my purposes here, primarily because I am dealing with the mainly liberal and highly institutionalised discursive terrain of British multiculturalism.

While egalitarian populist discourses establish equality through a particular kind of exclusion, there is a kind of exclusion that is common to all egalitarian discourses. There will always be elements that cannot enter into the egalitarian space of the chain of equivalence – and thereby be counted as equals – because they are wholly at odds with the norm of equality. We are dealing here with elements that are at odds with the way in which equality is represented, that is, with the particular empty signifier representing the equivalence among those counted as equals. We could also say that they are elements at odds with the way in which the subject of equality is represented. An example is the exclusion of animals from being counted as equals according to a norm establishing the equivalence of human beings, and where human beings are defined in opposition to, or as different from, animals. Another example would be the exclusion of someone from 'the people' in a populist discourse because that person or group has historically been identified as part of the elite.[16] Thus, any egalitarian space will be limited because it must be represented and must be represented by a particular signifier – 'human beings', 'the people', 'man', and so forth. There is only a subject of discourse or representation.

There is another constitutive exclusion – or, better, relative marginalisation – that is common to all egalitarian discourses, and that results from the fact that the egalitarian space must be represented through a particular and only tendentially empty signifier. Here we are dealing with identities that have a place within the egalitarian space established through the chain of equivalence. The egalitarian space is defined not only by exclusions, as just explained, but also by an inequality internal to it, an inequality which is also a relative marginalisation of some identities. For instance, the signifier 'human' may define an inclusive egalitarian space where men and women, whites and blacks can all be counted as humans. Yet, the signifier 'human' is not entirely empty. Not only can certain subjects not be counted as equals (because they do not count as humans), but the signifier 'human' may also have connotations of manhood and whiteness. The result is not outright exclusion, but inequality and relative marginalisation where some subjects are more equal than others, because of how they are represented, and because of how the norm of equality is represented. That sort of inequality and marginalisation may take different forms, for example a discrepancy between formal and substantial equality. Or it may be that, as Parekh argues, allegedly difference-blind rules are not actually blind to differences, and not only that, but also that the very abstraction from differences may itself be prejudiced against certain cultural identities – in short, that difference-blind equality relies on a particular liberal image of the subject of equality.

The inequality arises from the fact that the egalitarian space must be hegemonically instituted – that is, it is only possible through a particular representation of the subject of equality. Not only does the egalitarian space (the chain of equivalence) have a limit, it is also structured as concentric circles around a defining image of the subject of equality. Inclusion through equality is not simply a matter of either/or, even if it may also be that for some subjects.

Thinking of equality in this way makes it clear how equality cannot be dissociated from identity or, to be precise, from representations of identities, both the representations of particular identities to be included and the image of the subject of equality. Identity is not simply opposed to difference, however. While there is clearly a tension between the two – and, in many instances, also a direct opposition – equality is not a discourse that simply erases or excludes difference, but one that establishes equivalences among differences, while excluding others (Laclau in Butler and Laclau 2004: 331).

This is important for the dilemma identified above. Claims to equality – such as those by de Gouges and Mandla – are claims to sameness: women are like men in relevant respects because both men and women are humans and have reason, and so on. Yet, as Joan Scott points out, the claim also reproduces women's difference at the very moment when claiming it to be irrelevant to equal rights: 'If Woman is not specified, she is excluded; her inclusion requires that her difference from Man be acknowledged in order to be rendered irrelevant from the point of view of political rights' (Scott 1996: 42). As long as 'woman' is not mentioned, the assumption is that 'human' equals 'man'; but once 'woman' is mentioned, she is included as 'woman' in a chain together with 'man'. 'Woman' therefore retains her difference from both 'man' and 'human', all the while the identification of 'human' with 'man' remains operative, if also hidden. The norm of the equality of humans remains based on an image of man, while women continue to struggle with their difference from that norm.

Likewise with Sikhs and racial discrimination legislation. The Race Relations Acts introduced a number of categories – race, ethnicity, and so on – and the question is then to what extent particular identities can be recognised through those categories. In some cases, identities are included through a particular category, as was the case with Sikhs and the category of ethnicity in *Mandla*. However, even here we must ask whether those included through the category of ethnicity, to take that example, are included in the same way and to the same degree. When formulating the Race Relations Act 1976, the legislators had in mind Jews as an example of an ethnic group which was not, in their view, a racial group in the strict physical and biological sense. In that case, one must ask to what extent is the legislation, and the court decisions, shaped by taking Jews as the exemplary ethnic identity? And are Sikhs an ethnic group in the same way as Jews? (Herman 2011: 142–9). A subject of equality defined by ethnicity understood on the basis of a representation of Jewishness is going to be more or less biased against subjects that do not completely fit the bill. But here we must remind ourselves that *any* egalitarian space – any norm or subject of equality – will be limited because it will be defined by a particular representation of the subject of equality.

Gays and lesbians today face the same dilemma in relation to marriage: should they claim the same rights to marriage as straight couples (because they are the same kind of relationship), thereby reproducing a heteronormative institution? Or should they insist on their difference vis-à-vis those norms, thereby reproducing the relationship between norm and difference? Both are strategies of equality, and both *also* reproduce inequality.[17]

Importantly, the image of the subject of equality does not remain intact – it is rearticulated, however slightly, through (recognised) claims to equality. The dilemma of equality and difference, and the way in which both horns of the dilemma reproduce inequality, remains operative: whether claiming sameness or difference, the claim to equality is made in a discursive terrain already marked by inequalities that appear as given. Those inequalities – and the norm of equality, and the existing identities – are never simply given, but ultimately contingent and open to rearticulation. There is nothing automatic about this, though. Just as the very possibility of making a claim to equality, and having it recognised as such, instantiates a rearticulation of the norm of equality, so the claim to equality may not even be recognised as a claim, let alone a claim to equality, because the subject making the claim is excluded from the egalitarian space to such an extent that the claim cannot even be registered. This is what de Gouges experienced when making her claim, ending her life on the scaffold.

In the case of a rearticulation of equality that extends the chain of equivalence to include new constituencies, or to include already included ones in new ways, the extension does not leave the norm of equality intact. It is not left intact because it is not a universal norm that has merely been misapplied; it is a norm that is constituted on the basis of what is included and what is excluded from it. This is why conservatives are opposed to gay marriage: although they might be happy to see the norm of marriage gain ground, it is now no longer *their* norm of marriage.

To see how the rearticulation of equality might proceed, take the example of the equal rights of men and women. If equal rights are extended to women, the norm for what kind of person – and for who can count as a person – must change. Previously the norm may have been constituted on the basis of the exclusion of women as insufficiently rational. This may change in one of two ways, or a combination thereof: by reproducing the difference but abstracting from it (irrespective of their rationality, all humans are equal), or by negating the difference (women are rational beings like men). In the first instance, the definition of the subject of equality changes (we move from 'rational human' to 'human'); in the second instance, the identity of the included changes (women are now no longer represented as irrational). In order to extend the equivalence, what previously counted as a defining difference must be rendered irrelevant from the perspective of the norm of equality.

Consider now the *Mandla* case and British anti-discrimination legislation. The House of Lords decision rearticulated the meaning of ethnicity in such a way as to make it more inclusive. Since ethnicity is one part of what constitutes race for the purposes of the Race Relations Act 1976, the Lords decision effectively rearticulated the meaning of race. The meaning of race was rearticulated in such a way that more differences may be counted as racial.

Specifically, Sikhism was now a racial identity for the purposes of the Act, and racial discrimination could now be identified in relation to a new identity (Sikhism). The inclusion of Sikhs happened by likening Sikhs to Jews (as equally ethnic) and likening ethnicity to race.

In *Mandla*, equivalence is articulated in two interconnected ways. It happens through the rearticulation of the categories at the basis of the anti-discrimination legislation (ethnicity, race, equality). With the rearticulation of 'race', more identities can count as racial and be included within this category; this changes what identities are represented as includable. At the same time, equality is rearticulated through analogies. An identity is added to the chain of equivalence because it is 'like' identities already included in the chain; this is what happens, for instance, when Jews are taken to be the exemplary ethnic identity, and Sikhs are taken to be ethnic in a way similar to Jews.[18] This changes the image of race or ethnicity.

Just as 'black' has traditionally been taken as exemplary of what it means to have a race, so Jews and Sikhs have been seen as not sufficiently racial but as obviously ethnic and more than 'just' religious. And Muslims have been seen as not sufficiently racial or ethnic, but as obviously religious. The categories of race, ethnicity, religion, and so on, are articulated through analogies and exemplars. The opposite is also the case: a particular identity is articulated when it is associated with a category, for instance when Sikhs are taken to exemplify the category of ethnicity as opposed to, say, the category of race (in a narrower sense) or religion. The norm of equality is rearticulated, but so are the identities of those who can claim racial discrimination. After *Mandla*, when someone claims a racial identity, this identity need not be a matter of physical differences; to claim a racial identity for yourself or for others now means something different. And, after *Mandla*, Sikhs could claim racial discrimination, but not religious discrimination, and this limited the effectiveness of certain self-representations of Sikhism (as religious) with regard to equality.

The articulatory practice of equivalence is further evident in what happened to anti-racial discrimination after *Mandla*. Lord Fraser's test of ethnicity was subsequently taken to authoritatively and unambiguously establish the meaning of ethnicity, yet when it came to concrete cases, the test was not straightforward. In cases involving Rastafarians, courts applied Lord Fraser's test from *Mandla*, but in most cases found that Rastafarians did not constitute an ethnic group and so were not covered by the Race Relations Act 1976. In most cases, the judges accepted the *Mandla* definition of ethnicity and race, but did not find that Rastafarians were sufficiently ethnically and racially different (Poulter 1998: 351–4). Both the interpretation of ethnicity and the interpretation of Rastafarianism were in dispute, and Rastafarians could have been included in two ways. They could have been included by interpreting 'ethnicity' in a more abstract and inclusive fashion; here the emphasis is on rearticulating the categories that form the basis for equality. Or they could be included by interpreting Rastafarianism in a way more in line with Lord Fraser's definition of ethnicity; here the emphasis is on rearticulating what it means to be a Rastafarian in order to conform to existing categories.

Another possibility would be to add religion to race as a relevant difference to be taken into consideration in the context of equality and discrimination. Assuming that Rastafarianism could count as a religion, this would make possible a claim to equality without having to fashion Rastafarianism as an ethnicity or a race. This is the route taken by Muslims who were not protected (as Muslims) by the Race Relations Act 1976 because they could not count as an ethnic, national or racial group even under Lord Fraser's revised definition of ethnicity. Muslims were faced with a definition of ethnicity and race so sedimented that the only way to achieve the kind of equality afforded to ethnic, national and racial groups was to argue that discrimination on the basis of religion is like – that is, equivalent to – discrimination on the basis of ethnicity, nationality and race. The argument rests on the possibility of doing two things at once: distinguishing religion from race (if they were not distinct, there would be no need to add religion as a category), and arguing that religion is equivalent to race in relevant respects. Race and religion become two different ways of being identified as equal (in relevant respects), but two different instances of the same, namely discrimination or equal treatment.[19]

Conclusion

The theory of hegemony serves to explain debates about equality, whether academic debates, such as that between Barry and Parekh, or debates in law, such as the one in *Mandla* or in British race relations legislation. Hegemony also serves as an explanation of how equality is constituted: through the creation of a chain of equivalence, where the equivalence is represented through an empty signifier or an image of the subject of equality. Equality is representational in the sense that it is constituted through representation: representations of the norm of equality, of the subject of equality and of the identities who are taken to be equal. That, in turn, means that equality and identity, and equality and difference, are intrinsically linked, and that there will always be a tension between identity and difference. The upshot is that there is no equality without exclusion and inequality.

The politics of equality consists in the dis- and rearticulation of chains of equivalences – of what, and who, can count as equals. That struggle over equality is situated at the tension between identity and difference, articulating differences as relations of oppression, for instance. The politics of equality is also a politics of representation: a struggle in the terrain of representation (understood as the terrain in which equality and identities are constituted), and a struggle over representations, whether the representation of the norm and subject of equality, or the representations of particular identities. As equality is always limited – the limit to equality is simultaneously what makes it possible – we might speak of an economy of exclusion and inequality. We must not simply ask: equality or inequality? Inclusion or exclusion? But rather: which equality and which inequality? Which inclusion and which exclusion? It would be an an-economical economy though. It is only possible to choose the lesser exclusion and the lesser inequality from within a discourse of equality, from the perspective of a norm of equality. As Derrida writes of violence and non-violence, 'every philosophy of nonviolence can only choose the lesser violence within an economy of violence' (Derrida 1978: 313 n.21; see also 1978: 117; Menke 2006: 65, 84). What we are left with are struggles over how to negotiate inclusion and exclusion, equality and inequality, where the former part of the pairs is constituted through the latter part. And here there can be no guarantees that rearticulations will be progressive.

I suggest a radical democratic approach to equality. Following Laclau and Mouffe, I take radical democracy to be a radicalisation of the democratic imaginary and, specifically, the values of equality and freedom. To quote Laclau and Mouffe:

> a left alternative can *only* consist of the construction of a different system of equivalents . . . the alternative of the Left should consist of locating itself fully in the field of the democratic revolution and expanding the chains of equivalents between the different struggles against oppression. (Laclau and Mouffe 1985: 176)

There are two things I would like to stress here. First, it is possible to conceive of the articulation of equality and freedom in ever new ways and new spheres once one has moved away from a conception of human nature where equality and freedom are connected to a human essence and have a determinate meaning. We can then think of equality on the model of what Laclau and Mouffe (1985: 167) call 'a radical and plural democracy', as 'the struggle for a maximum autonomization of spheres on the basis of the generalization of the equivalential-egalitarian logic'. It is then a matter of articulating differences as relations of equality or inequality, and of articulating new representations of equality, the subject of equality and particular identities. For instance, 'the production of *another* individual, an individual who is no longer constructed out of the matrix of possessive individualism' (1985: 184).

The second thing worth stressing here is the relationship between equality and freedom. With Laclau and Mouffe, we can think of this relationship as one of an ineradicable tension where equality and freedom are not simply opposed. In a discussion of democracy, Derrida (2005: 48) opposes equality to freedom: 'equality tends to introduce measure and calculation (and thus conditionality) whereas freedom is by essence unconditional, indivisible, heterogeneous to calculation and to measure'. This is a widespread view of equality and freedom and their mutual relationship. However, he then goes on to argue that freedom and equality are not simply opposed, but stand in an internal relationship, at least when it comes to the democratic value of equal freedom:

> equality is not always an opposing or rival term *beside*, *facing*, or *around* freedom, like a calculable measure (according to number or according to *logos*) beside, facing, or around incommensurable, incalculable, and universal freedom. Not at all. As soon as everyone (or anyone . . .) is equally . . . free, equality becomes an integral part of freedom and is thus no longer calculable. (Derrida 2005: 48–9)

Not only are freedom and equality not merely opposed, but equality is not simply measurable and calculable, not simply homogenising. Likewise, freedom is not simply immeasurable and incalculable. The reason is that equality (as equal *freedom*) cannot be reduced to a given norm or measure of equality; and freedom (as *equal* freedom) requires some measure of who is counted as equally free. As a norm determining who can be counted as an equal, equality enters into freedom; and freedom – resisting all attempts at determining singularities – enters into equality.

This idea of equal freedom as a self-limiting concept and practice is particularly relevant for the concept of equality as equal opportunity. We can think of the latter in terms of equal freedom: those who count as equals enjoy equal freedom understood as the negative or positive opportunity to realise that freedom, for instance the freedom to live as one thinks a Sikh ought to live. The equality rests on a certain measure (norm, representation, and so on) of the kind of person who can take advantage of the freedom; in short, it is conditional. At the same time, affirming the freedom of equal freedom unconditionally extends that freedom to the norm of equality, thus opening the possibility of challenging it.

Thinking of the relationship between equality and freedom in this way opens the possibility of articulating them in different ways. The aim is not to overcome the tension between them, or to overcome the subjectivation involved in both equality and freedom (which I have identified with the help of Rancière, Menke, and Laclau and Mouffe above). Rather, the aim is to open the possibility of thinking the equality–freedom relationship in ever different ways. It is because the relationship between, and the meaning of equality and freedom are contingent that it is possible to articulate them in ways different to the dominant and liberal articulation of them as equal opportunity.

The view of equality defended here is opposed to three alternative views of equality (Menke 2006: 175). First, equality is realisable neither here and now nor in any future; and it is not an ideal to strive for or to use as a critical yardstick, because there is no ideal or concept of equality that is not perspectival. Equality is to-come, with a phrase from Derrida (2005: 86). What we have are particular negotiations of equality and inequality, inclusion and exclusion. There is no equality without inequality, marginalisation and exclusion. This is the aporetic character of equality: its condition of possibility (namely, inequality) is simultaneously its limit; inequality both makes possible and limits equality. Yet, and although we will never have equality without inequality, inclusion without exclusion, there is no reason why we should accept one negotiation of equality and inequality over another.

Although equality is neither an essence nor an objective yardstick, it can nonetheless be effective. Accordingly, the approach to equality defended here also breaks with Marxist accounts of equal rights as merely epiphenomenal and as a distortion of an unequal reality, where the illusion of equality reproduces the reality of inequality. Discourses on equality – even liberal discourses of formal and legal equality – cannot be reduced to a more real reality, whether a reality of natural (in)equality or underlying structures of society.

Finally, this view of equality also challenges the liberal attempt – for instance, in Barry and Parekh – to calculate just those limits between freedom and equality, and between objective and subjective opportunities, that will guarantee both freedom and equality and, thereby, equal opportunity. When theorists and practitioners of equality believe they have struck the right balance between freedom and equality, their mistake is not to have drawn their distinctions in the wrong place, but to believe that it is possible to get them right.

This does not amount to another definition of equality, but to something less and something more. Less because it does not amount to a theory of equality, only to an account of how equality is constituted. More because it amounts to a claim about how any definition or theory of equality is constituted.

Notes

1. While not the subject of this book, the discursive terrain, and the discourses and discursive sites characterising it, can be examined through a genealogical enquiry in order to see how we have come to think the way we think, and how certain signifiers became hegemonic.
2. In his concurring opinion, Lord Templeman concludes that 'the Sikhs remain a group of persons forming a community *recognisable* by ethnic origins within the meaning of the 1976 Act'. Lord Templeman in *Mandla* HL 1983, my emphasis. Representations of identities – whether other- or self-representations – only have effect if recognised. I explore this relationship between recognition and representation in the next chapter.
3. For critiques, see Mendus 2002; Miller 2002.
4. See also Barry 2001a: 36. Here I am not interested in whether Barry can square this with the image of a chooser facing a choice set.
5. Here there are clear parallels with the early Rawls 1971.
6. Having said that, I shall argue below that the dilemma is not so clear-cut if the claim making is marked by what Derrida calls iterability – if, in short, claims to equality always also rearticulate, even as they also reproduce, existing norms and representations.
7. Here I am not interested in whether this is a correct interpretation of Rancière. See Chambers 2012.
8. As I shall argue in the next chapter, something similar can be said about recognition, which also binds subjects to particular identities and representations.
9. For the sake of simplicity, I am speaking here of groups and members of groups, and I put to one side the differences that exist within groups, including differences over how to represent the group and the identity. I return to this in the next chapter.
10. Here there is a clear divide between, on the one side, Habermas and, on the other side, Foucault and Rancière. For Foucault and Rancière, equality and freedom always come together with inequality and unfreedom. See, for example, Rancière 1999: ch. 3.

11. One could describe this in terms of Derrida's (1988) notion of iterability where the rearticulation, or signification, proceeds as a combination of repetition and alteration.
12. Following Derrida and Butler, we might think of this as 'sedimented iterability' (Butler 1995: 134).
13. Laclau and Mouffe (1985: 153–4) distinguish subordination ('in which an agent is subjected to the decisions of another') from oppression ('those relations of subordination which have transformed themselves into sites of antagonisms'). Relations of subordination can also become relations of domination when judged to be illegitimate from the perspective of an external agent. I prefer the terms difference and inequality. The term subordination already assumes too much about the agents and decisions, and therefore it seems to me better to start from differences or relations, which may already be articulated as, for instance, subordination. I want to stress though that *all* relations are articulated in one way or another – that is, part of a meaningful social practice – as difference, relations, subordination, oppression, domination, and so on. What interests me is how, in the discursive terrain of British multiculturalism, some differences become articulated as relations of inequality and discrimination, while others do not.
14. For Laclau, the equivalence goes hand in hand with the construction of an antagonistic frontier dividing the chain of equivalence from a common enemy. However, in the case of equality I believe that aspect is less important, if important at all. On the notion and role of antagonism in the theory of hegemony, see Thomassen 2005.
15. By putting quotation marks around 'man', and so on, I do not mean to suggest that there is a natural man who is sometimes articulated as 'man'. The quotation marks are only meant to make clear that we are dealing with articulations, and they should not be taken to suggest a distinction between articulated meanings and non-articulated meanings.
16. Strictly speaking we need to distinguish between two different forms of exclusion here, both resulting from the fact that the empty signifier is not really empty but only tendentially empty, which in turn means that the chain of equivalence is necessarily limited. There is, first, the exclusion of those elements that are represented as at odds with the empty signifier. This is an antagonistic exclusion. Second, there are elements that do not even enter into the representational space of the egalitarian discourse and are therefore heterogeneous to it (Laclau 2005: ch. 5; Thomassen 2005). In both cases, there is

nothing natural or intrinsic about the identities of the excluded that prevents their inclusion into the chain of equivalence.

17. On this dilemma of equality and difference, see Butler and Laclau 2004; Minow 1991; Scott 1996.

18. In *Mandla*, this happens in a subtle way when Lord Fraser quotes the New Zealand case *King-Ansell v Police*. This case concerned a Jew and established Jews as an ethnic group for the purposes of New Zealand anti-discrimination legislation. From *King-Ansell*, Fraser takes his definition of ethnicity as social rather than physical or biological, and, in doing so, he assumes that Sikhs are an ethnic group in the same way as Jews (Herman 2011: 142–9).

19. See the Equality Act 2010, which also replaced existing anti-discrimination legislation.

3   (Not) Just a Piece of Cloth: Recognition and Representation

Begum and the politics of recognition

On 3 September 2002, the first day of the school year, Shabina Begum showed up at her school, Denbigh High School in Luton, dressed in a jilbab, a version of the hijab which, when combined with a headscarf, covers the whole body except the face, hands and feet. Since the jilbab did not conform to the school uniform policy, she was sent home to change. A two-year stand-off followed during which Shabina Begum was not allowed to attend school in the jilbab, and during which she refused to attend school without it. In 2004, her case came before the High Court which ruled against her (*Begum* HC 2004). The following year, the Court of Appeal overturned the ruling (*Begum* CA 2005), but in 2006 the House of Lords reversed that decision (*Begum* HL 2006).[1] The case concerned schooling, one of the central discursive sites for debates about the character of multicultural Britain and about what it means to be a Muslim. The case is also the most commented upon among British legal cases involving the hijab, both in the media and in the academic literature.

Begum is useful for interrogating the concept and practice of recognition in a way that escapes the opposition, and restrictive choice, of liberalism and communitarianism, of individual and collective identity. As in the case of the discussion of equality in the previous chapter, the discussion of *Begum* allows me to interrogate and challenge conceptions of identity and inclusion that cut across distinctions traditional to political theory.

Although it could have been articulated that way, the case did not pit liberals against communitarians and multiculturalists. Neither the school nor Shabina Begum argued for the distinctions that one finds in liberalism and in much of constitutional and human rights law between private and public, and between belief and practice. Both parties stressed the importance of recognising religious identities within the public sphere; we are firmly in the terrain of British multiculturalism where culture is taken to be important and relevant for public institutions. For Shabina Begum, the jilbab is a public manifestation of her religious identity: 'The jilbab', she wrote in an online chat, 'represents Islam as way of life rather than Islam as a few personal rituals and actions. It is a public expression of Islam as a way of life or ideology' (Begum 2005a). Here we have someone who, given her religious beliefs, cannot privatise her beliefs, whether by leaving them at home, at the school gates or in her heart and mind. The school's response was not to insist on the distinctions between private and public and between belief and practice. Instead the case concerned the specific identities that should be recognised in the school uniform policy, and this boiled down to the difference between the jilbab and a shalwar kameeze. The latter was one version of the school uniform designed to accommodate Muslim, Hindu and Sikh female pupils, but it covers less of the arms and legs than the jilbab. Together with a shirt and skirt version, the school had included the shalwar kameeze as an option within the school uniform after consultation with local mosques. Shabina Begum insisted that her minority view of Islam – which she had arrived at after study of Islamic texts and scholars – should also be publicly recognised; if not, it would amount to discrimination.

In the United Kingdom, multiculturalism emerged in the context of racial discrimination and race relations legislation. Only later did 'culture' come to the fore as a marker of identity and difference, and more recently 'culture' is often displaced by 'religion'. That does not mean that race and culture have disappeared; indeed, the terms are often conflated so that, for instance, religion is racialised. Recognition is only one vocabulary and conceptual lens through which multiculturalist concerns have been articulated.

In North America and Australasia, the vocabulary of recognition is used in connection with (non-white) immigrants and cultural diversity as well as indigenous groups, and in Canada also in the context of national identity. In the United Kingdom, the vocabulary of recognition has been restricted to the context of immigrants (but see Kenny 2012), and the debates around recognition echo the concerns of multiculturalists such as Bhikhu Parekh. Although the conceptual vocabulary is different, the recognition literature makes many of the same assumptions, for instance regarding the cultural embeddedness of individuals.

Although Shabina Begum articulated the case as one of 'the West' vs 'Islam' after winning in the Court of Appeal (Begum quoted in Aslam 2005; Begum 2005b), the case could not be reduced to this opposition between 'the West' and 'Islam'. The nature of Islam and its role in British society were central to the case, but rather than for or against Islam, the parties disagreed over which, and whose, Islam should be recognised in the school uniform policy. The case pitted a mainstream Islam against a minority Islam, and both the school and Shabina Begum claimed to speak for Islam. In this way, the case also draws attention to the relationship between recognition and representation.

When probing the practice and concept of recognition through the *Begum* case, I argue that it is necessary to look at the relationship between recognition and representation for three reasons. First, both recognition and representation bring into being what is simultaneously being recognised or represented. They share a structure whereby they proceed in two modes at once: a constative mode (reflecting already existing identities) and a performative mode (constituting what is recognised or represented). This structure has paradoxical and destabilising implications, which I exemplify with the *Begum* case. Second, I will argue that the politics of recognition is also a politics of representation in the sense that it always involves questions such as: which representations are recognised? Whose representations are they? For instance, in the context of *Begum*, the all-important question is which and whose representation of Islam is recognised as authoritative. Third, the reverse is also true: the politics of representation also involves recognition because representatives and representations must be recognised as representative, or authoritative, in order to gain authority. We can examine recognition as representation, and there is no recognition without representation, and vice versa. To understand the politics of recognition, we must conceive of it as a politics of representation. Shabina Begum's struggle for recognition is a struggle over which and whose representation of Islam shall be recognised, and it is a struggle to have her representations of Islam recognised as authoritative. There are clear continuities with the analysis of equality in the previous chapter: like equality, recognition is inherently connected with representation, and like equality, recognition is inherently ambiguous because we are at once emancipated and bound by equality and recognition.

What is more, I shall also argue that the politics of recognition should be understood as a politics of identity where identities are constituted and renegotiated through recognition, through demands for recognition and claims to recognise. As such, we should reject the view of recognition as identity politics where already constituted identities are recognised in public policy. This also has consequences for how we perceive of recognition as a practice and concept of inclusion. If the politics of recognition is to be understood as a politics of representation where identities are constantly renegotiated, then not only will there always be an element of exclusion involved (because recognition will be based on some representations rather than others), but the line between inclusion and exclusion will be constantly renegotiated. In *Begum*, the identities in question are Islam above all, but also multicultural Britain as concretised in the identity of Shabina Begum's school and, in turn, expressed through the school uniform policy.

My discussion of recognition is organised around the *Begum* case. While also drawing on the representations in the media and by the judges, I organise the analysis of the material around the school's and Shabina Begum's representations of themselves, each other and Islam.[2] This necessarily entails an element of simplification of the case, but this is balanced by attention to the paradoxes within their discourses. The aim is not to resolve the paradoxes, which are precisely constitutive of – that is, inherent to – the politics of recognition and representation. In this, I am analysing the case deconstructively in the style of what Joan Scott (1996: 16–8, 174) calls 'reading for paradox'. The aim is not to resolve the paradoxes, or to argue for a non-paradoxical alternative. I take the paradoxes to be like aporias in Derrida's (1993) sense: we can work through, but not resolve them. Normatively, the purpose is neither to decide the *Begum* case (who is right: the school or Shabina Begum?) nor to judge the correctness of the representations made by the different agents (does Islam require women to wear a shalwar kameeze or a jilbab?). Nor is the aim to argue for or against recognition as such. Instead the aim is to analyse and deconstruct the discourses of recognition – in this case the discourses of the agents in the *Begum* case – in order to better explain what is going on.

Reading for paradox may give rise to a different attitude to the concept and practice of recognition as well as a different approach to inclusion, identity and representation. If anything, the normative upshot is that, by showing the paradoxes of practices of recognition, we can challenge the assumptions as well as the representations involved in the politics of recognition in order to show what they foreclose and in order to open up new political possibilities. Thus, my sympathies are with attempts to challenge existing, and especially dominant, representations by showing their contingency, and I am critical of both the school and Shabina Begum to the extent they try to naturalise their respective representations of Islam. Put differently, I am critical of attempts to present recognition as identity politics where identities are taken as given. Instead I try to bring out the representational – that is, contingent – character of recognition, and to show that we are dealing with a politics of identity where identities are renegotiated through recognition as a means of inclusion.

The case for recognition

In the following, my focus is on theories of recognition as they pertain to identity politics, although I believe that many of the conclusions apply more generally to other kinds of recognition theories.[3] I focus on Anna Elisabetta Galeotti and Charles Taylor who have been making the case for recognition in the European and Canadian context respectively (Galeotti 2002; Taylor 1994).[4] Like communitarians, recognition theorists start from the premise that individuals are defined by identities that are collectively anchored. Although liberals often represent theorists of recognition as breaking with liberalism, Galeotti's and Taylor's own self-understandings are that they are taking liberal equality to its logical conclusion. Like Bhikhu Parekh, they believe that we are beings with particular identities of such importance that their non- or misrecognition affects our status as equal human beings.

Making the case for recognition, Galeotti argues that recognition is the logical extension of liberal toleration, and it is in the name of equal respect and inclusion into citizenship that she argues for the importance of public recognition. For Galeotti, the move to recognition is necessitated by the emergence of new kinds of cases that traditional liberal toleration cannot adequately address, for instance the French headscarf debates, same-sex marriage and racism. Equal respect and inclusion, Galeotti argues, cannot be secured by liberal tolerance and rights alone, among other things because of the public/private distinction in liberalism. Some differences and identities cannot easily be 'privatised'; this is the case with Islam, for instance. In political terms, many Muslims do not make a clear distinction between religion and politics, and in the *Begum* case we find an example of the importance of public manifestation of religious (Muslim) identity. Here we have someone who, given her religious beliefs, cannot privatise her beliefs. It is someone who cannot just leave her clothes at home, someone for whom her beliefs are 'public' and entail a practice, namely wearing a specific dress.

Furthermore, for Galeotti, the public is not really difference free. She illustrates this with the headscarf case from Creil in France (Galeotti 2002: ch. 4). There it was argued that religious identities have no place in state schools because they undermine the neutrality and cohesion of that public space. However, Galeotti argues that this overlooks the ability of the majority to define the norm in accordance with its own identity thereby making the latter invisible as a difference. The majority identity is not marked as a difference, but other identities are marked as different from the majority identity, and in this way they are 'othered'. Difference is defined by its distance to a norm and thereby problematised, while the norm remains unproblematised (Minow 1991). For instance, in the *Begum* case, only Shabina Begum's minority difference, and not the mainstream Muslim identity, is problematised.

For Galeotti, the solution to the marginalisation of minority differences is public recognition so that the otherwise marginalised identities get a place within the public spaces of society, and so that the norm is modified to include those marginalised groups. Liberal toleration understood as difference blindness – in the style of Brian Barry, for example – would leave intact and reproduce existing norms and inequalities. Only through public recognition of their group identities can individuals belonging to these groups become full members of society and take full advantage of their citizenship on a par with the majority (Galeotti 2002: 6, 11–12). Importantly, what is recognised is group identity. This is so because discrimination and marginalisation occurs on the basis of group identities that are either invisible (non-recognition) or represented in a negative light (misrecognition). Individuals belonging to those groups are discriminated and marginalised because they are taken by the rest of society as belonging to those groups, and because they are not themselves in control of the value ascribed to their identity (2002: 67).

Here we find a key tension in the practice and concept of recognition. On the one hand, public recognition is supposed to secure equal respect and inclusion for individuals so that they become full citizens and can exercise their freedom. On the other hand, they will achieve this recognition as members of groups whose identity and limits are relatively fixed, and which are further entrenched through the process of recognition. Recognition becomes recognition of already recognised and determined identities. They must first identify with these group identities, which are determined at least in part by the state and the majority population, that is, by others. They must be Muslims, gays, and so on, and be recognised as such, before they can be included and enjoy equal liberty as individuals. This is similar to what I argued in the previous chapter in the context of equality: you can only be counted as an equal if you have already been subjectivated in ways whereby you can be recognised as a potential subject of equality. The same applies to equality, or redistribution, and recognition: emancipation is only possible in a way whereby the extension of equality or recognition at once contributes to, and takes away from it. In the context of recognition, the emancipation from ascribed negative group identities happens in a way that simultaneously binds the individuals to those very group identities, even if these are no longer negatively valued. Moreover, the recognised groups are bound to the state through a relation of dependency (García Düttmann 2000; Markell 2003; Brown 1995: chs 3, 5; Povinelli 1998). Recognition is torn between emancipating and binding agents, including them and positioning them in a hierarchical relationship of dependence. This is one of the two central tensions or paradoxical structures of recognition that I want to investigate through a reading of the *Begum* case.

For Charles Taylor, the politics of recognition involves two kinds of politics. There are, first, policies aimed at cultural survival, aimed at the creation of future bearers of the culture or identity in question. His example here is language politics in Quebec (Taylor 1994: 58–9). Second, there are multiculturalist policies of equal worth, for instance, in the context of education and the teaching of a canon. Here one should, according to Taylor (1994: 64–73), presume that cultures have equal worth at the beginning of a dialogue aimed at a fusion of horizons that also changes our own standards.[5] The *Begum* case would fall into this second category of the politics of recognition.

Making his case for recognition, Taylor (1994: 26) writes: 'Due recognition is not just a courtesy we owe people. It is a vital human need.' In the case of political recognition, the state or representatives of society recognise the value of the identity of a group through symbolic or institutional measures. The objects of the politics of recognition are group identities, and Taylor's examples of group identities are mainly established and large-scale cultures, for instance Quebecois linguistic culture (see, for instance, Taylor 1994: 66, 72). Taking group identities as the basic units of public recognition obviously raises the liberal objection that it is a threat to individuals and minorities. In the *Begum* case, this is an issue because the school recognises a mainstream representation of Islam, whereas Shabina Begum belongs to a minority at odds with mainstream Islam. Where *Begum* differs from most other cases concerning minorities within minorities is that the minority within the minority (Shabina Begum) is more conservative than the majority.

Withholding due public recognition would result in harm for two reasons, according to Taylor. The first reason is authenticity. The claim is that subjects have an inner truth, one that only they have access to and can express. Thus, it is a matter of self-realisation, of living out one's authentic and true self. Shabina Begum, for instance, says that, by studying her religion, she has learned what kind of Muslim she is (*Begum* HC 2004: §67). Her clothes become a public manifestation of this, and she wants to be recognised as this kind of Muslim by others and to be included as such within the school community. The second reason why, for Taylor, recognition is important is that identity is 'dialogical'. We acquire the language for our self-representations through interaction with others: 'We define our identity always in dialogue with, sometimes in struggle against, the things our significant others want to see in us' (Taylor 1994: 32–3). Similarly in *Begum* where Shabina Begum finds out what sort of Muslim she is through study of Islamic texts and scholars. Taylor concludes, linking the two arguments for the importance of recognition:

> Thus my discovering my own identity doesn't mean that I work it out in isolation, but that I negotiate it through dialogue, partly overt, partly internal, with others. That is why development of an ideal of inwardly generated identity gives a new importance to recognition. My own identity crucially depends on my dialogical relations with others. (Taylor 1994: 34)

There is a tension here around the constitution of identity, a tension between discovery and dialogical creation (Markell 2003: ch. 2). My true identity is there for me to discover, but at the same time identity is purportedly created through dialogue with others. I can discover my true identity, which is 'proper' to me, but to the extent that this happens through a dialogue with others, it undermines the idea of an identity that is proper to me because it places the source of my identity outside me in the dialogue. The tension is reflected in the *Begum* case. Shabina Begum discovers what she believes to be her true identity, but she does so through interaction with others, primarily through others' representations of Islam, the Koran and what it means to be a Muslim woman. In addition, while her claim for public recognition of her identity is based on the authenticity of her beliefs, it is precisely a claim for *public* recognition. The assumption is that an identity cannot stand alone, as it were, but relies on the recognition by others – in short, that dialogue and interaction are constitutive of one's identity and of a sense of self-worth. However, this invariably undermines the claim to inward authenticity, to an identity that must be recognised by others but precedes their recognition of the identity.

There are then two tensions inherent to the practice of recognition. Identities are at once prior to recognition (waiting to be recognised by others) and a result of recognition. Identities are at once taken as given, as the ground for the politics of recognition, and performatively constituted through recognition. By implication, and this is the second tension, inclusion and equality through recognition come at a price – the price of being attached to (collective) identities, or representations of them. You can only be recognised as this or that (kind of Muslim, for instance), you can only be recognised as long as you are already recognised and represented (by others, by yourself) as this or that. Galeotti and Taylor and their likes miss these two tensions, and, in this chapter, I want to examine recognition as a practice of inclusion through the lens of these tensions as constitutive of recognition.

Recognition and representation

In order to analyse the concept and practice of recognition, I draw on Alexander García Düttmann's (2000) and Patchen Markell's (2003) deconstruction of recognition. Here I shall only highlight some of the points they bring to bear on the concept of recognition; these are points that I will develop through the analysis of the *Begum* case.

Both García Düttmann and Markell draw attention to the fact that recognition proceeds in two modes, a constative and a performative. Recognition involves a claim to recognise an authentic and already constituted identity. Recognition that is true to the identity in question consists in the congruence between that identity and the act of recognition. As such, recognition proceeds in the register of cognition and knowledge, which García Düttmann and Markell express as 're-cognition'. García Düttmann adds that recognition also involves 'repeated re-cognition' because recognition only works as the recognition of an already determined identity, an identity that has already been recognised as this or that (García Düttmann 2000: 120). In Markell's terms, agents become bound by recognition because they become bound to their recognised identities.

However, recognition must also add to what is recognised. The demand for recognition only arises because of a lack that recognition is meant to ameliorate, and so recognition also performatively constitutes what is recognised. This is the paradox of recognition: recognition at once reflects and constitutes what is recognised, and must proceed in both a constative and a performative mode. The recognised is at once prior to and an effect of the act of recognition. Although recognition is bound to proceed in both modes, they are also mutually contradictory: recognition must at once reflect a full identity and fill a lack in that identity. Recognition is structured like the Derridean infrastructure of supplementarity, at once substituting for and adding to what is recognised or represented (Derrida 1997). It is no coincidence that Derrida developed that argument in the context of representation: both recognition and representation share the double claim of reflecting some already existing identity and adding to it in order to realise it more fully.

Practices of recognition are paradoxical because they are caught within this structure, proceeding at once in a constative and in a performative mode. Given this structure of recognition, no act of recognition ever achieves the completion of the recognised identity, and so it must be repeated, even if always differently. As García Düttmann (2000: 44) notes, the act of recognition and its effects must themselves be recognised as recognition in order to have their desired effect. The dissemination of recognition cannot be put to a halt with reference to an essence (because the act of recognition is also performative) or to an achieved complete identity (because recognition must be recognised). The upshot is that the effects of recognition, and its success, are constantly deferred; they cannot be controlled from any particular point, including the intentions of the recogniser. In *Begum*, this is shown most clearly in relation to the identity of Islam, which is represented in different ways by different agents (who are differently positioned). The claim to recognise Islam, or to have Islam recognised, is therefore intrinsically linked to disputes over which representation, and whose representation, of Islam is to be recognised. Recognition and representation are inherently open as they depend on their uptake, on being re-recognised and re-represented. This is not to say that everything is possible, because the web of recognition and representation is marked by power differentials, for instance between an individual (Shabina Begum) and an institution (Denbigh High School).

Representation shares the constative and performative structure with recognition. As argued by, among others, Ernesto Laclau (2005: ch. 6), Lisa Disch (2011) and Brian Seitz (1995) in the context of political representation, there is more to representation than a transparent reflection of already constituted identities, interests and wills.[6] Representative claims proceed at once in a constative and a performative mode, and neither mode ever completely disappears behind the other. Representation at once follows and precedes, reflects and constitutes, what is represented. If representation is not transparent, but constitutive, then we must examine what happens in the process of representation – that is, we must treat representation and recognition as sites of political struggle. Here it is not enough to examine recognition as a struggle over which, and whose, representation will form the basis for recognition in law and policy. One must also pay attention to the ways in which identities are constituted through recognition understood as representation.

Just as the agents in the *Begum* case are engaged in representation and recognition, so are academic and non-academic commentators when analysing the case. Consider first how, by highlighting particular details of the case, one can represent the case and Shabina Begum in a particular light. This is so, for instance, when some commentators mention that Shabina Begum's older brother, who was also her legal guardian, was a member of the radical Islamist group Hizb ut-Tahrir (for instance, Tarlo 2010: ch. 5; Morey and

Yaqin 2011: 185–6). The reference to Hizb ut-Tahrir serves to associate Shabina Begum and the jilbab with more extremist and political interpretations of Islam. It goes to show that there is no neutral way of representing the case, and that the descriptive and the normative cannot be completely distinguished. The representation of the case is not just a reflection of established facts in a constative fashion, but also serves to establish the facts of the case and to establish the facts as facts. Here representation involves recognition insofar as (the representation of) a fact must be recognised as a fact in order for the representation to be authoritative.

Likewise, the case is represented as a particular kind of case – resonating with existing representative frameworks – when identified as a hijab case (see, for instance, Baroness Hale in *Begum* HL 2006: §§92–9; Joppke 2009: ch. 4) or as a case of 'Islam vs. the West' (for example, Joppke 2009: ch. 4; Begum quoted in Aslam 2005). Here the representation works as re-cognition: the case – as well as the jilbab and Shabina Begum – is recognised as this or that, for instance as a case of 'the clash of civilisations'. However, given the variety of ways in which we can recognise the case, the representation or recognition cannot simply be a reflection of the case, but also constitutes it as this or that kind of case. Again, the representation of the case is not just descriptive, but also normative, and this applies equally to the representations by the agents in the case and to the representations of the case by the researcher analysing the case. The case and the facts of the case do not exist as objects independently of their recognition and representation. In short, recognition and representation are constitutive.

The convergence of methodological and substantive issues surrounding recognition becomes more apparent when we consider the naming of the main protagonist of *Begum*. Shabina Begum is named in different ways by the other agents in the case and by commentators on the case. Most notably, she is referred to with her first name only and as a 'girl'. What we have here goes to the heart of the structure of recognition and representation: naming Shabina Begum at once has a constative dimension (referring to an already named – that is, identified – person) and a performative dimension (naming her one way rather than another). The name is neither a pure constative nor a pure performative. Furthermore, referring to Shabina Begum as 'Shabina' or as a 'girl' is significant because, like similar cases, *Begum* also concerns the autonomy of Muslim girls and women: was Shabina Begum acting on the basis of her own free and reasoned will, or was she a passive subject? To take just one example, one of the Law Lords refers to her as 'Shabina, not yet 14 years of age' when implying that, if left to her own devices, she would not have chosen a confrontational approach towards the school, and that she must have been under the influence of her brother who was also her legal guardian (Lord Scott in *Begum* HC 2004: §80; see also Begum HL 2006: §68).[7] The issue cannot be reduced to a matter of misrecognition or to a matter of the correspondence, or not, between a name and what is named. 'Shabina' is no less correct than 'Shabina Begum', if by correct is meant congruent with a non-representational reality. This is so because representation, recognition and naming are also performative acts, and 'Shabina Begum' is an effect of these rather than prior to and independent of them. With these caveats, I shall continue to refer to 'Shabina Begum', mainly to avoid infantilising her by referring to her only as 'Shabina'.[8]

Those on the receiving end of representations may feel misrepresented and misrecognised as does Shabina Begum when she objects to the representation of her as a pawn in the hand of her brother (for instance, Begum 2005a). From the perspective of autonomy, the problem with other-representations is paternalism; from the perspective of authenticity, the problem is misrecognition of an authentic self. This may suggest that we should let the agents speak for themselves, and rely on self- rather than other-representations. For instance, Gareth Davies argues that the courts in *Begum* rule on prejudice when they rely on others' representations of the jilbab. His alternative is to go through the agents' self-representations, although he still wants to hold on to a notion of 'objective' meanings which 'all reasonable people' will accept (Davies 2005: 519–22). However, if we accept that representation at once reproduces and produces what is represented, then there can be neither an objective reality nor autonomous or authentic selves independent of representations of them. The 'reality' of these autonomous and authentic selves should be seen as effects of recognition and representation. What is more, an agent must draw on others' representations to make his or her self-representations intelligible, and the agent cannot control how others take up his or her self-representations. Thus, the distinction between self- and other-representations is blurred.

Although we must be critical of agents – whether community leaders or commentators – who claim to represent others, we should not be searching for an autonomous or authentic self behind, or beyond, recognition and representation. There is no self or identity that is not constituted through representation and recognition or does not stand in need of further representation and recognition. If anything, subjectivity and identity – including the autonomous and authentic self – are effects of representation and recognition.[9] There is no non-representational reality and no non-representational autonomous or authentic self that we can use as a yardstick against which to compare the truth of different representations.

This should not be read as if the self were merely a cog in a big discursive wheel. To think so might lead to the misunderstanding that any particular act of recognition merely reproduces the dominant representations and the power of the dominant. Although the subjectivation at work in recognition may involve subjection, the latter cannot be total. This goes to the heart of recognition as a concept and practice. It may be said that recognition rests on an inherent asymmetry between someone asking for recognition and someone (perceived to be) able to grant recognition, most often the state. These asymmetries are present in *Begum* where an individual (Shabina Begum) faces an institution (the school) and the state, and where there is the additional asymmetry at work between a minority and a majority Islam. It could be argued that recognition reproduces the asymmetry between recogniser and recognised as well as the power of the recogniser, creating a relationship of dependency so that the recognised becomes bound by recognition (Markell 2003).[10]

This may certainly be the case, but it cannot be the whole story. In order for A to be able to recognise B, A must already be recognised as an agent capable of recognising, just as the act of recognition itself must be recognised as such. The relation of recognition thus goes both ways. Recognition reproduces the power of agent A to recognise, but only in a way that goes through B's recognition, over which A cannot have full control. B must have the power to recognise A, but this must also be the power not to do so, as the act would otherwise be empty. Thus, A's power to recognise depends on the dissemination of that power beyond his or her control (García Düttmann 2000: 111; Ferrarese 2009).[11] The roles of recogniser and recognised change back and forth, each agent must be both at the same time, and the process cannot be controlled from any one point. Recognition must be recognised, and it cannot be a unilateral relationship. We may never move beyond recognition and its reproduction of asymmetrical power relations, but because recognition is always disseminated, there will always be openings for resistance against the dominant representations. As a result, we must both examine how the politics of recognition reproduces and perhaps reinforces existing representational structures *and* examine the openings for resistance that exist in those structures.

Before moving on to *Begum*, it is necessary to briefly address the status of the subjectivity of 'Shabina Begum'. In the following, I will bracket questions about the unity of Shabina Begum as an agent. Both she and her brother and their lawyers speak in the name of 'Shabina Begum', but I shall treat them as a single agent. The same goes for 'the school', which also consists of a number of agents: the head teacher, the deputy, the teachers, the governors, their lawyers, at least some parents and sometimes the other children who (are made to) speak in the name of the school. Here I shall also abstract from the fact that Shabina Begum was not legally an adult, which in itself raises a number of issues. Parents, family, state authorities, peers, advertising and religion all exert pressure on Shabina Begum, but the real issue is which pressures are seen as legitimate and which are not.

However, the questions surrounding Shabina Begum's subjectivity go beyond this. The law requires a singular subject capable of representing him- or herself or of being represented, yet Shabina Begum is only a subject by virtue of her subject position within often conflicting representational frameworks or discourses. Put differently, the condition of possibility of Shabina Begum's subjectivity consists in her subject position(s) within discourses whose effects she cannot master. Her self-representations do not originate in a subjectivity located outside representational frameworks. Her subjectivity is an effect of representations even if she cannot be reduced to a passive effect, as if she were merely parroting representations entirely beyond her control. This much also follows from the fact that representation proceeds at once in the constative and the performative mode. It also follows that Shabina Begum's subjectivity is paradoxical: at once taken as given and constituted through her self-representations and others' representations of her.[12]

The dilemma of difference I: 'just a piece of cloth'

Recognition naturally concerns identity and difference, which are in turn linked to exclusion and inclusion. The *Begum* case must be examined in terms of how the school and Shabina Begum deal with difference, specifically how they argue for and against recognition and inclusion of Shabina Begum's difference. Here I take my cue from what Martha Minow (1991) calls the dilemma of difference, which means, first, that the inclusion of Shabina Begum's difference through recognition is only possible in a way that simultaneously reproduces her difference; second, that the difference is defined vis-à-vis a norm; and, third, that there is a hierarchical relationship between norm and difference.[13] As a result, when arguing for recognition of her difference, Shabina Begum at once insists on and plays down her difference.

Denbigh High School believed that the jilbab 'would lead to divisiveness within the school and would threaten cohesion within the school' (*Begum* HC 2004: §84 no. 27), thus introducing division within an otherwise unitary and harmonious space. According to the school, the school uniform was one of the reasons for the school's academic success, an argument that the judges accept (2004: §82 no. 51).[14] The uniform had supposedly helped create a common identity and undo differences that had previously threatened to erupt into open conflict, and it had done so by literally and figuratively covering and 'uniformalising' those differences. It is easy to see the analogies between this argument about the effects of a school uniform and arguments about the need for some homogeneity or shared identity for a society as a whole. The shalwar kameeze, which was one of the uniform options for girls at the school, was meant to hide differences between Muslim, Hindu and Sikh female pupils, for all of whom the shalwar kameeze was allegedly adequate. The deputy head teacher states:

> the school adopts a uniform policy that does not allow pupils to identify themselves *obviously* as belonging to a *particular* religion or race. The school uniform is designed to identify pupils as part of the inclusive community of the school and avoid the possibility of subgroups identified by dress developing as might be the case if a school were to adopt a dress code that was non-uniform. (*Begum* HC 2004: §83 no. 17, my emphasis)

In order to include pupils equally from different religious or racial backgrounds, the school excludes signs of those differences, at least insofar as those signs are 'obvious'. Although it comes in different versions, the uniform is supposed to represent the school community as a single community, at once reflecting and instituting this community.

Not all differences are undone by the uniform. There are, first, those differences that are visible despite the uniform, for instance, skin colour and class. Second, there are differences inscribed into the uniform because it comes in different versions for girls. While the different versions of the uniform share the same colour and the school logo, the school recognises some (religious) differences as significant and as worthy of recognition within the school uniform. The school neither can, nor wants to, do away with differences, and, as mentioned earlier, the *Begum* case did not pit difference-blind liberalism against a multiculturalist politics of difference. No one in the legal dispute takes the position of difference-blind liberalism; multiculturalism and the recognition of cultural, religious and racial difference are taken as given. *Begum* does not concern whether difference can be recognised in public policy, but *which* differences can be recognised.[15]

Where there is a school uniform policy, lines will have to be drawn to distinguish the uniform from other clothes, otherwise the policy would be meaningless. Where there is some community, identity or norm, there will be difference, and that difference is constituted through its relationship to the norm. The question is how the school construes Shabina Begum's difference, and how it establishes the line between inclusion and exclusion, between what differences can be recognised and what differences cannot be recognised.

The school qualifies its argument that the jilbab would introduce division, because the problem is not division or difference as such. It argues that it is the particular content of Shabina Begum's difference that is the problem. The school represents the jilbab as extremist, a view that is reflected among the judges and, especially, in the media, where it is also associated with the slide down a slippery slope towards ever more extremist practices (*Begum* HC 2004: §82 nos 15–16, §83 nos 17, 20; *Begum* HL 2006: §65). For instance, the school claims that other pupils have said that they might be forced to wear the jilbab if it were allowed in the school, and that they fear the extremism with which they associate the jilbab. To give the jilbab a stamp of approval by recognising it within the school uniform would be to change the nature of the uniform and, consequently, of the school community. The recognition and inclusion of a difference does not leave the community's identity unchanged (García Düttmann 2000: 3–4). The school is afraid of the consequences for the identity of the school community if it were to accept Shabina Begum's claim for recognition, and so they play up this aspect. It is right to think that it would have consequences for the identity of the school community. In contrast, Shabina Begum plays down the effect of the recognition of the jilbab as a legitimate version of the school uniform.

The school's construal of the jilbab as the expression of an extremist and marginal form of Islam through metonymical associations of the jilbab with extremist practices turns into metaphorical substitution when the jilbab comes to stand in for extremism, division, and so on (for instance, *Begum* HC 2004: §84 nos 23–4).[16] *Begum* is precisely a struggle over the meaning of the difference of the jilbab. To the school, the jilbab is more than just the jilbab, let alone a piece of cloth; similarly, the school uniform is more than just a school uniform or a piece of cloth. The school uniform becomes the site of a struggle over the identity of the school community. At the same time, the school implies that the shalwar kameeze uniform only signifies religious modesty and no particular religiosity, and so that the uniform is a way to include religious persons who, like Shabina Begum, believe modesty to be important. By casting the shalwar kameeze as inclusive, the school makes Shabina Begum's rejection of the uniform appear more extremist. This is supported by the argument that the choice and design of the shalwar kameeze was made in consultation with representatives from the local Muslim community, a fact that I shall return to below when dealing with the question of the authority of representations of communal identities. The argument is self-reinforcing: a norm is used to establish a difference as different, and the difference is used to support the normality of the norm. The representation of something as different is a performative act that simultaneously establishes the difference as difference and the norm as norm, and it does so in a way that establishes difference and norm in a relationship that is at once mutual and hierarchical (Minow 1991: 53–78).

While the school is mainly concerned with establishing Shabina Begum's difference as an extremist difference, Shabina Begum herself oscillates between emphasising and playing down her difference. On the one hand, Shabina Begum insists that the jilbab is important to her and that she cannot wear the shalwar kameeze – that the 'just six inches' of extra cloth are essential and make a difference, and should be recognised as such (Begum 2005a). 'The jilbab is not simply about a piece of cloth', she says (Begum quoted in Press Association 2006). She insists that her religious beliefs distinguish her, and that they mean that she must wear something different from non-believers and other kinds of believers (Begum quoted in Press Association 2006). So she also states that 'the better Muslim . . . wears the jilbab'.[17] Other Muslims and others in the media jumped on this and argued that it was evidence of Shabina Begum's arrogance and fanaticism (for instance, Alam 2006). Yet, she cannot trivialise the difference. If she did not believe that, by wearing the jilbab, she would be a better Muslim, there would be no point in wearing it, let alone having it recognised as part of her identity.

On the other hand, Shabina Begum at times plays down, and literally be*little*s, her difference, referring to the jilbab as 'just a piece of cloth'. Likewise, one of her solicitors says: 'I don't see why it is a big issue . . . this is a dispute over 11 inches of hem' (quoted in Asthana 2006). This should make her difference easier to recognise and tolerate, and, since the school does not do so, it just goes to show how unreasonable they are. Caught in a paradox, she both insists on her difference and makes light of it. She must insist on the significance of her difference, because otherwise recognition would not be necessary, but this also makes recognition more difficult to achieve. Playing down her difference makes recognition easier, but also inconsequential. Accordingly, when Gareth Davies (2005: 530) defends Shabina Begum by saying that 'they're only clothes', this simultaneously undermines her case for the significance of recognising the jilbab.

Difference (vis-à-vis a norm) is not a fixed relation, but is itself an effect of the way in which actors – here, the school and Shabina Begum – negotiate it. Difference and norm are established and renegotiated through a performative politics of in-/exclusion that must be understood as a politics of representation, that is, as taking place in the terrain of representation. Recognition and, as I will argue in the next chapter, tolerance must be analysed as practices of articulation of the relationship between norm and difference.

The dilemma of difference II: sexual difference

Shabina Begum encounters a final important version of the dilemma of difference. Like other hijab cases, *Begum* also concerns the female body and sexuality, and the sartorial focus of the case connects recognition and difference to the female body. While the male body is sometimes problematised – as in *Mandla*, for example – it is usually the female body that becomes the discursive site of cultural struggles, whether abortion or sexual freedom, or the female Muslim body as a body to be governed by men, family, community or the state.

Shabina Begum articulates her demand to be able to wear the jilbab as a requirement in Islam for modesty (hijab) for girls and women from the age when they start to menstruate. The jilbab is supposed to hide the shape of the female body and protect the woman from the male gaze, that is, prevent her from being reduced to an object of male sexual desire. The hijab is supposed to desexualise the woman's relationship to men, except her relationship to her husband and close male relatives, which are unambiguously sexual and asexual respectively (and here there is no question of homosexuality). Conversely, opponents of the hijab often link it to repression of sexuality, especially female sexuality. Sexuality is at once natural and civilised, and veiled women can then be saved from their culture, their religion and their men, who are in turn represented as both unnatural and uncivilised.

The hijab is meant to disambiguate; yet, by covering the body, the hijab simultaneously reveals it as (hetero-)sexually significant. Wittingly or unwittingly, Shabina Begum at once covers and draws attention to her sexual difference.[18] The jilbab both covers and reveals. Or, to be more precise, it reveals by covering because the sexuality that must be veiled is performatively construed through the very act of veiling it. There is a fabulous retroactivity at work whereby, through the act of veiling, Shabina Begum's body will have been what needed to be covered. The performative act masquerades as constative (Derrida 1988; Derrida 1986).

Boris Johnson, then MP and editor of *The Spectator*, rightly noted the 'paradox' whereby Shabina Begum's veiling had drawn attention to her sexuality. But he then wrote of 'this exceedingly good-looking and confident young woman . . . batting her (rather beautiful) eyes through her visor [sic], and thereby exciting the interest of millions of otherwise apathetic viewers, who are not only infidels but very possibly male infidels at that' (Johnson 2006). Jilbab or not, Shabina Begum's body is reduced to an object for enjoyment by the male gaze. Perhaps we must qualify the idea that it is the veiling of the body that sexualises it. Even if the veiling of the body sexualises it, it seems equally to be the case that both Islamic and 'Western' discourses on the hijab tend to be marked by a sexual difference whereby women are always sexualised, veiled or not (Scott 2007: ch. 5; Ahmed 1992: chs 8, 11, Conclusion).

The jilbab would have allowed Shabina Begum to stay in a mixed school; instead she ended up in an all girls' school. Whether she goes to a mixed school or not, the jilbab reproduces her (hetero-)sexual difference and, it might be argued, the inequality implicit in Islamic regulation of women's bodies as a solution to the male gaze. The hijab may allow women to take part in public life like men, but only on the condition that they cover their womanhood and sexuality, and yet this very covering also symbolises their womanhood and their sexual difference. Thus, the recognition of the jilbab in the school both has egalitarian effects (through the recognition and inclusion of another difference), but also reproduces certain differences that are simultaneously marks of inequalities.

Men's bodies are sexualised too through injunctions to wear loose clothes that cover an adequate part of the body, but the injunctions concerning dress bear more heavily on women.[19] And while the male gaze is sexualised, the solution lies in covering the female body. Some – including some Islamic and non-Islamic feminists – argue that covering the female body makes possible a gaze reversal (see Abu-Odeh 1993: 29–31). Covering the body facilitates gaze reversal, thereby liberating women from the male gaze and making them less passive and more active. This may be the case, and veiling may have a welcome emancipatory effect, but it still problematises the female body and sexuality at the expense of the male gaze. The jilbab and other forms of the hijab may empower the woman wearing them, but the empowerment comes at the price of accepting the problematisation of the female body and sexuality.

Recognition is a way to integrate those who are otherwise marginalised, but it also reproduces existing identities and inequalities. To recognise the jilbab as a legitimate difference is *both* to allow Shabina Begum equal access to a public space, as equal to men and other women, *and* to reproduce a certain representation of Islam and women, a representation that rests on an inequality between the sexes. That representation is neither set in stone nor all-dominating, and more than one representation of Islam, of women and of (different forms of) female veiling compete for hegemony. While this should not draw attention away from the subjection that takes place here and now through injunctions to cover or uncover, it does draw attention to the contingency of representations and their openness to renegotiation. Here my aim has been to show how female veiling may at one at the same time empower and subject, just as recognition both includes subjects as equals and reproduces existing differences and inequalities.

Individual and community, autonomy and compulsion

In her struggle for recognition of her difference, Shabina Begum takes recourse to the law and the courts, specifically Article 9(1) of the European Convention on Human Rights, which is included in the British Human Rights Act:

> Everyone has the right to freedom of thought, conscience and religion; this right includes freedom to change his religion or belief and freedom, either alone or in community with others and in public or private, to manifest his religion or belief, in worship, teaching, practice and observance. (Council of Europe 2010: 10–11)

It is with one foot squarely inside the law and the discourse of rights that Shabina Begum is able to make her claim for recognition. The claim can be articulated in terms of the rights of the Convention, and the rights to non-discrimination can be articulated in terms of equal recognition. But the law also restricts the form her claims can take. Her claims are made in a particular discursive terrain (legal discourse and, more specifically, the Convention) that shapes the claims that can be registered as meaningful claims. More precisely, her claims oscillate between individual and community and between autonomous choice and compulsion.

On the one hand, the subject of the relevant human rights law is an individual, and so Shabina Begum's claims can only be heard as the claims of an individual, and she must cast her religious beliefs as her individual beliefs. The nature of the law is liberal in the additional sense that she must cast her beliefs in terms of autonomous choice, which is to say that she must not have been forced to wear the jilbab; her beliefs must be 'genuine' in this sense. There was no challenge to the genuineness of Shabina Begum's religious beliefs, although at times the judges and others insinuate that she was under the influence of her older brother (for instance, *Begum* HC 2004: §68; *Begum* HL 2006: §§79–81).

Shabina Begum responds to the widely circulating view that the hijab cannot be freely chosen and is a sign of women's oppression. In 'Western' discourses on Islam and women, the length of a woman's dress is often taken as a measure of her agency and unveiling as a measure of choice and emancipation. The result is that you can only choose to unveil, but not to veil.[20] Against this kind of discourse, Shabina Begum insists that she is not a passive subject: 'all this [about being forced to wear the jilbab] is a lie and I feel that it belittles me and other Muslim girls by suggesting that I cannot think for myself' (Begum 2005a). And elsewhere she states: 'I do have a mind of my own and I can choose what I want to wear' (quoted in Rozenberg 2006). Her claim for recognition is only possible insofar as she insists that her beliefs and the jilbab are her individual and autonomous choice, yet this opens her to two counter-arguments from the school. First, it stresses that she was alone in her views, thus reinforcing her extremism and marginality (*Begum* HC 2004: §17, §82 no. 45).[21] Second, it plays into the argument that, rather than being excluded from the school, Shabina Begum had effectively excluded herself because the jilbab was a choice, and because she could have chosen a different school in the local area where the jilbab was allowed (for instance, *Begum* HC 2004: §§60, 73, Annex nos 16–17).

On the other hand, individual autonomous choice is not the whole story. The law not only allows for a communal dimension to religious beliefs and practice ('in community with others') but indirectly requires it. The religious beliefs protected under the law must be recognisable as religious beliefs, that is, they must correspond to what are recognised as religious beliefs and to existing, recognised religions (see *Begum* CA 2005: §§31–49).[22] Thus, Shabina Begum's claim for recognition of her difference immediately raises questions about the identity of Islam. Here we are dealing with what García Düttmann calls repeated re-cognition, whereby recognition works as the re-cognition of an already recognised identity, and whereby, to use Markell's phrase, the recognised becomes bound to the recognised identity. The recognition is not just cognitive in a descriptive sense, but also normative because certain religions are authorised as protected by the law. For these reasons, Shabina Begum's beliefs cannot simply be individual or personal. Indeed, Shabina Begum herself becomes embroiled in discussions about the identity and essence of Islam in the course of her claim to have her difference recognised. Most notably, she stresses how she has arrived at her beliefs through careful study of the scriptures and of Islamic scholars (*Begum* HC 2004: §67; Aslam 2005; Begum 2005a). The reference to established and recognised authorities is supposed to show that her beliefs are genuinely Muslim, but they also mean that her beliefs cannot simply be her individual beliefs.

When it comes to autonomous choice, if Shabina Begum's religious beliefs are to be taken seriously in court, they cannot be the result of 'mere' choice as if they were the result of a lifestyle choice. Shabina Begum can respond to this by stressing how she has arrived at her beliefs after careful study of authoritative texts. Likewise, she can argue that her beliefs have forced themselves upon her through revelation, making it compulsory for her to wear the jilbab. It is revelation that distinguishes her religious choice from a mere lifestyle choice and from a choice that could be the subject of rational deliberation. She herself says: 'Islam truly liberates her [that is, a jilbab-wearing woman] because it . . . makes her a slave to the Creator and not to man or her desires' (Begum 2005a).[23] In these terms, it must have been her religion that made her do it. Here the paradox becomes evident: on the one hand, Shabina Begum insists that the jilbab was not forced upon her; on the other hand, she writes that 'Muslim women do not wear the jilbab out of a choice of modesty or culture but because it is an obligation' (2005a). She must at once be a sovereign individual and refer to something beyond her control, whether a communal identity (of Islam) or religious injunctions.

Begum cannot be reduced to a case of individual versus community or autonomy versus compulsion, and the parties appeal at once to individual choice *and* communal identity, autonomy *and* compulsion. Neither individual choice nor communal identity or compulsion are unambiguous discursive strategies, and the struggle for, and against, recognition of the jilbab is marked by this ambiguity. Here the discourse of recognition is not simply opposed to liberalism and individual rights. Recognition is articulated in a wider discursive terrain shaped by competing discourses – the terrain of British multiculturalism.

To point to ambiguity and paradox here is not to criticise Shabina Begum, for instance, for being incoherent. Consider how, reflecting more widely held beliefs, one commentator, Madeleine Bunting, finds it

> intriguing . . . that Begum and her brother used Western concepts of individual human rights and choice to fight their case against the school and the local community. Traditionally, Islam has put a strong emphasis on conformity to the community's rulings – the rights of the collective trump those of the individual – but the Begums were turning this on its head to argue against the majority. (Bunting 2006)

Expressing a widely held belief, Bunting reinforces the opposition between 'Western' and 'Islam' with her surprise that, *qua* her religion, Shabina Begum is naturally alien to individual human rights and choice. The suggestion is that human rights have been hijacked for ulterior motives and for a discourse where they do not naturally belong. Here paradox is considered to be against the nature of things and so can be criticised on that basis. My point is that, on the contrary, paradox is inherent to the way in which Shabina Begum articulates the different discourses available to her; in short, if anything is 'natural', it is paradox.

Pluralism, homogeneity and representational authority

Perhaps the most important question raised by the *Begum* case and by the politics of recognition concerns the relationship between recognition, representation and authority: if recognition relies on representations, how is the authority of those representations established?[24] This touches upon the key issue at stake in liberal critiques of the politics of recognition: if recognition relies on group identities, someone must define those identities and must do so at the expense of heterogeneity within the group.

Throughout the legal process, the school emphasised that it had arrived at its uniform policy through a consultation process with Muslims. The judges also emphasise this in their decisions, and during the trials there were further rounds of consultation with British Muslim authorities. When the school developed the uniform policy, it consulted staff, parents and pupils as well as several local mosques, who all agreed that the shalwar kameeze fulfilled Islamic requirements for female dress. By being asked for their views on Islam by the school, the local mosques are recognised as authoritative representatives of Islam and authorised to speak in the name of, and for, Muslims.[25]

The recognition, or not, of Shabina Begum's religion comes to rely on a prior act of recognition, namely the recognition of those representatives as authoritative representatives of Islam and, by implication, the recognition of the authority of their representations. What we have is another case of what García Düttmann calls repeated re-cognition. When it comes to the authority of the representations of Islam, recognition relies on and repeats a prior determination – which is to say, recognition – of the identity in question. An identity has been determined (here, Islam), and it is now a matter of the identity between this recognised identity and the one that claims recognition (here, Shabina Begum's representation of Islam). Recognition becomes a matter of recognising in Shabina Begum's identity the identity that has been determined as Islam through the representations by the local mosques and the school. Two representations are compared, one of which is taken as authoritative and as the basis for the comparison.

To the extent that recognition relies on a correspondence between one identity and another, recognition proceeds in a constative, and cognitive, fashion. The recognition gets at least part of its authority from appearing as a reflection of something taken as given, and something that can therefore be taken as the basis for a judgement about the act of recognition. What is more, the representation gets its authority from being repeated, and when others repeat it in different contexts, this shores up its authority by confirming it as the correct representation of, for instance, Islam. The representatives of Islam are authorised as such because they are recognised as representatives of Islam. More generally, authority is constituted performatively through recognition of it as authority.

The performative dimension never disappears completely. Although recognition relies on repeated re-cognition, the former cannot be reduced to the latter. Although we cannot have recognition without repeated re-cognition, recognition also implies a normative dimension when deciding which identities should be included through recognition. This normative dimension is precisely what is at stake when it comes to the authority of the representations and, hence, of the recognition, because here we are dealing with the question of which, and whose, representations form the basis for recognition. Representations need to be recognised as authoritative in order to be so; the representations need to be taken up by others as authoritative or correct representations. In this way, a particular representation may become authoritative when it comes to policy making. However, the repetition by others in other contexts introduces alteration. This is so because to repeat is to repeat in a (however slightly) different context, and if meaning is relational – which is to say, contextual – then repetition also implies alteration. There is no point at which the process of recognition comes to completion, or where someone can prevent the continuation of the process of recognition.[26]

Together with the impurity of repetition, this undermines the ability of the recogniser to control the meaning of the act of recognition, and *Begum* precisely concerns who is able to control the meaning of the jilbab and the identity of Islam. Shabina Begum's struggle for recognition of her Islam is possible because there is no pure repetition, and because the recognition of the school's Islam is therefore not a closed matter. This is not to say that things are entirely open to resignification. On the contrary, the representations of Islam and the jilbab rely on, and take place within, existing representational structures and inequalities. This includes the inequality between majority and minority Islam and the repetitions of certain images of Islam in the media associating the jilbab with extremist Islam. I return to these media representations of the jilbab in the next chapter.

In *Begum*, the consensus in and around the school is disrupted by the change in Shabina Begum's religious views and her subsequent challenge of the school's representation of Islam. Where previously the consensus expressed everybody's recognition of the school's representation as authoritative, the authority of the representation is now put into question. The consensus comes about when everybody recognises Islam in the same way, that is, when the representations of Islam are repeated in a constative fashion and taken to refer to the same. Insofar as a representation of Islam is not disputed, it will tend toward a homogenisation of Islam. Insofar as the school is able to garner a consensus around its representation of Islam, this representation does not appear as one contingent and contestable representation among others. On the basis of this sort of naturalisation of a representation, alternative representations are rendered incorrect, marginal or extremist, which is precisely what happens in *Begum*. Hence it is important who is able to hegemonise the representation of Islam and to hegemonise the representational field. Shabina Begum's struggle for recognition of her Islam is possible because there is no complete consensus. Still, although the consensus on Islam is partial, the school was successful in representing her difference as extremist and thereby excluding it in a way that can be rationalised by the school, the community, the judges and most of the media.

The school and the courts rely on not only the authority of the local mosques to represent Islam, but also the authority of the head teacher. The school and the judges make references to the head teacher's background: she is a Bengali Muslim and, *as such*, she is taken to be in a privileged position to speak on behalf of Muslims (*Begum* HC 2004: §§37, 43; *Begum* HL 2006: §§5, 43, 74–5).[27] As with the consultation process involving the local mosques, the argument rests on the recognition of the head teacher as Muslim. The head teacher is authorised as a representative of Muslims on the basis of recognisable facts (her ethnicity and religion), and her Islam is recognised as the identity vis-à-vis which Shabina Begum's claims are recognised or not. Making the head teacher stand for Islam not only presumes but also reproduces an identity between her Islam and that of other Muslims, except those who differ and who are therefore marginal or extreme. One part of Islam (the head teacher) stands in for the whole in a synecdochic relationship, which assumes the homogeneity of the whole so that the part can substitute for the whole. However, if we insist on the heterogeneity of the whole and on the non-transparency of the representational relation, then the synecdoche is catachrestic in the sense that it also constitutes what is represented, namely the whole. What is more, the catachresis is normative in that it is only possible by picking one part over other possible parts to stand in for the whole.[28] Taking the head teacher as standing in for, and representative of, Islam, the latter is represented in a particular way.

The claim to be able to stand in for Islam is also a claim about the identity and limits of Islam. Shabina Begum's claim for recognition is a challenge to the representativeness of the head teacher and to the Islam she is said to represent. Indeed, Shabina Begum's disruption of the consensus shows the partiality of the school's view of Islam. One important way in which Shabina Begum does this is when making a distinction between culture and religion, when she and her brother argue that the shalwar kameeze is in fact a Pakistani cultural dress rather than an Islamic religious dress (*Begum* HC 2004: §67; see also Begum quoted in Alam 2006). For Shabina Begum, the shalwar kameeze is a particular cultural dress that is neither universal to Islam nor essentially Islamic; for her, 'nothing else is Islamic' but the jilbab (quoted in Alam 2006). Her argument rests on a homogenising and essentialising representation of Islam. She refers to a true Islam based on references to scriptures and classical scholars. This is also what is involved in her claim, mentioned above, that 'better' Muslims wear a jilbab. It is an Islam that can be distinguished from what are then merely local, cultural differences. The culture/religion distinction helps Shabina Begum exclude the cultural (the shalwar kameeze) as contingent and non-essential to the religious (Islam), which she can then claim has a core truth common to all Muslims (Tarlo 2010: 114–15).

Although Shabina Begum allows for pluralism within Islam, this view competes with her assertion of a single true Islam. And although the school appeals to pluralism within Islam (*Begum* HC 2004: Annex no. 10), it also appeals to consensus: 'All opinions were that the Shalwar Kameeze satisfies the Islamic dress code' (2004: §25).[29] Both the school and Shabina Begum want to be on the side of pluralism and tolerance. They operate in the discursive terrain of British multiculturalism where these values are important, but their claims for and against recognition are also based on representations of a single, true Islam. They need the language of pluralism and tolerance in order to appear reasonable and tolerant, but they must also claim to represent Islam in the right way. The latter is necessary because the dispute is not over the recognition, or not, of Islam, but over *which* Islam is to be recognised in the school uniform policy. There is a tension built into their arguments because, even if they were only paying lip-service to the language of pluralism and tolerance, these values undermine the representation of a monolithic Islam. While the different agents – the school, Shabina Begum and the judges (2004: §23)[30] – all declare that they do not want to judge the truth of religious beliefs, the case is necessarily also about the identity and limits of Islam.

The school's solution to its apparently paradoxical assertion of both pluralism and homogeneity is to defend the exclusion of Shabina Begum's difference on the basis of a defence of pluralism. It may seem paradoxical to defend pluralism at the price of excluding some pluralism (here: Shabina Begum's minority Islam). But the exclusion is rationalised as the exclusion of an 'extremist' difference that threatens pluralism. Among other things, the school states that other girls at the school have said that they would feel forced to wear the jilbab, which the girls associate with an extreme form of Islam (*Begum* HC 2004: §82 nos 15–16). In this way, Shabina Begum's difference can be excluded in a non-paradoxical way; indeed, on this line of reasoning, it would be paradoxical to include Shabina Begum's difference because it is said to threaten the inclusion of other, legitimate differences. 'I have been given the firm impression', the head teacher states, 'that there is a number of girls in the school which [sic] relies on us to help them resist the pressures from the more extreme groups', in order 'to preserve their freedom to follow their own part of the Islamic tradition' (2004: §82 no. 16). Not only can the school exclude Shabina Begum's difference, it must do so if it is serious about pluralism and tolerance. To exclude Shabina Begum's difference becomes the condition of possibility of others' freedom and a pluralistic school. Logically, there is nothing wrong with this argument, because there is no recognition without a limit to recognition. There can be no unlimited pluralism, and at the limit one difference will be recognised and included at the expense of another. However, this is not enough to rationalise the exclusion of *particular* differences. In order to exclude Shabina Begum's difference, the school relies on a representation of it as marginal and extreme. The flipside of that difference is a norm about what it means to be Muslim, a norm that appears all the more normal – mainstream, tolerant, and so on – as a result.

The tension between pluralism and homogenisation is also visible in the consultation process that takes place during the trial. The two parties submit statements from various representatives of the Muslim community in the UK, the school to the effect that the shalwar kameeze meets Islamic requirements, and Shabina Begum to the effect that a jilbab is required. Again the consultation process takes certain representatives and certain representations as authoritative. However, at certain points the authority of the representatives and representations is disturbed. First, some of the Muslim representatives stress that there are interpretive differences within Islam, and the school to some extent accepts this (for instance, *Begum* HC 2004: §16, Annex no. 10; but compare *Begum* HL 2006: §15). Second, the school treats the representations in a way that undermines their authority. When some of the representatives provided statements to both sides and with contradictory conclusions, the school 'could see no good reason for the local mosques apparently changing their minds' (*Begum* HC 2004: Annex, §8). Their response to the interpretive differences among the representatives is to refer to these differences as 'opinions':

> All that can be said now is that there appears to be a difference of opinion between no doubt learned gentlemen as to the proper interpretation of the Islamic dress code. The school is not required to become involved in any such learned discussion. (*Begum* HC 2004: §23)

Yet, the school does rest its case on representations of Islam, and not only when referring to supposed experts on Islam. This is the case when it argues that one can be a good Muslim while wearing the shalwar kameeze, basing this on statements by representatives from local and national representatives of Islam and on references to the head teacher's identity. Whether or not the school wants to get involved in disputes over the interpretation of Islam, it is forced to do so. This is so because the dispute is one of how to recognise Islamic belief in the school uniform, and so the dispute concerns what it means to be a Muslim in the first place, and what is proper to Islam. Recognition, representation and authority are closely connected, and one must always ask how the authority of recognition is established, and how authority is recognised. The discourse of recognition is, at least here, marked by several tensions or paradoxes: playing up and playing down difference; taking identities as given and constituting them; reproducing relations of power, yet also inherently open; homogeneity and heterogeneity, and consensus and pluralism. These are unresolvable paradoxes – they are aporias in Derrida's terminology – and 'reading for paradox' is a way to make better sense of the discourse or recognition marked by these aporias.

Contesting representations and recognition

If the politics of recognition can be understood as a struggle over representations, it is important who gets to represent what and whom, and how the authority of the representatives and representations is established. The authority of representations can be contested in two ways. One strategy is to argue for the contingent and partial character of a particular representation as opposed to an alternative non-contingent and true representation of, for instance, Islam. Another strategy is to argue for the contingent character of all representations. While both strategies may highlight the contingency of the contested representation, the second strategy does not substitute a supposedly non-contingent representation for a contingent one. The first strategy proceeds in a constative mode in that it claims that the true representation corresponds to something prior to, and independent of, the representation. The strategy is felicitous insofar as the performative aspect of the representation remains hidden from view. The second strategy, however, can be linked to the view defended here that representation and recognition proceed simultaneously in a constative and a performative mode. Here there is no claim to the independence and priority of the represented vis-à-vis the representation; any particular representation at once takes as given and constitutes what is represented.

In *Begum*, the two parties pursue both strategies. We have seen how the school rests its case on the view that there is a single authoritative Islam *and* on the view that no particular representation of Islam can be privileged, because those representations are mere 'opinions'. And we have seen how Shabina Begum is engaged in similar moves when she is at once talking up what she holds to be a true Islam and paying respect to the pluralism within Islam. It is tempting to ascribe these contradictions in their strategies either to confusion or to the self-serving pursuit of otherwise contradictory strategies, as when the school, very conveniently, only insists on interpretive pluralism when some of the Muslim representatives contradict the school's position. Nonetheless, although the parties may be both confused and self-serving, they cannot entirely avoid paradox, and this is due to the double constative and performative structure of both representation and recognition. Since representation must proceed at once in a constative and a performative mode, they must take the represented as both independent of and dependent on the representation. Likewise with recognition, which at once takes an identity as given and constitutes that identity performatively.

When Lord Justice Scott Baker complains 'that it is not for school authorities to pick and choose between religious beliefs and shades of religious belief' (in *Begum* CA 2005: §93), the answer must be that it could not be otherwise. Like Shabina Begum, the school authorities necessarily 'pick and choose' one representation of Islam over another. What must be analysed is how one representation becomes hegemonic, and what must be criticised are attempts to erase the representational and contingent character of a particular representation.

Insisting that recognition is marked by the constative/performative structure would undercut attempts to fix identities in time, whether it is the identity of a community (say, Islam) or of an individual. In *Begum*, for instance, the school argue that no further consultation was needed because 'appropriate consultation with relevant bodies has taken place' (*Begum* HC 2004: Annex, §11). They also argue that the policy was known to Shabina Begum, and that she had previously accepted the policy (2004: Annex, §§3, 25). These arguments fix the identity of Islam and of Shabina Begum at a certain point in time, but this is only possible to the extent that the identities are taken as stable and as re-cognisably identical over time.[31] This is problematic. Not only do identities change, but the process of recognition cannot be closed because identities are articulated through repeated recognition. It is precisely this insatiable need for recognition that keeps the process open to contestation.

Following the argument about the constative/performative structure of representation and recognition, we should pursue the second of the two strategies of contestation and posit representation against representation without claiming a non-representational – and, hence, uncontroversial – status for our favoured representation. One way to pursue the second strategy in the *Begum* case is to highlight the interpretive pluralism within Islam, thus rendering Islam internally divided to the extent that we can no longer talk of one Islam, and thus undermining the ability of anyone to set themselves up as authoritative representatives of Islam in the singular. Bringing pluralism and contingency to the fore pits (contingent) representation against (contingent) representation.

Insisting on pluralism and contingency is not an innocent or neutral strategy though, and it does not get us out of the paradoxical constative/performative structure of recognition and representation. For instance, in the case of Islam, interpretive pluralism can act as an implicit argument for a moderate interpretation of Islam that does not insist on a particular dress code. The pluralisation of Islam itself rests on a certain interpretation and identity of Islam. We do not get out of the bind of recognition and representation. What is more, the contestation of representations does not happen in an open market place of representations.[32] This liberal image of contestation ignores the ways in which the space of contestation is itself constituted on the basis of particular exclusions and biases.

Conclusion: beyond recognition and representation?

To understand the politics of recognition, one must conceive of it as a politics of representation. Recognition shares with representation the paradoxical structure of proceeding at once in a constative and in a performative mode. What is more, the politics of recognition draws upon representations, and representatives and representations must be recognised as authoritative. Since there is no recognition without representation, when we examine the politics of recognition, we must ask who gets to represent what, and how the representatives and representations are authorised. The politics of recognition is usually associated with identity politics. This is certainly true if by identity politics we understand a form of politics that proceeds from already recognised identities that are taken as given. But it is also the case that recognition involves a politics of identity where identities are rearticulated through the way that the discourse of recognition negotiates inclusion and exclusion.

Here my aim has been to call attention to and analyse the tensions – what I have called paradoxes or aporias – in the discourse of recognition. My argument is not against recognition as such. Recognition binds us to identities and representations that are often determined by agents in relative positions of power, something amply illustrated in the *Begum* case. In this sense, and to paraphrase Markell (2003), we become bound by recognition and representations. Like Markell, and their differences notwithstanding, Elizabeth Povinelli (1998), Wendy Brown (1995: chs 3, 5), Lois McNay (2008), Kelly Oliver (2001) and Drucilla Cornell and Sara Murphy (2002) stress the power relations involved in recognition, including the ways in which recognition itself helps reproduce these power relations (critically, see Malloy 2014).

This is not the whole story though. For the reasons given by proponents such as Galeotti and Taylor, recognition can be a way to include otherwise excluded and marginalised groups. What is more, although we become bound by recognition, we are never completely bound by it. Recognition requires that it be recognised in order to be effective. Like representation, no particular act of recognition can be the last word, because recognition is an open-ended process. This is a result of its paradoxical constative and performative structure. The upshot is that recognition and representations can always be contested, even if always in partly determined contexts of relative inequality.

Just as it is doubtful that we should simply reject recognition, it is questionable if we can and should move beyond recognition. We cannot escape the paradox of recognition or the way it binds agents to particular identities by substituting it with a different concept and practice. In the previous chapter on the concept and practice of equality, I showed how, although equality is inherently open-ended, it nonetheless involves recognition of the other as someone who can be counted as an equal and, thus, a representation of what it means to be an equal. It is also often noted how tolerance binds the tolerated party in an asymmetrical relationship to the tolerating party, and, in the next chapter, I show how tolerance involves the creation and negotiation of circles that distinguish a norm from those who are different. Finally, in the last chapter of the book, I show how hospitality implies an unconditional opening to the other, yet is simultaneously conditional and aimed at a particular, determined other. Thus we are dealing with a general structure: any inclusion involves representation, and any inclusion involves exclusion. Inclusion is always inclusion of a particular other, and it goes hand in hand with a degree of exclusion. Although my argument dovetails with that of Markell, this is also where we differ. For him, the bind of recognition is 'probably' unavoidable even when substituting acknowledgement and potency for recognition and sovereignty (Markell 2003: 188); for me, the bind is constitutive and also marks the alternatives to recognition. In any discourse of inclusion, gains cannot be dissociated from losses, and we will never have full recognition or inclusion without exclusion.[33]

What the sort of deconstructive analysis pursued here can contribute is a different attitude to recognition and inclusion. This alternative attitude is to challenge representations, thereby denaturalising them and revealing their contingent and contestable nature, and emphasising the open-ended character of recognition. This alternative attitude would help show that identities are effects of representations, and that their apparent authenticity is an effect of naturalisations of those representations. Even if the

resulting unbinding is never complete, it facilitates the contestation of existing – that is, recognised – representations. It would
also facilitate what William Connolly (1995: ch. 6) calls pluralisation as opposed to the pluralism of already recognised differences.
This is analogous to Markell's (2003: 188–9) proposal to multi-
ply the sites of political recognition in order to weaken the reproduction of the sovereignty of the state through recognition. With
Connolly, I would insist that sovereignty, power and inequality
cannot be done away with, only negotiated differently. It would
be a politics of recognition that takes neither what is to be recognised nor the parameters of recognition as given, and it means
treating recognition as an ongoing and open-ended process.

This sort of pluralisation may make us more sensitive to those
marginalised or excluded constituencies that have not yet passed
the threshold of recognition into mainstream society. In *Begum*,
that threshold is construed as an antagonistic frontier signified
by the sartorial difference between the jilbab and the shalwar
kameeze. Although a strategy of pluralisation will not take us
beyond recognition and the problems associated with it, it nonetheless contributes to opening up possibilities within the politics of
recognition and representation, making possible a *politics* of recognition based on the agonistic struggle over representations. The
politics of recognition and multiculturalism are steps towards such
a pluralisation of social and political spaces – imagine a Britain
without multiculturalism! – but we must be aware of the internal
limits to the discourse of recognition, and how it negotiates the
relationship between inclusion and exclusion.

Notes

1. For a good summary of the case, see McGoldrick 2006: ch. 6. Subsequent to the case, the government issued guidance to schools on
   school uniforms in which *Begum* was cited. In Chapter 4, I return to
   the debate about *Begum* as well as three later legal cases where both
   the judges and the media made reference to *Begum*.
2. In analysing the case, I have relied on the court decisions, newspaper articles, material from the internet and academic literature. The

school's views are mainly found in the court decisions. The bulk of Shabina Begum's self-representations are found in electronic media, including the online chat at IslamOnline.net (Begum 2005a); a TV interview with *GMTV Today* (Begum 2006a); and two public statements to *BBC News* (Begum 2005b; Begum 2006b). See also the radio programme 'Symbol-ed Out', presented by Shabina Begum (2008).

3. For instance, that of Axel Honneth (Fraser and Honneth 2003). See also McNay 2008.
4. For critiques of Taylor, see the contributions in Gutmann 1994; Markell 2003: ch. 2. For critiques of Galeotti, see Jones 2006; Lægaard 2008.
5. Note that the presumption of equal worth is only that: a presumption, which can be challenged through dialogue.
6. For this view of representation more generally, see Derrida 1982; Derrida 1997; Thomassen 2007a. For related treatments of representation in different contexts, see Spivak 1988; Alcoff 1991–2.
7. In the legal context, these arguments suffer from a fundamental bind: because autonomy is tied to age in the legal discourse, representing Shabina Begum as a child takes away from her autonomy, which it is claimed that the family (here her older brother) is wrongfully interfering with. The trouble is that you cannot both claim that she is just a child and complain that her family is trying to influence her.
8. More generally, recognition and representation are acts of naming and conceptual subsumption, but can be reduced to neither. They are not simply performative acts of naming because they draw upon existing representations and must be repeated; and they are not simply acts of conceptual subsumption because they are constitutive of what is recognised or represented.
9. On recognition and autonomy, see García Düttmann 2000: 214–16. There is something improper about recognition: both authenticity and autonomy refer to something that is proper to the self, but neither of them can function as origins or teloi of recognition. See Markell 2003: 63–4.
10. For this critique of recognition, see also Brown 1995: chs 3, 5; Povinelli 1998. Critically, see McNay 2008.
11. Cf. also the classic formulation in Hegel 1977: §§178–96.
12. For this view of the subject, see Adams and Minson 1990.
13. See also García Düttmann 2000: 125–6; Scott 1996; Scott 1999: chs 8–10. Neither Minow nor Scott links her analysis explicitly to the constative/performative structure; however, their analyses stress

how (claims for) rights do not merely reflect pre-existing identities, but also constitute these, in particular in the context of the hierarchical relationship between norm and difference.

14. For the judges' confirmation of this view, see *Begum* HC 2004: §§39–40; *Begum* HL 2006: §34.

15. This is distinct from the newspaper debates about the case where there is a wider array of views. I return to these debates in the next chapter.

16. Shabina Begum (2008) is 'symbol-ed out'. In the next chapter, I return to a fuller analysis of the ways in which Shabina Begum's jilbab is signified in the media.

17. This is how it is referred to in the deputy head teacher's statement (*Begum* HC 2004: §84 no. 26). When pressed on the issue, Shabina Begum (2005a, in online chat at IslamOnline.net) is ambivalent about whether other forms of dress are good enough for Muslim women.

18. For Shabina Begum's views on how veiling contributes to Islam's economy of interaction between men and women, see online chat at IslamOnline.net (Begum 2005a).

19. Blair and Aps (2005: 15–16) point out that the discrimination against the jilbab could be considered intersectional discrimination because it happens at the intersection between religion *and* sex. Both the Islamic injunction to veil the female body and the prohibition against veiling put heavier burdens on women.

20. In Islamic discourses, the length of dress is often taken as a measure of religiosity and modesty. In both types of discourses, (Muslim) women are reduced to what they wear. For a critique of this in the context of *Begum*, see Eltahawy 2005.

21. It also reinforces the image of her as aggressive, the other side of widely circulating representations of hijab-wearing women as simultaneously passive and aggressive.

22. Compare *Begum* CA 2005: §93; *Begum* HL 2006: §21.

23. Here I am not interested in the meaning of 'kul' of which 'slave' is the translation, but which could also be translated as 'subject'; what is important is the way Shabina Begum uses this idea. See also Tarlo 2010: 117. On Islam, the hijab and agency, see Ahmed 1992: ch. 11, Conclusion; Scott 2007: ch. 4; Hirschmann 1997; Hirschmann 1998; Norton 2013: ch. 2; Abu-Odeh 1993; Mahmood 2005: chs 1, 5, Epilogue.

24. For media discussions of the authority of the representations of Islam by the school and Shabina Begum, see Eltahawy 2005; Alam 2006; and the discussion at IslamOnline.net (Begum 2005a).

25. For instance, in *Begum* HC 2004: §15, my emphasis, the judge refers to the '*independent* advice' by the representatives.
26. The process can be described in terms of the Derridean notion of iterability, which is another way of saying that there is no pure repetition and no pure constative (Derrida 1988; García Düttmann 2001: 84–95).
27. However, see *Begum* HC 2004: §2. In *Begum* HC 2004: §12 and *Begum* HL 2006: §§4, 43, 74, they also highlight the fact that several of the school governors were Muslim.
28. I return to the rhetorical aspect of representation in the next chapter. See also Laclau 2005: 72–3; Laclau 2008.
29. Note the reference to '*the* Islamic dress code'.
30. Similarly Justice Bennett in *Begum* HC 2004: §71: the school 'was not determining whether the Claimant's beliefs were legitimate'.
31. Note that the European Convention on Human Rights, Article 9(1) stipulates a right 'to *change* [one's] religion or belief' (Council of Europe 2010: 10). For a defence, in the context of *Begum*, of the view that agents develop over time and that the law must reflect this, see Leader 2007.
32. As suggested by Tarlo 2010.
33. As a result, Markell's (and others') scepticism about the state as a source of recognition and inclusion may be well placed, but this should not lead to a flight from the state, but to pursue different and simultaneous strategies, some of which may involve the state. This is also where Malloy (2014) goes wrong when she reproduces the opposition between state and non-state in an inverted form in her critique of Markell and Brown.

4 Tolerance: Circles of Inclusion and Exclusion

Introduction: circles of tolerance

It is often noted that tolerance, or toleration, always involves a limit. There is no tolerance without limits, no tolerance without intolerance, and this is all the more so because tolerance is a self-limiting practice that must be protected against those intolerant of it. Tolerance, then, draws a circle that shuts out; it draws a circle, or a threshold, of tolerance around me, or us, protecting us from that which threatens us in one way or another. What is shut out is different from me, or from us or a norm, so different that I object, and so objectionable that I cannot tolerate it. As is also often noted, I can only tolerate that to which I object; this is the so-called objection requirement. I cannot tolerate what I like or that to which I am indifferent. Tolerance is precisely a means to deal with and include difference, a way of relating to difference in a manner that is not simply hostile or excludes what is different. Tolerance, then, also draws a circle that shuts in: it shuts me up with some difference that is not to my taste, but without which I would not be exercising tolerance. The practice of tolerance at once reproduces and reinforces identity *and* opens it up to what might undermine it (Forst 2013; King 1998; Stolzenberg 1993).[1]

When we practise tolerance, we include and exclude at one and the same time. It is not a question of either/or: either inclusion or exclusion. Rather, as is the case with equality and recognition, tolerance is always a combination of both inclusion and exclusion. If tolerance shuts out and shuts in, it is perhaps better to think of the circles of tolerance as concentric circles around a subject, whether an individual or a collective identity. What is more, there is no tolerance without the inequality between tolerating and tolerated, between the ones in a position of extending tolerance and the ones asking for tolerance. In this, too, tolerance shares a common structure with equality and recognition. Although included, the tolerated is not included into an egalitarian space, but into a further set of circles, where the tolerated is continuously reminded of his or her marginal and precarious position (Brown 2006; Fish 1997; Hage 1998; Marcuse 1969). For all these reasons, tolerance is an ambiguous practice and concept of inclusion, and it may be better to speak of marginalisation and relative inclusion and exclusion rather than a dichotomy of inclusion and exclusion. On top of that, in any society, and at any particular point in time, there will be more than one (competing) representation of the circles of tolerance and of who we and they are, the tolerating and those who are tolerated or not tolerated.

Some limit to tolerance is necessary. If tolerance were normatively empty, and if there were no limit to it, we would be forced to tolerate those intolerant of tolerance. Tolerance would turn into its opposite. Tolerance is necessarily a self-limiting discourse, and it requires us to distinguish between the tolerable and the intolerable – without intolerance there is no tolerance. But if we only tolerate those who are reasonable or morally acceptable, this merely replaces the distinction between tolerance and intolerance with another distinction: between reasonable and unreasonable, or between moral and immoral. Tolerance, then, only works if there is a limit to it, and if that limit is articulated in some way. What we need to examine is how the distinction between what should be tolerated and what should not is articulated: what are the normative distinctions, values and identities that are brought into play in order to articulate tolerance and its limit in one way or another? And that is why it is useful to analyse tolerance – as discourses about tolerance – through the lens of hegemony understood as articulation and representation (Laclau 1996b: 50–2).

Tolerance starts from difference, but it also differentiates. It produces and reproduces difference, sometimes as inequality, marginalisation and exclusion. Tolerance does not overcome difference and exclusion because these are constitutive of it. Tolerance also binds. In a way similar to recognition (Chapter 3), it binds the tolerated party to the tolerating party in a relation of hierarchy and marginality, and it binds those who are not tolerated in an antagonistic relation vis-à-vis those who refuse them tolerance. But the bind also goes in the reverse direction: the tolerating party is bound by their tolerance or intolerance of those who are different from them, and their identity is in part constituted through the relationships of tolerance and intolerance. Through the practice of tolerance, we become 'we the rational, tolerant, and so on' and others become 'they the irrational, intolerant, and so on'. This is important to keep in mind because of the way in which Britishness is usually represented as tolerant, and in both its liberal and conservative versions, Gordon Brown and David Cameron being good examples. Yet, the image of a tolerant nation only goes so far: from Locke to Cameron, through the early debates about multiculturalism and Brown's Britishness, tolerance is not extended to those who are represented as dangerous to the state and the nation. This is equally visible in the (post-)colonial aspect of British tolerance discourse that usually reproduces a relationship between we white, civilised and tolerant and the coloured and unruly other.

Through the articulations of circles of inclusion and exclusion, tolerance also rearticulates identities, for instance when representing ourselves as tolerant and others as tolerable or intolerable. This is most obvious when we claim to be tolerant. Not only do we claim to be tolerant – open-minded, generous – but we also situate ourselves in a position to be capable of extending tolerance. To claim to be tolerant is also to claim to be sovereign, just like the claim to recognise (Chapter 3) or be hospitable (Chapter 5). At the same time, our claim to be tolerant places the others in a position of being tolerated, or not. They are different, and at best they are placed in a position of minority and marginality; at worst, they are placed in the position of intolerable. Tolerance invokes subjectivities and identities, and not only as formal relationships between tolerating and tolerated parties, positions that can be occupied by one subject or another. Invoking a 'we', and the positioning of a 'we' and a 'they', is always connected to more concrete identities, as when we tolerate turban-wearing Sikhs who are deemed to be different yet tolerable and somehow part of a British imperial history that we cherish. And often those who are deemed intolerable are so because they are said to be intolerant – fundamentalists and extremists and *as such* intolerant; intolerant and *as such* fundamentalists and extremists – thus justifying our intolerance of them. The *Begum* case and the debate about it are good examples of this. Engaging in tolerance means engaging in identity formation. And if, as I suggested, there is more than one representation of tolerance at any one time, then there will also be different and competing representations of the identities involved. This is what I want to analyse: how is the relationship between inclusion and exclusion articulated through practices of tolerance, and how are identities articulated, and rearticulated, in the process?

This chapter also provides an opportunity to revisit Laclau's theory of hegemony. Looking at tolerance through the analytical lens of hegemony makes me able to argue that tolerance is not simply a one-way hierarchical relationship of power where the tolerated are placed in a position of marginality and inferiority with no power to resist. This is the danger of the approach of some critics of tolerance – for instance, Herbert Marcuse (1969), Stanley Fish (1997), Ghassan Hage (1998) and Wendy Brown (2006) – for whom tolerance may not in the end be reduced to domination, but there is nonetheless a strong tendency to do so in their works (see also Tønder 2013). Through the lens of hegemony, tolerance can be shown to be a practice articulated in a discursive field of competing discourses and representations of tolerance and of identities. This is not to suggest that everything – including the hierarchical relationship of tolerance – is (equally) open to easy rearticulation. This much will become clear through the analysis and discussion of the cases in this chapter; any articulation and representation happens in a discursive field that is already partially sedimented, and sometimes more so than at other times. And, while it is better to be in a position of tolerator than tolerated, tolerance is better than intolerance, even if tolerance and intolerance – inclusion and exclusion – are not diametrically opposed.

Tolerance discourse also provides an example of a kind of discourse that does not work only by way of the articulation of a chain of equivalence, an empty signifier and an antagonistic frontier. While these are important elements of the representation of tolerance in the discourses analysed here, tolerance and the different identities are also articulated through circles (rather than only antagonistic frontiers), nodal points (rather than only empty signifiers) and by placing subjects within an intricate institutionalised hierarchy (rather than only a populist discourse of 'us' and 'them'). This is particularly important for the way tolerance has been articulated in the terrain of British multiculturalism.

Discourses of tolerance

There is no concept of tolerance that can be analysed at a purely formal or structural level; there is only tolerance as particular discourses of tolerance, and it is these discourses that one must analyse. As in other chapters, I therefore analyse a concept – here: tolerance – through an analysis of the way in which it is articulated and used in particular discourses. But it is with the caveat that the particular discourses are not instantiations of some universal and essential concept of tolerance that can only be indirectly appropriated in this way; there is no concept of tolerance as such to be appropriated.

I discuss the circles of tolerance through analyses of the debates about four British court cases from the first decade of the twenty-first century. The cases all concern religious symbols and clothing worn by schoolgirls in state schools: *Begum* (a Muslim jilbab), *X v Y* (a Muslim niqab), *Playfoot* (a Christian chastity ring) and *Watkins-Singh* (a Sikh *kara* or bangle). The court cases occurred in this chronological order between 2004 and 2008, although the *Begum* case started in 2002. The three later decisions all make reference to *Begum*, which was the only case to go to the House of Lords, and in the journalistic coverage and in the debates, there are several cross-references among the cases.

The four cases all concern religious difference, and we have become used to thinking of tolerance first and foremost in the context of religion, and to thinking of the solution to religious difference as tolerance (Forst 2013; Zagorin 2003). The cases all concern female pupils. Cases involving religious symbols and clothing in the public sphere almost always involve women, the main exception being Sikh males (as in *Mandla* discussed in Chapter 2). Female sexuality and bodies provide a privileged site for struggles over identity, whether the identity of the majority or the identities of minorities. I will not go into a wider discussion of this here, and, as evidenced by the discussion in Chapter 3, the literature is vast. The cases all involve state schools. Schools – and in particular state schools – are supposed to teach the children to be full and equal citizens in a pluralistic society. Schools are key sites of struggles over the meaning of citizenship, Britishness and tolerance, and this was no less so during the New Labour years, with the Crick Report, the Parekh Report, David Blunkett's interventions and Brown's Britishness discourse being prominent examples.

The cases are all from the first decade of the new millennium. While multiculturalism had been a staple of the first years of the New Labour government – with, among other things, the Parekh Report (Commission on the Future of Multi-Ethnic Britain 2000) and the Human Rights Act 1998, which came into effect in 2000 – multiculturalism was increasingly challenged, and, after 9/11 and 7/7, Muslims were increasingly singled out as suspicious.[2] The first decade of the twenty-first century was also a time of religious revival, with religion and religious symbols gaining increased significance in the public sphere, especially among fundamentalist Christians and Muslims. This gave added importance to religious dress and symbols as markers of difference and identification. This much is also evident in other similar cases and debates from the last decade, whether cases concerning schoolchildren or employment disputes or debates about Islam and veiling.

The four cases concern different religions and different forms of dress and symbols: different versions of Islam (*Begum* and *X v Y*), Christianity (*Playfoot*) and Sikhism (*Watkins-Singh*). One of my aims is to see how the three religions, and different versions of them, are placed in relation to one another and in relation to those writing about them. Here the positions of atheist and secular are also important, and together these different cases contain a number of different positions and relations, above all: different versions of Islam; Christianity in opposition to two different minority religions (Islam and Sikhism); and secularists and atheists in opposition to religious people in general and in relation to particular religions, whether the majority religion (Christianity) or minority religions (Islam and Sikhism).

The question is then how, in and through the circles of tolerance, inclusion and exclusion as well as identities are articulated and represented. Here, as elsewhere in the book, I take representation as constitutive. It is therefore not a question of adjudicating between different representations as to which one best mirrors a non-representational reality. Rather, that reality consists of representations, and identities are constituted at the level of representation. So I shall not be asking whether, for instance, Islam and Christianity are correctly represented in the material, or whether the views of the protagonists in the court cases are correctly represented by journalists and commentators. As such, my approach differs from the Critical Discourse Analysis (CDA) of John Richardson and others who have written about the misrepresentations of Islam and Muslims in the British media (Richardson 2004; Baker et al. 2013; Morey and Yaqin 2011).[3] For them, it is possible to distinguish correct from incorrect representations and to identify agents with already constituted interests and identities, agents who employ (mis)representations to exercise power. My approach is different in that I take representation as constitutive. Therefore we cannot compare the different representations with a non-representational reality, and the representations are constitutive of the identities of those who are represented, whether they are self- or other-representations.

I analyse the debates about the cases in two major broadsheets: *The Guardian* and *The Daily* (and *Sunday*) *Telegraph*.[4] The first is on the liberal left, the second is right-wing and conservative. My aim is not to cover all aspects and positions of the debates; in order to do that, it would be necessary to look at other newspapers, especially tabloids, and at television and internet material. Rather, *The Guardian* and *The Telegraph* give me an interesting slice of the debates. As agents and as discursive spaces of inscription, the two papers represent important, and contrasting, positions: the liberal and tolerant *Guardian* as opposed to *The Telegraph*, which is not necessarily intolerant but represents a certain conservative and nationalist view of the United Kingdom or, to be precise, England. Whether liberal or conservative, both newspapers are self-consciously tolerant. In each case I use the online versions, and I have analysed news articles written by journalists, columns and longer commentaries, letters to the editor and readers' online comments.[5] Following the order of this list of materials, the different kinds of material become gradually shriller and more xenophobic in both newspapers. Although I only look at broadsheets, there are plenty of the kinds of statement one would otherwise expect to find in tabloids.

I focus on debates about legal cases, and my interest is not in the legal proceedings and decisions as in Chapter 3 on the *Begum* case; instead my interest lies in the public debates and popular discourses. Having said that, there is no watertight separation between the decisions, the legal discourse, the media coverage and the debate in the newspapers; as described in Chapter 3, *Begum* was a good example of this. Signifiers and arguments travel from the court into the media through news reports and statements by the parties involved, and the parties make their case both in court and in the media. What is more, what goes on in court and what goes on in the media draw upon the same, more general discourses about Islam, religion and schools.

When analysing the newspapers, I am interested in them less as agents and more as spaces of inscription for other agents. As agents, the newspapers use different kinds of material to represent their self-understanding: there may be a journalistic line, and columns, letters to the editor and readers' online comments are authorised to different degrees by their inclusion in the paper. This gives rise to differences between the two papers, and I shall highlight those significant differences below.

However, I am more interested in the newspapers as discursive spaces that express – and are representative of – larger societal discourses about religion, schools and British identity. Those discursive spaces function as spaces of inscription that are always already partly shaped and framed. Although I am more interested in the two newspapers as discursive spaces of inscription than as agents, it should be stressed that the two things cannot be wholly separated. The discursive space and discourses do not 'speak' by themselves, but nor do subjects, because they draw upon, and place themselves within, existing discourses, and because they are only speaking subjects insofar as they are recognised as such within a discursive space. And to place oneself and speak from within a particular discursive space – for instance, *The Telegraph* – is also a way of performing one's identity.

Treating the newspapers as discursive spaces of inscription within which different discourses compete for domination means that, as far as possible, I disconnect the statements analysed from enunciating subjects and connect them to wider discursive structures within and outside the papers. This has important consequences for the individuation – which is also to say identification and representation – of the subjects, discourses and discursive spaces. Identifying subjects (newspapers, journalists, commentators, and so on) is less important than identifying the discursive space temporally and spatially, and also less important than identifying the dominant discourses within that space. By no means do this discursive space and its structure lend themselves to be simply discovered, as if passively; rather, the identification of the discursive space and of the discourses is an active act of representation that, while claiming to discover an object of analysis, simultaneously construes it as an object that can be submitted to analysis. And here the individuation of the discursive space and the discourses cannot be distinguished absolutely from the choice and analysis of the material.

If, as I have argued throughout this book, representation is constitutive, this also applies to the researcher's representation of his or her material, and it applies to the relationship between the material and what it is supposed to represent. The analysis proceeds in a quasi-self-referential manner, at once pointing towards an object and constituting it, and as a result methodological questions remain – and must remain – open. Take just two examples.

First, what are the units that I analyse – discursive spaces, discourses, newspapers, journalists, readers, individual articles, comments for individual articles, individual comments, statements within articles or comments? I am drawn towards smaller – concrete and citable – units for evidence in support of my conclusions, yet they only provide support if they are representative of something bigger – discourses about British identity, for instance. Put differently, the individual statements that I quote can only be interpreted as evidence of the existence of a larger discourse insofar as the latter has already been identified, which is in turn only possible through the interpretation of individual statements. The analysis is caught in a hermeneutic circle that cannot be closed.

Second, and more concretely, I identify a discursive space temporally as roughly the first decade of this century, starting with 11 September 2001, and spatially I limit it to the UK, two newspapers and the debates about four legal cases. Those are the limits and starting point of my analysis, yet those limits can surely only be identified through the analysis itself. Just as one might ask whether the discursive space should not be broadened out (taking 9/11 as a limit is both obvious and problematic), one might ask whether this discursive space is indeed a single space and not several.

When analysing the material, I impose on it the language of 'tolerance'. The cases are articulated as cases of tolerance by the parties and by the commentators, and often this is linked to representations of British identity and history. There are good reasons for treating the material as illustrative and representative of the concept and practice of tolerance, but when I use the language of tolerance, it also follows a certain logic of the book as a whole. According to this logic, tolerance is an important concept in political theory and an important practice and concept of inclusion. The analysis of the material is situated in this hermeneutic circle that never closes, between a logic foreign to, and imposed upon, the material and the representations 'discovered' in the material – representations that only appear as representations of tolerance through the prism of a logic that emerges from a point partly outside the material.

When analysing the material, I ask two questions. The first is how someone positions themselves in what I have described as concentric circles of tolerance. Here I am interested in how agents position themselves and others as tolerating and tolerated, tolerable and intolerable, and so forth. I ask how they position themselves in relation to a norm and in relation to those who are different or other, whatever the content of the norm or the difference. Treating difference as relational – because defined in relation to a norm – brings out the contingent character of identity and difference (Minow 1991). The second question I ask is how they articulate their own identity and that of those who are different, for instance as moderate as opposed to fundamentalist and extreme, as tolerant as opposed to intolerant, as British or foreign, as religious or as secular or atheist, and as Christian or Muslim or Sikh. Although it is possible to analytically separate the two questions, they are not separate questions in the material, and I will not separate them in the presentation of the material. This is so for the simple reason that the positioning vis-à-vis a norm and a difference is always in relation to a particular norm and a particular difference (for example, 'British' and 'foreign') which are articulated as the norm and as what is different. To claim that someone is different is only possible in relation to a particular norm against which their difference can be identified. Any discourse of tolerance may involve the representation of a norm and what is different from it, but no discourse can be analysed at this abstract and formal level alone.

Modesty and extremism: *Begum*

As described in Chapter 3, the *Begum* case started when Shabina Begum came to school wearing a jilbab at the beginning of the school year in September 2002. This contravened the school uniform policy, which had different versions of the uniform for girls, including a shalwar kameeze, which Begum believed covered too little of her body. Begum took the school to court. She lost in the High Court in 2004, won in the Court of Appeal the year after, and lost in the House of Lords in 2006. Apart from being the first of the four cases I discuss in this chapter, and apart from being the case with most coverage in the media and in the academic literature, the case stands out because it went through three rounds of court hearings and decisions. However, there are no significant differences in the coverage of, and comments upon, the three different court hearings and decisions. Although the court decisions differ, the journalists and commentators take the same positions throughout.[6]

Begum's jilbab is articulated in two ways by commentators and by the parties involved. In the dominant articulation of the jilbab, it is articulated as a symbol of extremism, and, in a less prominent articulation, it is articulated as modesty. I shall refer to these as the extremism and modesty discourses respectively.

The school and its solicitors (through news reports) and the majority of commentators and readers in the two newspapers draw upon and position themselves within the extremism discourse.[7] The jilbab is associated with extremism, as being on one end of a continuum where the school has placed itself in the moderate middle. As extremist, it is deemed intolerable. The physical difference between the shalwar kameeze and the jilbab symbolises Begum's difference from a tolerable Islam. The school is said to have acted in a sensible and tolerant fashion, seeking to facilitate inclusion through the different versions of the school uniform and by consulting with representatives of the local Muslim community. The jilbab is assumed to introduce division into the school which had otherwise gained socially and academically from the school uniform. Begum's stance is taken to be provocative and the jilbab to express an extreme and radical form of Islam, and both the school and several commentators and readers see Begum's actions as politically (as opposed to merely religiously) motivated. Some link her to Hizb ut-Tahrir, of which her brother was a member (for instance, McCartney 2005).

In the extremism discourse, a distinction is made between moderate and extremist Muslims, with Begum and the jilbab belonging to the latter category. Having said that, there are a few examples of another version of the extremism discourse where Islam as a whole is represented as extremist and alien to Britain, for instance: 'Our traditions are the golden thread of freedom and a good piss-up every now and then; neither is compatible with Islam' (comment for Odone 2006).[8]

One of the main reasons for the extremism label being applied to the jilbab is that it is associated with the oppression of women; that is, one of the defining characteristics of the jilbab is that it is antithetical to freedom. The best example of this is the title of a commentary in *The Guardian*: 'Of course women have a right to choose. But agreeing to wear a jilbab is no choice at all' (Bennett 2005). Here Begum's freedom to choose to wear what she wants is first asserted ('Of course women have a right to choose'), but this freedom is immediately deemed shallow. The choice can then be described as 'no choice at all' but 'agreeing to . . .', implying that it follows from pressure from others. If the choice to wear the jilbab is 'no choice at all', then it is not self-contradictory to oppose Shabina Begum's so-called 'choice' in the name of free choice.[9] Intolerance is here articulated on the side of freedom, but it is the intolerance of intolerance, and so there is no contradiction between *this* intolerance and freedom.

Apart from the generally more nationalist and Islamophobic character of the material from *The Telegraph*, the only substantial difference between the two papers is that, in *The Telegraph*, the case is linked to human rights and the European Union (often referred to as 'Europe').[10] The case is said to show that human rights practice has gone awry, and this is in turn linked to multiculturalism and to the allegedly excessive influence of the EU on British society. Opposed to this are common sense and British values. A good example is 'We need common sense and justice – not "human rights"', where 'ordinary human feelings of justice and common sense' and 'British justice' are opposed to '[a]bstract and absolute' human rights imposed on the UK through the European Convention on Human Rights, 'the very opposite of British common law' (Utley 2005).[11] Human rights are also associated with 'lawyers' and 'courts':

> Six years of baffling, even perverse, rulings now serve as a reminder of what happens when carefully drafted laws are over-ridden with vague principles that can be interpreted in widely different ways.
>
> It is bad enough that lawyers are now making the law but . . . it is not always the courts themselves that are guilty of making barmy decisions: deprived of any clear rules, the Human Rights Act has created a climate of fear in which all manner of authorities give in to all kinds of outrageous demands, for fear of being sued and subjected to the lottery that the legal system has become following the Human Rights Act 2001. (Leapman 2006)

Lawyers, courts, human rights and the EU are – together with multiculturalism – part of a liberal elite and, as such, removed from ordinary British taxpayers, and it is this elite and these institutions that allow for extremists like Shabina Begum to take advantage of British freedoms. Absent from *The Guardian*, except in the readers' online comments,[12] this view is prevalent on the British right, but is also influential among many Labour voters. This populist discourse divides ordinary British people from elites and extremists and all things foreign. Importantly, because of the distinction between moderate and extremist Muslims, Islam is not simply excluded from ordinary British people.

The modesty discourse is represented by Shabina Begum, her brother and her solicitors as well as a minority of commentators and readers. It has a significantly smaller voice in the material than does the extremism discourse, including in *The Guardian*. Shabina Begum and her brother place the case in the context of the vilification of Muslims in Britain after 9/11, and they articulate the case as yet another attempt to exclude and marginalise Muslims. Thus, after winning in the Court of Appeal, Shabina Begum says that it was a victory against the 'prejudice and bigotry' of the 'atmosphere that has been created in Western societies post-9/11, an atmosphere in which Islam has been made a target for vilification in the name of the "war on terror"' (quoted in Aslam 2005). And a *Guardian* reader comments online:

> Interesting that everybody assumes that wearing the jilbab is necessarily a decision made under pressure. All teenagers come under pressure from parents regarding the clothes that they wear, but that's hardly a matter for the school to intervene in.
>
> It is somewhat patronising to assume that girls wearing the jilbab do this solely due to pressure from others. At a time when Islam is widely under attack in the Western world, isn't it understandable that this girl chose to make a strong statement about her faith? Wearing a jilbab certainly does that. (Comment for Bunting 2006)[13]

Whereas in the extremism discourse, the jilbab is represented as extremist and un-British, in the modesty discourse, wearing the jilbab is articulated as a matter of religious freedom, which is in turn represented as part of a British tradition of freedom and rights. 'I was just practising my religion', Shabina Begum says (quoted in *The Guardian* 2006). That it is *religious* freedom is important for Shabina Begum because it gives her a foothold within the Human Rights Act and Article 9 of the European Convention on Human Rights. It is also important because it dissociates the jilbab from the apparent threat of political Islam, and makes possible alliances with other religious people, even if it may at the same time antagonise secularists. In these ways, the actions of the school become associated with intolerance and oppression. In this discourse, wearing the jilbab is religiously, as opposed to politically, motivated, and the jilbab is associated with modesty, something which some of the agents of the extremism discourse openly reject. Conversely, Shabina Begum and her brother reject the extremism label attached to the jilbab and their views, and they reject that the jilbab is anything more than an expression of Shabina Begum's genuine religious beliefs. There is a tradition of thinking about tolerance as first and foremost religious tolerance. Going back to at least Locke, this tradition reduces the tolerated difference to a religious difference, thereby taking the danger out of tolerance. Treating the religious difference as *religious* difference assumes a distinction between private and public, church and state, thereby protecting the state and the national identity from what is now merely religious.

Each discourse is centred around a chain of equivalence where the elements are related through contiguity, whereby the meaning of each element is in part constituted through its association with the other elements (Laclau and Mouffe 1985: ch. 3; Laclau 2005: ch. 5).[14] In the extremism discourse, the chain includes the jilbab, extremism, oppression and, in the case of *The Telegraph*, also human rights and multiculturalism. In the modesty discourse, the chain includes the jilbab, modesty and freedom. We might refer to this as the metonymic aspect of the discourses, whereby meaning travels from one element of the chain to the others by way of association. The metonymy turns into metaphor, and the association into substitution, when the jilbab stands in for the other elements, both individually and collectively. The move from metonymy to metaphor happens as an equivalence is established between the different elements that come to make up the chain of equivalence. Thereby each element is split in two: on the one hand, it is a particular element and different from the rest; on the other hand, it is one element in a chain where all the elements share the same equivalential content. It is the latter that makes possible the move from association to substitution because the elements are now (also) the same in some respect and can substitute for one another. The consequence is that, in the extremism discourse, the commentators can debate Islam by debating the jilbab, even when insisting that they are only debating the jilbab, and that they do not mean their intolerance of the jilbab as intolerance of Islam as a whole.

Strictly speaking, we are dealing with a synecdoche here because a part of the chain (for instance, the jilbab) stands in for the chain as a whole (for instance, Islam). Insofar as the elements are elements in the same chain of equivalence, each and every element can, to some extent, stand in for the rest of the elements and represent the chain as a whole. However, there is nothing necessary about a particular part (here, the jilbab) coming to stand in for the whole. The articulation of the part and of the whole, separately and related, is contingent, which does not mean that it is accidental. In the *Begum* case, for instance, it is not accidental that the jilbab came to take up this role, because the legal dispute concerns the difference between the jilbab and the shalwar kameeze. The particular element that substitutes for the rest of the elements in the chain and, thus, structures the discourse will shape the discourse as a whole. In this sense, it matters which element comes to take up this quilting role in the discourse, that is, which element comes to play the role of a nodal point. The relationship between part and whole is therefore a relationship of articulation, or representation, in the sense that it is constitutive: the whole is constituted through this relation whereby a particular part of the chain of equivalence stands in for, or represents, the whole. We are dealing with a catachresis because the synecdoche does not establish a relationship between two already constituted elements (part and whole), but itself constitutes those two elements. In other words, the meaning and identity of 'jilbab' and 'Islam' are not simply given, but constituted in the moment when the jilbab is articulated as representative of Islam. To be precise, the meaning that is articulated is not simply the meaning of the jilbab and of Islam, as if those meanings were given, but a particular meaning of the jilbab and a particular meaning of Islam – and of course there are competing meanings of both jilbab and Islam in play here. This is why it matters which element comes to stand in for the whole. In reality, the contingent relationship between part and whole will often be naturalised to the extent that the parts are all and entirely defined by the whole of which they are a part, and to the extent that no internal divisions appear in the whole. In one version of the extremism discourse, for instance, Muslims are all defined by the extremism of the jilbab, even those who do not wear it.[15]

The two discourses stand opposed to one another with one negating the other's articulation of the jilbab. One's freedom is the other's oppression; where the jilbab stands for extremism in one, it stands for modesty in the other; and where the jilbab and Begum's actions are political in one, they are religious in the other. Here we can talk of an antagonistic frontier between the two discourses, where the two meanings of the jilbab are mutually exclusive. But the discourses are quilted around the same nodal point: Shabina Begum's jilbab. We have here two antagonistic or mutually exclusive representations of the jilbab. The mutual exclusivity is not a matter of logical contradiction, but arises from the representation of them as mutually exclusive.[16]

The antagonistic frontier is important for both discourses, but perhaps especially for the extremism discourse, at least insofar as it relies on a slippery slope argument. This is the argument of some of the columns, longer commentaries and letters to the editor. The argument is that if one does not draw the line between moderate and extreme Muslims, the shalwar kameeze and the jilbab, tolerating the former but not the latter, then this will lead to all sorts of imaginable evils. For instance, in *The Telegraph*, one reader asks: 'What now? Are polygamy and circumcision of females also rights?' (James 2005), and one commentator asks: 'would the next innovation in the uniform – for the truly devout – be the face-concealing burqa?' (McCartney 2005). And in *The Observer*, a journalist doubling as a commentator asks: 'But what if another 14-year-old girl decides that the jilbab on its own is too immodest and therefore opts to add the niqab?' (Anthony 2005). Allowing Begum to wear the jilbab would lead us down a slippery slope to even more 'extreme' practices with which the jilbab is then associated. The slide down the slippery slope is only halted by drawing an antagonistic frontier which is non-negotiable.

The antagonistic frontier is drawn with the help of the sartorial difference between the shalwar kameeze and the jilbab, and the frontier is necessary to stop the sliding down the slippery slope towards the things with which the jilbab became associated. For instance, the *Guardian* columnist Madeleine Bunting (2006) writes that, while the hijab is 'well within the comprehension of Western traditions', Shabina Begum's demand to wear the jilbab puts us on a slippery slope towards the 'nightmare' of the niqab.

A revealing example of the nature of the slippery slope argument is provided by a *Guardian* reader commenting online:

> I'm aware of invalidity of slippery slope argument, but the point remains; if she won the case, and people were allowed to wear what they like to school based on their own personal spin on their religious beliefs (and not what is considered 'mainstream' in their own religion), the sky would be the limit. (Comment for Alam 2006)[17]

What is important to note is that the slippery slope argument is not based on logical arguments, but works through association. I return to this below, but for the moment I just want to note the consequence of this, namely that these arguments cannot be countered with logic or evidence alone, but must be addressed at the level of rhetorical rearticulation.

Although the two discourses stand opposed to one another, they are nonetheless linked through the jilbab and certain key signifiers (freedom, above all). The same signifiers (the jilbab, freedom, and so on) are articulated differently in the two discourses, and the discourses struggle over the meaning of those signifiers (does the jilbab mean oppression or freedom? And so on).

The two discourses compete over who gets to name the jilbab and thereby constitute its meaning. The meaning of the jilbab is constituted discursively, as is the meaning of, say, 'freedom', and there is not some extra-discursive jilbab or freedom with which we can compare the different articulations. The texture of the jilbab does not make it any less discursive; discourses are material and the different versions of the hijab form part of hijab discourses. Likewise, there is no concept of freedom outside of discursive naming of freedom as freedom. Neither the physicality of the jilbab nor the conceptuality of freedom is extra-discursive. What they 'are' is the result of contingent articulations, that is, their being is discursive. There is no discursive distortion of the meaning of a pure concept or of a physical piece of cloth, because the representation is itself what constitutes the meaning of the piece of cloth and of the concept (and constitutes the concept as a concept). *Begum* is a struggle over the meaning of the jilbab, one which is not literal but is established through the struggle over the recognition and tolerance of the jilbab. A small sartorial difference is signified as significant. Small is represented as big, but it is not a question of opposing the representation ('big') to a non-representational reality ('small').[18]

If all we have are competing representations of the jilbab, where does that leave us if we want to criticise these representations and take a stand? Clearly critique cannot proceed on the basis of a comparison between a representation and an extra-representational truth. The only basis for critique is itself representational, and we can only compare one representation with another. Critique cannot be a question of whether it is the extremism or the modesty discourse that comes closest to some extra-representational truth about the jilbab. What we can do is to facilitate alternative representations, in particular counter-discourses that challenge dominant discourses. In the *Begum* case, this may consist in challenges to the dominant articulation of the jilbab as extreme.[19] At the same time, we must insist on the contingent character of meanings and identities. In the *Begum* case, we may for instance challenge Begum's articulation of the jilbab as the only proper dress for true Muslims as if there were something naturally modest about covering the body and covering it in this way, and as if Islamic texts gave just one answer to the issue (see Alam 2006).

Because representations are contingent, rearticulations are always possible. It is always possible to disarticulate particular elements of a given discourse and re-articulate them in new ways. Such dis- and rearticulation may latch on to a particularly overdetermined signifier. In the debate about the *Begum* case, this may, for instance, be 'freedom': in the extremism discourse, the jilbab is the antithesis of freedom, whereas Begum asserts freedom as a central British value in order to argue for her freedom to choose what to wear (in Aslam 2005). When doing so, Begum is trying to appropriate the signifier 'freedom', and she can do so because there is nothing essential to the meaning of that signifier. There is nothing necessary to the success of her attempt to articulate freedom in a particular way. Likewise, there is no guarantee that counter-hegemonic rearticulations will be any more progressive than the representations that dominate the social and political space.

The debates about *Begum* are typical of more general discourses about Islam in the UK and beyond. This is one reason to start with the *Begum* case. Another reason is that *Begum* frames the analyses of the debates about the other three cases because the people writing about and commenting on those cases do so having read and written about *Begum*. What is more, starting with the *Begum* debates frames my representations of the other cases, and the other debates at once confirm and render more complex the antagonistic lines of inclusion and exclusion drawn in the *Begum* debates.

British and moderate, foreign and extremist: X v Y

The debate about *Begum* was partly framed as a dispute between different representations of Islam. That facilitated contrasting images of moderate and extremist Muslims, although that distinction competed with representations of Islam as extremist as a whole. What emerged were two lines of exclusion. In one version – the dominant one – extremists such as Shabina Begum are excluded, and the including 'we' is defined by moderation. In another, less dominant version, Muslims are excluded as Muslims from a 'we British'; in this version, the including 'we' is Christian or non-religious, but it is defined by its opposition to Islam.

These lines of division are even more evident in the debate about the *X v Y* case (*X v Y* HC 2007).[20] X started wearing a niqab to school when she reached puberty, and after the school (Y) told her that she could not wear the niqab, and after a period of back and forth between the school and her parents, the latter filed for judicial review of the case. The case was decided in favour of the school in the High Court on 21 February 2007. According to the girl's solicitor, the case was a case about tolerance: 'This is a case about religious tolerance and the freedom to practice your religion as long as it does not interfere with others' (quoted in Press Association 2007).

From the very beginning, the journalistic coverage in the two papers and the readers' comments in *The Telegraph* are framed by an offer by Taj Hargey of the Muslim Educational Centre of Oxford (MECO) to raise money for the school to fight the legal case. This is the first mention of the case in the newspapers. Hargey and MECO position themselves – and are recognised by others – as moderate and British, and the newspapers go with their opposition between moderate Muslims (who may wear a headscarf) and extreme Muslims (who wear a niqab).[21]

Another more widely known organisation, the Muslim Council of Britain (MCB), who claim to represent Muslims in Britain, do not reject the niqab. Nonetheless, they agree that 'the hijab headscarf is "quite sufficient to meet Islamic requirements"' (Hooper 2007). Later, after the court decision, the MCB are more evasive and simply say that the niqab 'was not a significant issue for the Muslim community':

> Mr Alam [the MCB education committee chairman] said: 'As far as the niqab is concerned it wasn't an issue for us. It wasn't a relevant issue.'
>
> The Muslim Council of Britain spent last year developing its own guidance for schools and wanted to consider the most common issues raised by Muslim parents rather than 'some of the obscure ones', he said. (Andalo 2007)

Hargey and MECO are happy to have a debate about the niqab, while the MCB are reluctant to be drawn into this. Hargey and MECO can position themselves as the good (moderate) Muslims through the opposition vis-à-vis the bad (extremist) Muslims. For the MCB – who claim to represent all Muslims in Britain – this opposition is unavailable as a way to represent themselves and Islam. Hargey and MECO can position themselves as devout, but moderate, Muslims in opposition to fanatical and extreme versions of Islam. The MCB are bound by a claim and a wish to represent all Muslims; this is after all part of their *raison d'être*: for Muslims to speak with one voice and, thereby, gain political influence. At the same time, in order to be taken as a legitimate voice in the public sphere, they cannot be seen as defending an extreme Islam (condensed in the image of the niqab). This was all the more so at the time when the MCB's relationship with the Labour government was fraught after the Iraq war and the 7 July 2005 bombings. It is no wonder, then, that the MCB would rather not speak about the niqab, because no matter what position they take on the niqab, they lose.

Hargey and MECO represent the niqab as the expression of an extreme version of Islam, and this image is reproduced in the rest of the material. For instance, *The Telegraph* journalist Philip Johnston (2007) writes in an opinion piece: 'As Dr Taj Hargey, the director of the Muslim Educational Centre of Oxford, has pointed out, the veil is not a requirement of Islam but the manifestation of a particularly extreme interpretation.' And many readers' comments follow the same line, for instance: 'MECO have my admiration for standing up to the extremist trouble-makers. They have reminded all of us that moderate (normal!) Muslims exist, and that not all should be tarred with the terrorist brush' (comment for Johnston 2007).[22]

The niqab, and the version of Islam that it represents, is said to be cultural and political rather than religious, to the extent that it is a 'non-Islamic imposition' and not obligatory for Muslim women to wear (Hargey quoted in Orr 2007). It is also represented as foreign, specifically as an import from Saudi Arabia. Opposed to 'the full-face mask' of the niqab are religiously devout but 'sensible integrated British Muslims' who base their faith on the Qur'an rather than on the secondary sources used by the extremists (Hargey 2007). Insofar as the representation is recognised by others, it establishes moderate as normal, that is, as the norm vis-à-vis the extremist as an extremist. The identities of moderate and extremist are relational because only established in relation to one another.

Representing the niqab as foreign to both Islam and to the UK places Muslims and Brits on the same side, opposed to the same threat. Dividing and segmenting[23] Muslims in this way makes it possible for the moderate Muslims to position themselves as British, but it is also clear from the readers' comments that those (non-Muslims) who identify as British are ambiguous about this. Some make the distinction between moderate and extreme Muslims and represent the former as British or at least capable of being British. Others equivocate between opposing British to extreme versions of Islam (represented by the niqab) and opposing British to Islam as a whole. At issue is whether Islam can be included within 'we British', or at least tolerated, and this depends on the existence of a distinction between moderate and extreme Islam. At stake is the positioning of Islam vis-à-vis a 'we' identified as British.

In the debates about *X v Y*, there is hardly any space for the modesty discourse found in the debates about *Begum*. Apart from a couple of readers' comments, the only articulation of modesty and religious freedom comes from the girl's solicitor: 'My client and her family are not the extremists that they have been portrayed as by some elements of the press. All she wants is to be able to practice her deeply held beliefs whilst getting on with her daily life' (quoted in Press Association 2007). The extremism discourse dominates, but it is combined with the segmentation of Muslims into good and bad, moderate and extremist.

The 'we' invoked is always 'we British', but there are competing articulations of this 'we British' and of what it is opposed to. One representation is of moderate British as opposed to the intolerable niqab extremists. This is the way Hargey and MECO include moderate Muslims within a British 'we'; it is reproduced by many readers, but sometimes Muslims are rendered different, if includable, in the process. The latter is evident, for instance, when a reader makes the distinction between good and bad Muslims and welcomes the former:

> Way 2 go MECO! Thanks a million! You have restored my faith in the common sense of the vast majority of muslims in UK. Let us realise that it is only a tiny minority of trouble-makers and attention-seekers who give a bad impression of an otherwise welcome, hard-working and law-abiding community. (Comment for Johnston 2007)[24]

Although moderate Muslims are included and tolerated, they are marked as different from the norm of Britishness, as British and Muslim or as British Muslim. It is this difference that makes their tolerance possible (because they are different) and that makes it possible to welcome them (because they are only moderately different). Tolerating and welcoming them reproduces that difference.

The moderate Muslim may be included into a shared political and social space, but that space is itself differentiated between a centre and a margin defined by a norm and what is different from it. Through the discourse of tolerance, some are represented as at home; others as not quite at home. When moderate Muslims are represented as tolerable, they are both distinguished from intolerable extremist Muslims and from the tolerating non-Muslim 'we'. Although included, the inclusion is a matter of degree rather than a matter of either/or; difference is tolerated, but it is also reproduced as different from a norm about what it means to be British.

Another representation of 'British' opposes 'we the British' to Islam; here moderate Muslims are sometimes tolerable, but always as a suspicious element. The difference between the two representations of 'British' lies in the representation of Islam. In the first case, British is defined through the opposition to extremism; in the second case, British is defined through the opposition to Islam; and in both cases, 'British' is sometimes linked to 'Christian'.

The dominant lines of division between moderate and extremist Muslim, and Muslim and British, are also evident in the use of the saying 'When in Rome . . .', a recurrent refrain which is specific to the comments on the *X v Y* case. The saying is repeated by the commentators in different forms. One form is a version of the distinction between moderate and extreme Muslims:

> Thank goodness MECO have spoken out. Shame on the dumb idiot who allowed this case to be funded. The Shalwar kameez and hijab are prefectly acceptable muslim dress, seen universally. The jilbab and niqab is not . . . They are also being used to stick two fingers up to our country and customs. When in Rome and all that . . . (Comment for Johnston 2007)[25]

In another form, the UK is represented as a Christian country:

> Isn't this Racial Discrimination in reverse? We are a Christian Country, with The Arch-Bishop of Canterbury and the Queen being the principal authorities?
> . . .
> If the people who and wish to remain in the Country and use our services, then they must comply with our terms and conditions. If they

insist in breaking our dress codes, then they should seek an alternative county of residence. (Comment for Johnston 2007)[26]

And if not Christian, then the UK is at least represented as non-Muslim: 'Lets remember that this is GREAT BRITAIN and not a Muslim State. Respect our traditions or go' (comment for Johnston 2007).[27]

These different versions of 'when in Rome . . .' place some in the position of being at home and, therefore, able to tell others to leave. Sometimes this being-at-home is marked with different forms of the word indigenousness to oppose British to Muslims who are only late-comers.[28] The niqab-wearing Muslim – and sometimes all Muslims – is placed in the position of visitor, immigrant and foreigner. Here it does not matter that many such people – including X – are not in fact immigrants or foreigners; what matters is that they come to occupy a subject position of 'foreign', and, as such, they can be asked to leave or 'go back'. They are defined by their difference vis-à-vis a norm of Britishness. Even when the niqab-wearing Muslim is assumed to be a British citizen, she may nonetheless be undesirable: 'If this family are so insensitive to the society in which they live, I would suggest they are not desirable citizens and they should move somewhere else' (comment for Johnston 2007).[29] The antagonism is clear: you are either British or (an extreme) Muslim. Sometimes the opposition is due to the Christian history and identity of the UK, sometimes there is no mention of Christianity. The 'othering' of the niqab-wearing Muslim goes hand in hand with the representation of a British 'we' who share a common identity which the others should accept, and, if they are unable to do so, they should leave. The (niqab-wearing) Muslim is othered in two ways: she is represented as foreign (immigrant, and so on) and as extremist.

But the 'we' is threatened not just from without, but also from within. The threat from without is clear: a perverted form of Islam, backed by Saudi Arabia, is imposed on British Muslims and, as a consequence, on the UK. But, as in the debates about *Begum*, there is another threat to the UK and its values, and that is the threat coming from the usual suspects of the liberal elites: human rights, political correctness, lawyers and courts. The liberal elites induce a softness into Britain so that we cannot withstand the threat from without, in this case the threat from the niqab. This comes out well in several comments, for instance:

> Why are we here again? Because they know that by repeatedly kicking at the system the system will eventually yield. Because they know that White people are weak and degenerate, that they prefer to hide their weakness, their lack of conviction, behind a lot of guff about 'tolerance' and 'British cohesion'. (Comment for Johnston 2007)[30]

One reader sees a threat as: 'a result of a series of court challenges (ironically financed by legal aid aka the state) thanks to our ultra-PC Human Rights legislation which lets the minorities ride roughshod over the majority' (comment for Johnston 2007).[31]

Doubling up as a commentator, *The Telegraph* journalist Philip Johnston places the case within a narrative where even the 'most enthusiastic proponents' of multiculturalism are now turning against it. The theme of waking up to the realities and discovering that Britain is under threat is a common one:

> The sister [of X] started wearing the niqab in 1995. 'The school and staff were very supportive,' she said. 'I was even told I could wear the jilbab as well if I wanted.'
>
> This was the high-point of multiculturalism, that benighted concept now disavowed by its most enthusiastic proponents.
>
> Had the school put its foot down then – along with many other public institutions in thrall to a well-intentioned, but ultimately self-defeating, concept – we might not be in the mess we are now. (Johnston 2007)

The British have been too soft, and this has placed the UK in danger. Minorities have taken advantage of British tolerance and multiculturalism. Having said that, tolerance is not rejected outright because the very same commentators also wish to retain tolerance as a characteristic of British identity and history – they want to be able to speak in the name of tolerance and from the position of a tolerant subject.

The liberal elites occupy an ambiguous position; while they are perceived as a threat, they are not foreign to the UK in the same way as the niqab or Muslims. Instead they are foreign to a true and authentic Britain which is now threatened by the combination of the softness of the liberal elites and an aggressive Islam. This view is summed up in the following comment:

> We have the usual problem here – a weak, vacillating host culture drained of all belief in its own efficacy (and where everything is 'complex'), against a focused, powerful, unwavering creed (where everything is simple – i.e. we are always right). Why my own people have come to this craven pass is debatable, but we can only lament what has happened and what will now happen in the next fifty years or so. (Comment for Johnston 2007)[32]

There is an antagonism between an indigenous British culture and the twin threats of liberalism and Islam. The frontier between, on the one hand, British and, on the other hand, liberalism and (extremist) Muslims is antagonistic in Laclau's sense of the term: the other is represented as a threat to our identity, yet it is also this threatening other that helps define and sustain our identity. The threat is condensed in the image of the niqab-wearing woman to the extent that the debate about the niqab is a debate about British identity, liberalism and Islam. The two threats are connected, but they are not made equivalent. Different elements are made equivalent around liberalism (human rights, multiculturalism, lawyers and courts), and other elements are made equivalent around the niqab (extremism, terrorism, oppression of women, sometimes Islam as a whole). The niqab plays the role of an empty signifier in both chains of equivalences, and the two chains are connected through the nodal point of the niqab.

The focus on Islam and the opposition between British and Islam is typical of public discourses in the decade after 9/11, and it is not surprising that it is so present in the debates about *Begum* and *X v Y*.[33] In both cases, divisions are articulated between moderation and extremism, thus segmenting Muslims and making possible the inclusion of some as tolerable (because moderate) and the exclusion of others as intolerable (because extremist). However, in both cases, this articulation of the distinction between tolerable and intolerable competes with another, less dominant opposition between 'we British' and Islam as a whole. These two divisions – moderate versus extremist Islam; 'we British' versus Islam – are in many instances articulated together with a division between ordinary British people and liberal elites, and together with representations of what it means to be British. Although the definition of British through an antagonistic frontier vis-à-vis (extremist) Islam is not challenged in the debates about *Playfoot* and *Watkins-Singh*, the articulation of Britishness is nonetheless rendered more complex.

Christian fundamentalism, secularism and British identity: *Playfoot*

In 2004, at the age of thirteen, Lydia Playfoot decided to wear a so-called purity ring to symbolise her Christian commitment to celibacy before marriage. Her school – Millais School in West Sussex – treated the ring as jewellery which could not be worn with the school uniform. After a stand-off, the school decided she could not wear the ring, and she took the school to court, which decided the case in favour of the school on 16 July 2007.

The newspaper debate about *Playfoot* is a debate over the role of Christianity and religion in the UK in a way that it is not in the debates about *Begum* and *X v Y*. What is more, the minority asking for tolerance and inclusion is not a non-white or non-Christian minority, and this complicates the usual lines of division. I shall return to this below and start instead with another significant difference, namely that of the coverage of the case in the two newspapers. Whereas there are small differences in the coverage of the *Begum* case, there are no differences in the coverage of *X v Y*. However, the coverage of *Playfoot* is different and this frames the debate among the readers in the respective papers.

The journalistic coverage is different in two important aspects. First, in the initial coverage, *The Guardian* gives voice to representatives from the Secular Society who take the side of the school and see Lydia Playfoot's purity ring as an attempt to politicise education. *The Telegraph* makes no mention of the Secular Society position until the court case begins and then only in passing. Instead *The Telegraph* gives voice to Lydia Playfoot's backers among the clergy and conservative politicians – 'an impressive array of politicians and Church leaders' (Petre 2007a) – who are only cited in passing in *The Guardian*. Through the people they cite, the two newspapers position themselves as defenders of secular and Christian Britain respectively. At once spaces of inscription and agents, the papers frame their readers' views through the information they provide.

There is another decisive difference in how the debates among the readers unfold in the two papers. From the very beginning, *The Guardian* provides details that contextualise and frame the case in a particular way. The facts are not disputed: the purity ring that Lydia Playfoot wears is from the organisation Silver Ring Thing (SRT), an American Christian movement that launched its purity ring in the UK in 2004; Lydia Playfoot's father is a minister in a local evangelical church; and it so happens that the parents are involved in the British branch of the SRT.[34] *The Telegraph* also makes mention of the SRT, but not of the parents' jobs and roles.

As a result, what is an issue in the readers' comments in *The Guardian* from the very beginning only becomes an issue in *The Telegraph* after the verdict, and only because the readers get the information from sources outside the newspaper. It is only in the later readers' comments in *The Telegraph* that Lydia Playfoot is represented as manipulated by her parents using the case as a publicity stunt for SRT. This image of Lydia Playfoot is often combined with an image of her as an attention-seeking teenager who wants to show off her purity. In *The Guardian*, these two images are present from the very beginning, for instance:

> This seems like a carefully orchestrated PR campaign for a group that has managed to succesfully get lots of press coverage in the US and now wants some over here. Both her parents are listed as being on the UK 'team' for SRT, her father in particular runs the parents program for them. (Comment for *The Guardian* 2007)[35]

The representations of Lydia Playfoot here combine an image of her as a passive pawn in the hands of her parents with the image of her parents and fundamentalist Christians as aggressively using religious symbols to pursue their own interests. This is the way that Muslim girls and women are often represented.

Lydia Playfoot plays two roles in *The Guardian*. She and the purity ring are first of all taken as representative of a fundamentalist and extreme form of Christianity that has been imported from the US and is foreign to the UK. As such, the purity ring is deemed intolerable, at least as an attempt to influence education in state schools. The purity ring and the American fundamentalist Christianity with which it is associated are represented as foreign threats to the UK, and so an antagonistic frontier is drawn.

Apart from being extreme and a threat to secular schools, the purity ring is also represented as a commercial fad, and this also adds to its foreign nature. 'I'm interested to hear that her father the Pastor is behind the movement, and I'll be interested to hear her views on it in 10 years' time. It sounds like more American bullshit' (comment for *The Guardian* 2007).[36] The first role played by Lydia Playfoot in *The Guardian* comments is that of representative of a suspicious fundamentalist Christianity. When Lydia Playfoot is represented as such, the commentators speak from a British 'we' that is most often characterised as secular, although secular has different meanings here, from secular over non-religious to anti-religious. The secular UK is tied to a history of progress of enlightenment and of emancipation from religion, a history now under threat from a religious revival.

The second role played by Lydia Playfoot in the material from *The Guardian* is also as representative of a Christian religious worldview. However, this time her Christianity is not characterised as extreme; rather, she is part of a Christian UK that is under threat, and the commentators speak from this Christian UK:

> Isn't it funny how this secular school only has a problem with Christian symbols . . . yet more evidence of Christianphobia, which is alive and kicking in the UK today. It doesn't get more petty than this does it. Those spiteful politically correct liberals just can't leave Christians alone! (Comment for *The Guardian* 2007)[37]

Articulated in this way, Lydia Playfoot and the purity ring represent a religious culture under threat from secularism and atheism and from minorities, especially Muslims. It is a representation of a Christian UK tied to a particular Christian history under threat from secular liberals and non-Christian minorities. While this is a minority representation of Lydia Playfoot in *The Guardian*, this is the most common view in *The Telegraph*. A significant number of readers question the essential nature of the purity ring to Christianity, but the school's ban of the ring is also taken as an expression of the differential treatment of Christians. Unlike minorities – and especially Muslims who are represented as aggressive – who are protected by political correctness, the silent Christian majority is represented as intimidated. For instance:

> Of COURSE Lydia should be allowed to wear her Christian ring – if muslims and sikhs are allowed to wear their symbols why not Lydia? It is becoming one rule for muslims and another rule for the rest of us! Are the authorities here too afraid of upsetting the muslims, but it doesnt matter about Christians? (Comment for Petre 2007b)[38]

This line is also taken by the journalistic coverage in *The Telegraph* and by Playfoot herself: Muslims and Sikhs can wear headscarves, turbans and *karas* to school, but Lydia Playfoot cannot wear the purity ring because it is treated as a piece of jewellery. For instance, *The Telegraph* writes in its first article on the case:

> Although the school allows Muslim and Sikh pupils to wear headscarves, trousers and kara bracelets as a cultural expression of their religion, the chastity ring – small band engraved with a biblical verse, 1 Thessalonians 4:3–4 – is not allowed because it is considered to be jewellery. The school also forbids the wearing of crosses and crucifixes.
>
> 'I felt as if I was being picked on because I was a Christian,' said Miss Playfoot. 'People were around me from other faiths and they could wear trousers and bracelets and headscarves. . . .' (Petre 2007a)

Note the description of the different kinds of dress and symbol. The religious content of the ring is talked up with the reference to the Biblical verse, whereas the opposite is the case for Muslim and Sikh dress and symbols, which are described as cultural expressions of religion.

The backdrop to this representation of Lydia Playfoot is an image of a Christian country where Christianity is under threat, where it is the subject of negative differential treatment, and where morality is in decline. Morality is dependent on the existence of Christian values and institutions, and the decline of morality is linked to the rise of multiculturalism. To take just one example:

> I see no reason why someone should not wear such a thing. All Christians should take heed of the fact that the Christian faith is under attack all over the world. All ethnic minorities in the UK always win their case because of the right to practice their religion. The UK is a Christian country so it's about time ALL Christians stood up & fought for our rights to practice our religion without any interference. (Comment for Petre 2007a)[39]

The Playfoots also draw on this image, but there is a small difference between their way of representing Christianity and themselves and the self-representations by the self-declared Christians in the readers' comments. The difference is that whereas the latter place themselves in the role of passive victims, the Playfoots are much more assertive. Of course, this is what makes the Playfoots appear as representatives of an aggressive fundamentalist evangelicalism in the eyes of the secular *Guardian* readers. Whether they position themselves as passive or aggressive, an antagonistic frontier is drawn between themselves and the external threat of multiculturalists, Muslims, liberals, and so forth.

In the comments on the later articles in *The Telegraph*, the focus moves from Christianity to Lydia Playfoot herself. These comments are more divided, because Playfoot is now no longer taken automatically as representative of Christianity. Instead some of the commentators represent her in a way similar to the *Guardian* readers: manipulated by her parents and representative of an American and a foreign form of Christianity. The synecdochic substitution of Lydia Playfoot for Christianity is no longer automatic, and a fault line opens between a moderate (British) Christianity and an extremist (foreign) Christianity.

The journalists and commentators draw different circles of tolerance in the debate about *Playfoot*. Some draw a circle around a Christian UK, placing themselves and Lydia Playfoot within the circle and the threat from secularism and minorities outside the circle. Others draw a circle around moderate Christians and others who defend secularism against the establishment of religion within state schools. These readers speak from a 'we' inside this circle and opposed to Lydia Playfoot's fundamentalist Christianity, which is placed outside the circle and beyond tolerance. Finally, a common circle is the one drawn by many *Guardian* readers around a secular 'we' under threat from religious groups in general and fundamentalists such as Playfoot in particular. In all three instances, the 'we' is represented sometimes as a minority and sometimes as a (silent, passive) majority within the UK; although the 'we' and the UK are not necessarily identical, the 'we' is always represented as properly British and under threat.

The debate about *Playfoot* is a debate about British identity in a way that the debates about *Begum* and *X v Y* are not. In *Begum* and *X v Y*, the issue was the extent to which some form of Islam was tolerable and includable. In *Playfoot*, the issue is similarly whether Lydia Playfoot's Christian fundamentalism is tolerable and includable, but it is just as much a matter of whether the UK is a Christian or a secular society (where secular implies that religion – and especially Christianity – can have no place within a state school). That line of division between secular and Christian was almost absent in the *Begum* and *X v Y* debates because it was overdetermined by the preoccupation with Islam. In those debates, the question was if Muslims could be considered British, and, if so, what kind of Muslims could be tolerated. The question of British identity therefore only arose in an indirect way as the question whether the UK is inherently and exclusively Christian. Muslim is only opposed to British in one form of what I have called the extremism discourse where Islam as such is represented as foreign, whether because it is represented as extreme or as non-Christian.

Another difference between the *Playfoot* debates and the debates about the Muslim cases concerns the articulation of human rights. Typically, multiculturalism is associated with liberal elites, human rights, Europe and political correctness and opposed to a Christian and (more or less implicitly) white British majority. This is also the case here, albeit with one exception: human rights. In the debates about *Begum* and *X v Y*, when a Muslim minority draws on human rights discourse, it is interpreted as an abuse of hospitality and tolerance, and human rights themselves are represented as a foreign element introduced into the UK by liberal elites in general and the legal profession in particular. Human rights are represented as a perverted form of tolerance. In the debates about *Playfoot*, the signifier 'human rights' is not used by those who speak from a position of a Christian UK under threat. The reason is that Lydia Playfoot makes her case with reference to human rights, and although 'human rights' does not sit well with the usual suspects of multiculturalism and liberal secularists, it is equally awkward for this kind of discourse to appropriate 'human rights' as part of a defence of a Christian UK. Instead it is taken up by readers criticising Playfoot in *The Guardian*. Echoing the critics of Shabina Begum and X, Playfoot's use of human rights discourse is articulated as a perverse exploitation of human rights threatening secular society. Whatever the angle, the signifier 'human rights' is thus on the 'wrong' side.

Note that all the representations of Lydia Playfoot, her chastity ring and the other elements of the case are restricted by existing representations, which may be contingent but are also more or less sedimented. In the debates about *Playfoot*, tolerance is organised as different and competing circles. Those circles are in turn articulated through different and competing representations of Playfoot, Christianity, secularism, human rights and British identity. Moreover, those representations compete in a discursive terrain where these signifiers – Christianity, human rights, British, and so on – already have a more or less fixed meaning. This complicates matters because the *Playfoot* case cuts across some of those established meanings in ways that the *Watkins-Singh* case also does, but in ways that the *Begum* and *X v Y* cases do not. The cases involving Muslims are easily represented within already established and recognised representations of Muslims and of Britishness.

Cricket tests and slippery slopes: *Watkins-Singh*

Sarika Watkins-Singh was a fourteen-year-old schoolgirl of Welsh and Punjabi Sikh background who wore a Sikh *kara,* or bangle, to school at Aberdare Girls' High School in Wales. When she refused to remove it, she was isolated from the other children at the school and taught in a separate room. Upon taking the school to court, she won the case in the High Court on 29 July 2008.[40]

In her argument for tolerance for her bangle, Watkins-Singh introduces her own cricket test. She makes an analogy between herself and Monty Panesar, the first Sikh cricketer to play for England. She makes the analogy showing a picture in court of Panesar playing cricket and wearing the bangle, and the image is reproduced in the media. The cricket test helps Watkins-Singh prove something that she assumes is, or would be, questioned, namely her Britishness. It familiarises the bangle, and if a cricketer can represent England wearing the bangle, there seems to be no contradiction between the bangle and being English/British.

Watkins-Singh also states that she is 'a proud Welsh and Punjabi Sikh girl', a statement that is repeated in several media reports (quoted in Gammell 2008). Whether deliberate or not, identifying herself as *Welsh* (and Punjabi Sikh) and not as *British* (and Punjabi Sikh) bypasses the way in which these issues are usually articulated, namely as a tension between being British and being from a non-white and non-Christian minority. Bypassing this dominant image of a clash between Britishness and minority identities, Watkins-Singh does not have to defend her difference in a game of Britishness that she can never win because her difference will always mark her out from what is truly British. Highlighting her Welshness is a way of decentring Britishness, and her Welshness makes her Sikhness less foreign.

There is also a reference to Britishness in Watkins-Singh's self-representation. It is there in an indirect form in her reference to an English cricket player, and it is there in her invocation of a British tradition of freedom and tolerance when, after the court decision, her lawyer states: 'Our great British traditions of religious tolerance and race equality have been rightly upheld today' (quoted in Gammell 2008).[41] Invoking this tradition represents the tradition in a particular way, most of all as tolerant. At the same time, invoking this tradition places Watkins-Singh in an ambiguous relation to it. On the one hand, she speaks from within the tradition, placing herself within a British 'we' ('*Our* great British traditions . . .'). On the other hand, it reinforces her difference from a norm: it is only because she is different that there is a need for tolerance.

166

This ambiguity is also evident in another argument used in the debate about the case. This is the argument that 'them Sikhs fought and died for Britain' (comment for Rai 2008),[42] and therefore they should be tolerated. The argument echoes an analogy made in earlier debates about Sikh turbans, motorcycle crash helmets and hard hats for builders: if Sikhs could risk their lives wearing turbans instead of steel helmets when fighting for Britain, they should also be allowed to ride a motorcycle or work on a construction site wearing only a turban.

However, these arguments are ambiguous. The call for tolerance places Sikhs as different from the norm of those who are truly British and, therefore, in a position to decide whether Sikhs should be tolerated. While deserving of inclusion and tolerance, Sikhs are also marked as different: 'them Sikhs' fought *for* Britain, but not *as* British.

Together these representations of British history and of Sikhs serve to make Sikhism and the bangle less foreign. Although still marked as different from British – because they are at best British Sikh rather than just British – Sikhs are placed within a history shared with the British in a way that only rarely happens with Muslims. The history of race discrimination legislation may also play a role here. Sikhs were some of the first to gain exceptions and protection from discrimination under the Race Relations Acts in the 1970s as evidenced in the *Mandla* case.[43] Thus, (white, Christian, and so on) British people had already been exposed to, and got used to, legal disputes about Sikh dress and symbols.

Watkins-Singh's religion and her bangle are problematised, but they are so in a way that distinguishes this case from the other cases. With very few exceptions, there is no problematisation of Sikhism, of her particular religion, and she is not represented as fundamentalist or extremist. This is so whether she is positioned vis-à-vis a norm of a secular or a Christian 'we'. While not seen as part of that 'we', her particular religion is seen as a tolerable difference. Nor is she represented as a fundamentalist or extremist in relation to a norm about what Sikhs look like or how they behave.

However, her particular religion is problematised in one specific way when commentators debate what Sikhism requires of its followers. At issue is whether Watkins-Singh's bangle is a compulsory

part of Sikhism. This is similar to the other cases where the obligatory character of the religious symbol or dress is put into question,
and this is where the issue emerges of who gets to represent, and
speak for, a particular religion. It is important to note, however, that
whenever the issue is raised in this form, it is not the tolerance of the
particular religion that is at stake. What is problematised is the difference between the religious symbol – here the bangle – and a norm
about the particular religion, rather than the difference between the
religion and the norms of the rest of society.[44] Watkins-Singh's Sikhism does not correspond to the received images of Sikhism.

In the debate about *Watkins-Singh*, the problematisation of
Watkins-Singh's Sikhism takes a particular form. Watkins-Singh's
Sikhness is problematised by representing her as picking and choosing the parts of Sikhism that she likes because she only wears the
bangle (*kara*) and not the other four Ks of Sikhism (*kesh*, *kanga*,
kirpan and *kaccha*). Sikhs and non-Sikhs alike argue that this is
inconsistent, and that therefore she cannot be a true devout Sikh.
For instance:

> the bangle (kara) is part of the 5 K's. If it meant so much to the girl to
> show her Sikh identity, why is she not following all the 5 K's? Is it okay
> for her to pick and choose which ones she does not want to follow and
> the others she will disregard? (Comment for Lipsett 2008)[45]

The image of an inconsistent believer assumes a coherent belief
and practice, the norm of which can be defined by believers or
observers who are recognised as authorities (as true believers or
as scholars). Whatever position the commentators take on this
issue, the issue is not whether or not Watkins-Singh's Sikhism is an
extreme version of Sikhism, but whether her Sikhism is authentic.
This is one of the ways in which the debate about *Watkins-Singh* is
different from the debates about the other cases where it is a matter of both the authenticity and the extremism of the girls.

The issue of the consistency and authenticity of Watkins-Singh's
religion is often linked to a portrayal of her as an attention-seeking
teenager or, in a different version, an attention-seeking teenager
who has been manipulated by her parents or the Sikh community.
This is also a common image in the debates about the other cases.
Whatever the case, it is not her particular religion (Sikhism) that is

problematised, but instead her claim to be a devout and true Sikh: either because her bangle is not essential to Sikhism, or because she (or someone behind her) is using Sikhism instrumentally to further some other agenda: 'This girl obviously isn't as devout as she would have us believe and I'm not judging her . . . However she has misused her religion, in this case to her advantage' (comment for Lipsett 2008).[46] And:

> What is a school supposed to do when faced with a deliberately disobedient and truculent child who will not be reasonable and insist on flouting the uniform standard and challenging the rules?
>
> The school from all reports bent over backward to compromise with a difficult child. I don't blame the child, its her parents fault and they are to blame for not supporting the school and the teachers but instead undermining them and encouraging her to be disobedient. (Comment for Hundal 2008)[47]

Whatever the case may be, the problem is not Sikhism as a difference; there is no issue whether Watkins-Singh can be tolerated *as a Sikh*. Contrast this with the debates about *Begum* and *X v Y* where the issue is whether the girls and their dress can be tolerated *as (extremist) Muslims*, and where there is the important distinction between moderation and extremism which is completely absent from the *Watkins-Singh* debate.

Although Sikhism as a particular religion is not problematised, in some cases Sarika Watkins-Singh's religious difference is problematised as a *religious* difference. Echoing the *Playfoot* debates, religion is problematised in relation to representations of the UK as 'secular' and 'atheist' (and it is significant that these commentators refer to 'religion' rather than 'faith').[48] Only in relation to these identities is Watkins-Singh's religiosity problematised, but it is problematised as religion, not as Sikhism. The recurrent theme here is the perceived special treatment for religion: religion is given a special place in society as a form of appeasement. The secular UK is threatened by religion and by the kind of concessions given to Watkins-Singh. For instance: 'What is so special about religion? Why should we promote the flight from reason as being somehow so worthy and admirable that it trumps all other considerations?' (comment for Rai 2008).[49] There is a sense of being under siege, and that those who once were, or ought to be, in the majority are now a threatened minority: 'We have had this all before – surely atheists are now a minority and allowed to wear a bit of jewellery that signifies their non-belief . . .' (comment for Lipsett 2008).[50] The different articulations of the 'we' and of the UK are part of a struggle over the identity of that 'we' and over what it means to be British, in particular whether the UK is Christian or secular/atheist.

In this struggle there are two lines of division that look different depending on which side of the line you find yourself; these lines of division were also present in the debates about *Playfoot*. The first line of division looks like a threat to a secular majority or minority from religion from one side, and like a threat to a Christian majority or minority from anti-religious attacks on religion from the other side. This is by far the most prominent line of division in the debate about *Watkins-Singh*, in particular in the version where religion is articulated as a threat to secular society. The other, and less prominent, line of division is a division among those who identify themselves and the UK as religious. From one side of the line, this looks like a Christian UK under threat from (non-Christian) minority religions; from the other side of the line, it looks like special status for Christianity and discrimination of minority religions.

As with the debates about the other cases, regardless of which identity they speak from, everybody represents themselves as under threat: British from foreigners; secularists and atheists from religious people; religious people from secularists and atheists; Christians from minorities; and minorities from Christianity. In the debate about *Watkins-Singh*, two threats dominate: threats to religious people from secularists/atheists and, especially, threats to secularists/atheists from religious groups, thus confirming that this case is more about religion than a particular religion. What is more, in the *Watkins-Singh* debate, the usual suspects of multiculturalists, lawyers and other softy liberals are not very present, but when they are, they are opposed both by those who defend the UK as Christian (because on the side of minorities – as in the debates about *Begum* and *X v Y*) and by those who defend the UK as secular (because on the side of religious groups – as in the debate about *Playfoot*). This confirms how, in this case, the representational space is dominated by an antagonism between religious and secular, and that other lines of division are secondary to this antagonism. Representations and discourses are articulated within a given discursive terrain, yet both reproduce and rearticulate this terrain.

The final important aspect of the *Watkins-Singh* debate is the omnipresence of slippery slopes. This is also present in the debates about the other cases, but much less so. The slippery slopes take two forms. In one version, allowing Sarika Watkins-Singh to wear her bangle will lead other Sikhs and other religions to demand similar concessions. This *ad extremis* slippery slope takes us towards ever more extreme forms of religious belief and practice:

> This was a stunt, plain and simple. It is a thin edge of the wedge thing, if this then why not a full Burqa for a Muslim girl? Can a Sikh boy carry a ceremonial knife? How about a Scottish one? If you allow this, you must allow those. (Comment for Hundal 2008)[51]

In another common version, the slippery slope takes the form of *ad absurdum*: if Sikh bangles and other religious symbols are allowed in the school, tolerance will take us down a slippery slope towards jewellery, Jedi light sabres and swastika T-shirts. For instance:

> All Scottish males at English schools should henceforth insist on asserting their racial identity and stuff a knife doon their socks. Try stopping that one. English boys should of course retaliate by buckling bells around theirs, what jollies eh what? (Comment for Rai 2008)[52]

In this articulation of the slippery slope argument, religion is just one form of superstition and should have no differential treatment; religious symbols should be treated as other kinds of private follies. What is construed by others as common-sense tolerance, is now construed as the opposite of common sense, as silly if not outright dangerous.

The rhetorical logic of these arguments is that if you have said A, then you must also say B . . . and Z, and consequently there is only one solution, namely to avoid saying A in the first place. The very introduction of difference and exception – whatever the particular content may be – creates a society characterised by tribalism, sectarianism and Balkanisation. In these arguments, there is only one way to avoid the slippery slope to extremism and absurdity, and that is a total ban on religious symbols, and a completely uniform school uniform. It is all or nothing, and there is little to no room for compromise. A line is drawn: on one side there is uniformity – we are all the same, at least as citizens or as schoolchildren – and on the other side there is a slide towards ever more extreme and/or absurd forms of difference. Drawing an antagonistic frontier like this becomes the only way of securing the continuing existence and unity of the UK. The differences on the other side of the antagonistic frontier are not necessarily treated as equally and immediately dangerous. However, through association, they are all contaminated by the differences further down the slippery slope. This is so to the degree that, to some extent, one difference (say, the bangle) comes to stand in for and substitute other differences (say, the *kirpan* or swastika T-shirts). Slippery slope arguments work something like a chain of equivalence.

The slippery slope arguments do not go unchallenged, and they are challenged from two sides. They are challenged, first, by those whom we might characterise as libertarians and who reject uniformity in the name of individual freedom. For them, the slippery slope is not a problem because they believe that it should be up to the individual to decide what to wear. In fact, it is only just that the exception for Sarika Watkins-Singh becomes a general rule.

Second, the slippery slope argument is challenged by those who want to give religion a place in the public sphere, whatever the particular religion. This takes the form of a rejection of anti-religious discourse, for instance, referring to 'the so called secular . . . lobby', one reader writes: 'They see anything related to religion with hate deep down in their minds, they are NOT liberal even though they pretend to be. It is the hatred in their minds that drive their whole discussion regarding religion' (comment for Cohen 2008).[53] For this group of readers, religious difference and exceptions are not problematic because religion is not a threat to national unity or to other people's freedoms. As far as religious differences are concerned, the slippery slope disappears; in fact, it is only natural that the inclusion of one religious difference (for example, the *kara*) is extended to other religious differences.

Slippery slope arguments are notoriously difficult to counter. One can ignore them and ask 'so what?' Or one can try to articulate a clear break in the slope (that is, in the chain of equivalence); for instance, one can try to argue that the bangle is different from the other symbols with which it is associated. This is difficult, however. As I noted above in the section on the debate about *Begum*, slippery slope arguments do not necessarily rely on logic or knowledge about causal relationships. They work at a rhetorical level where they are difficult to neutralise because they draw on fears that are present in existing discourses. Those fears are often implicit, but all the more effectual for that reason; had they been explicit, they would have been easier to reject as irrational or racist. The slippery slope arguments work because they draw on these often hidden fears of disorder and otherness (Borovali 2008–9). At the same time, they can be a way of rejecting what is different while retaining an air of tolerance. Whether sincere or not, the slippery slope arguments do not concern Sarika Watkins-Singh's particular difference. On the face of it, the slippery slope arguments reject the bangle not because it is itself a ridiculous or dangerous symbol, but because of what tolerating it might lead to. The intolerance of the bangle (and of Sikhism) can be hidden behind the religious symbols and practices further down the slippery slope towards extremism.

Conclusion

In the debates about *Begum*, *X v Y*, *Playfoot* and *Watkins-Singh*, tolerance is articulated in different ways. In each case, the articulation of tolerance goes hand in hand with the representation of particular identities and the articulation of particular values that are said to be ours or theirs – for instance, Britishness, moderation and extremism and reason. In each case, the representations of tolerance and identities draw on existing representations while also being limited by these. In each case, tolerance is articulated sometimes in terms of an antagonistic frontier – us versus them, moderate versus extremist, tolerant versus intolerable – but also as circles of relative proximity to a norm, for instance an identity of Britishness. In each

173

case, tolerance is articulated both in terms of either/or, inclusion or exclusion, *and* in terms of circles of more or less: more or less included and excluded. Where tolerance is articulated in antagonistic terms, there are often competing antagonistic frontiers, say between Islam and British, and between moderate and extremist. As a result, any particular identity can be articulated in different ways and in relation to different antagonistic frontiers and nodal points – all at the same time.[54] Hegemony understood as articulation can take more than one form. It need not proceed through the articulation of empty signifiers and an antagonistic frontier between us and them. It can also take the form of the articulation of nodal points and a less populist and a more institutionalist discourse.

This point about the theory of hegemony is also important for tolerance. Tolerance is not a practice that simply includes or excludes. There are times when tolerance is articulated in this way, although even then the picture is often a murkier one. One way to make sense of this is to say that tolerance positions subjects in particular ways in relation to one another and in relation to values and institutions. In this case we must ask how those subjects become articulated as particular identities, and how values and institutions are articulated. For instance, subjects are positioned as more or less moderate or extreme. Or they may be positioned in different ways in relation to the state, as foreign to it or as sharing with it a common history. This is the approach taken by, among others, Ghassan Hage (1998) and Wendy Brown (1995; 2006). Drawing on Michel Foucault, they argue that tolerance – and rights and recognition and multiculturalism – can be viewed through the lens of governmentality. This is a suggestive and insightful analysis of tolerance. It is not one that I can develop here, but I see it as complementary to, rather than competing with, the account that I have given of tolerance here.

Relative inclusion – like relative exclusion and antagonistic exclusion – are different ways of dealing with, and managing, difference. They are also different ways of articulating identities, whether 'ours' or 'theirs'. Hegemony works through this positioning of identities, and governmentality is a way to understand this; governmentality works through the representation of identities in one way or another, and the category of hegemony is a way to make sense of this. The practice of tolerance always starts from, and is shaped by, existing identities and the relationships among those identities. At the same time, tolerance does not leave those identities unaffected. The identities are articulated as tolerant or intolerant, tolerable and intolerable, and they are positioned in old and new ways in relation to other identities and in relation to values and institutions. One upshot of this is that we must pay critical attention to how some identities are consistently placed in particular positions of marginality and exclusion, while other identities are consistently articulated as those of the majority or those sharing a history with the state – those positioned, and able to position themselves, as tolerating and tolerant subjects at the centre of concentric circles of tolerance. Here tolerance and identity formation are intrinsically linked.

I have argued how the theory of hegemony can make sense of how tolerance and identities are articulated and represented. Thought of in this way, tolerance always involves exclusion. Phrased in terms of the often noted paradox of tolerance, there is no tolerance without intolerance, and as a result tolerance and intolerance cannot simply be opposed. This distinguishes my approach from the sort of – usually analytical – approach that takes tolerance to be a question of establishing the essence of tolerance and the just – fair and precise – distinction between tolerance and intolerance.[55]

In contrast to this view, I have argued that there is no conceptual essence to tolerance independent of its particular articulations. We can recognise tolerance when we see it, but only because it has been articulated as what we have come to recognise as tolerance. Tolerance, then, can be articulated in different ways, as in the debates about *Begum*, *X v Y*, *Playfoot* and *Watkins-Singh*. And no identities are inherently tolerable or intolerable. The distinction between tolerant and intolerant, and between tolerable and intolerable, is the result of hegemonic articulation. It is articulation all the way down. This also has consequences for the attempt to draw a just distinction between tolerance and intolerance. The distinction between what should be tolerated and what should not be tolerated cannot be drawn independently of a discourse of tolerance and justice. We are dealing with competing discourses of tolerance, discourses that may be more or less hegemonic and more or less institutionalised.

In itself tolerance is neither good nor bad, but, even if the two cannot simply be opposed, it is better to be the subject of tolerance than intolerance. Turning to other concepts and practices – equality, recognition or hospitality, for instance – will not solve the problem that exclusion is constitutive of inclusion. That is not to say that alternative practices may not, on the whole, address the problem in more fruitful ways; one example here would be William Connolly's notions of pluralisation and agonistic respect, either as alternatives to tolerance or as inspiration for a different approach to tolerance (Connolly 2002; Connolly 1995; see also Tønder 2013). At this point it is important to stress that tolerance does not simply reproduce existing exclusion and marginalisation. It does so, but there is no practice of tolerance that does not open up to that which is different and other, that which may pose a threat to the identity of the tolerating subject. There is no tolerance without a threshold, no tolerance that does not shut difference out. But it is equally the case that there is no tolerance that does not shut us in with difference, even as we try to manage that difference and position it as marginal and dependent. Accordingly, there are already resources within the discourse of tolerance with which to challenge the exclusion and marginalisation that results from tolerance, and with which to challenge the ways identities and differences are reasserted through tolerance. The same is the case with the discourses of equality and recognition, as argued in Chapters 2 and 3.

Tolerance cannot be reduced to power with power in turn reduced to domination. There is a tendency among some theorists to do so, for instance Hage (1998) and Brown (1995; 2006), who both draw on Foucault.[56] Here tolerance becomes the strategic exercise of power, the reproduction of inequalities and the domination of the less powerful by the more powerful. For instance, Brown (2006: 9) writes that she 'aims to comprehend political deployments of tolerance as historically and culturally specific discourses of power with strong rhetorical functions'. She adds that 'the invocation of tolerance, and the attempt to instantiate tolerance are all signs of identity production and identity management in the context of orders of stratification or marginalization' (2006: 14). My objection is not to 'the complex involvement of tolerance with power' (2006: 9) – on the contrary – but tolerance emerges as an ideological discourse that serves to mask stronger relations of power and domination. Hage, Brown and others are right to identify the nexus of tolerance and power as key to understanding tolerance as a discourse; the analyses in this chapter also suggest that much. This point is not restricted to the critical theory literature on tolerance. Others also identify power as central to tolerance, although it is usually referred to as a paradox: to be tolerant is to have the power to be intolerant too, thus making of tolerance an act of grace (Forst 2013; King 1998).

Tolerance does indeed reproduce a relation of inequality and relative power between tolerator and tolerated, and it does so in a way similar to recognition and hospitality. The tolerating party can only tolerate insofar as they have the power to withdraw tolerance. The tolerated party comes to depend on the tolerance of the tolerating party; their inclusion through tolerance is conditional on the reproduction of this relationship of dependence and power. Without power and inequality, and without exclusion, there is no tolerance. This is the point rightly made by, among others, Hage and Brown.

However, as is the case with equality, recognition and hospitality, this cannot be the whole story. The hierarchical relationship between tolerator and tolerated is interrupted by the way in which the tolerator becomes hostage to tolerance and to the tolerated. It is clear how the tolerated becomes hostage to tolerance: with tolerance comes dependency, but without tolerance comes intolerance and exclusion. But the tolerator also becomes hostage to tolerance. Power can only be exercised through tolerance if the object of tolerance is not simply that: a passive object with no power at all. There is no tolerating party without someone who asks for tolerance, no tolerance without the inclusion of something sufficiently different that we cannot stay indifferent to. There is no tolerance, in short, without the recognition of the tolerating party as tolerant and tolerating – and that recognition has to come from others, including those who are tolerated. Tolerance cannot be reduced to power understood as the one-way domination and manipulation of a passive subject (see also Thomassen 2006).

How does the relationship between tolerator and tolerated become articulated in particular discourses? That is the question to ask. Likewise, we must ask how some subjects become positioned as tolerant or intolerant, and as tolerable or intolerable, and how patterns are reproduced over time and across discourses. The tensions of tolerance – like those of equality and recognition – can neither be resolved through definitional fiat (as attempted by analytic philosophers above all) nor dissolved by reducing representations and discourse to underlying structures (as attempted by Marxists such as Marcuse). Tension, or paradox, is constitutive of tolerance discourse and, more broadly, of any concept and practice of inclusion.

Notes

1. I will not distinguish between tolerance and toleration in the following.
2. On the representation of Islam and Muslims in the UK, see Poole 2002; Richardson 2004; Morey and Yaqin 2011; Baker et al. 2013.
3. For a contrast, see Poole 2002.
4. I also include material from *The Observer*, the sister paper of *The Guardian* published on Sundays. When analysing the material, I do not distinguish between *The Guardian* and *The Observer* or between *The Daily* and *Sunday Telegraph*.
5. There were no leaders about the cases. I have looked at every text in the two papers that mentions the four cases even if just in passing, although there are only a few of those. Something is lost and gained by using the online versions of the newspapers. I use them for ease of access, but I thereby miss part of the framing of the cases in the papers: their place within the paper and on the page. On the other hand, I read the material as do those who read and comment online, and using the online versions of the newspapers makes me able to include the online comments.
6. There is less coverage of the High Court decision than the decisions in the Court of Appeal and the House of Lords. While there is a lot of coverage of the *Begum* case in *The Guardian* and *The Telegraph*, there are only online readers' comments in *The Guardian* and only very few of those. This contrasts to the debates about the later cases – especially *Playfoot* and *Watkins-Singh* – where there are hundreds of online comments.

7. There is one example of the association of the jilbab with extremism in the academic literature: Joppke 2009: 94–100.
8. On 3 September 2006 at 9.50 p.m., by DevilsAvocado. When quoting from the readers' comments, I reproduce exactly the readers' pen names as well as any typos and other errors in the comments. The comments that take Islam to be extremist and intolerable as a whole are limited to the online comments (in *The Guardian*).
9. A *Guardian* reader comments online: 'not for the first time muslim women have basked in their oppression by calling it their own personal choice' (comment for Alam 2006, on 22 March 2006 at 5.28 p.m., by shellshock).
10. There is one other but less substantial difference: compared with *The Guardian*, journalists, commentators and readers in *The Telegraph* more often get the facts of the case wrong.
11. An example of the ridiculing of multiculturalism is Steyn 2005.
12. For instance: 'I'm sick of them and I'm sick of the do good wet liberals who encourage them in their pursuit of "rights"' (comment for Bunting 2006, on 22 March 2006 at 2.12 p.m., by Mashud). And in *The Observer*: 'And let's not forget another unpleasant female who fought the school in Luton – Cherie Blair. At least Shabina wasn't stabbing her own people in the back too' (comment for Odone 2006, on 3 September 2006 at 2.01 a.m., by Persian).
13. On 22 March 2006 at 3.50 p.m., by vickyhall.
14. For Laclau's reformulation of the theory of hegemony in rhetorical terms, see Laclau 1998; Laclau 2008; Laclau 2014.
15. Drawing on Richardson 2004, Baker et al. 2013: ch. 5 refer to this as differentiation and collectivisation: an identity is differentiated in an antagonistic manner, and everybody who is said to belong to that identity is treated as identical.
16. Which is why antagonism should be understood as a representational effect and not as the limit of representation as was the case in Laclau and Mouffe's earlier work. See Thomassen 2005.
17. On 23 March 2006 at 10.53 a.m., by Setanta.
18. In rhetorical terms, the representation is catachrestic, because there is no tropological displacement from a literal to a rhetorical term. Thus it is a catachrestic – which is also to say performative – operation. More generally, if we understand catachresis as a rhetorical act where there is no tropological displacement from a literal to a rhetorical term, then representation is catachrestic, and catachresis is a general trait of all discourse because discursive articulation has a performative aspect to it (Laclau 1998; Laclau 2008; Laclau

2005: 71–2, 101–10). The quotation marks I have placed around
freedom in one instance should not be understood to signify a
distinction between a pure concept of freedom and a particular,
discursively articulated concept of freedom. Any word or concept
is quoted and framed by the quotation marks of a particular discourse. Yet, the use of quotation marks facilitates the point that I
want to make. My deconstruction of the distinction between discursive and extra-discursive must go through that distinction, at
once quoting and discarding it.

19. For a reading of the hijab and the *Begum* case that emphasises the
contingency and pluralism of the meaning of the hijab, see Tarlo
2010.

20. Among the four cases, this is the one with least coverage in *The Telegraph* and *The Guardian*, and there are very few readers' comments
in *The Guardian* material.

21. Joppke 2009: 102–4 uses $X v Y$ together with the *Begum* case as
examples of what he calls the 'extreme veil'.

22. On 9 February 2007 at 11.50 a.m., by Mike Bibby. Note that
the subject in the name of which the reader speaks ('all of us')
does not include Muslims – tolerance here marks two divisions:
one between 'all of us' and moderate Muslims, and one between
tolerable, because moderate, Muslims and intolerable, because
extremist, Muslims.

23. On the segmenting of Muslims into moderate and extreme, see Baker
et al. 2013: ch. 6.

24. On 8 February 2007 at 10.17 p.m., by gabbathehut.

25. On 5 February 2007 at 1.12 p.m., by CM. Most often the representations of the UK and Islam are abstract, but in a few cases the
representations are linked to everyday life experiences. Consider, for
instance, the way in which this particular reader links their views to
feelings arising from an everyday occurrence:

> Just last week I saw a large group of young muslim girls some of
> whom were pre-pubescent and others who were adolescent. These
> girls were obviously returning from some religious ceremony and
> all were wearing a jilbab and niqab. Needless to say they stood
> out and looked threatening despite their innocent youth.

Although they are perceived as a threat (and so obvious a threat that
it goes without saying), their inclusion remains possible. This is so
because the reader makes a distinction between the girls' innocence

and their clothes, and, the reader adds later on, the girls 'are being used as pawns in the name of making political statements'. While the niqab is intolerable, the girls wearing it are not.

26. On 5 February 2007 at 10.18 a.m., by Chris Richards.
27. On 12 February 2007 at 9.19 p.m., by Nelly. Another reader of the same article writes:

> When will we learn that we must stop appeasing this monstrous religion, and learn that it is not racist (Islam is a religion) to assert Britishness. Those who do not want Britishness will find that some other countries will probably be glad to accommodate them. (Comment for Johnston 2007, on 12 February 2007 at 4.34 p.m., by Andrew Armitage)

28. For instance, one reader writes:

> If you wish school attendees to be required to wear your kind of uniform please attend a school where this is the required norm. It is incredible, no, totally unacceptable, that you or any other culture, would attempt to impose its own culture upon any other indigent society! You want to live under sharia law – great! Go to those countries that support it! (Comment for Johnston 2007, on 5 February 2007 at 4.53 a.m., by yer man abroad)

29. On 12 February 2007 at 8.22 a.m., by JP.
30. On 12 February 2007 at 6.48 a.m., by Edward.
31. On 5 February 2007 at 1.58 p.m., by simon coulter.
32. On 12 February 2007 at 7.55 a.m., by Mike Collins.
33. On representations of Muslims in the UK, see Poole 2002; Richardson 2004; Morey and Yaqin 2011; Baker et al. 2013.
34. *The Guardian* describes the rings as 'American-style "purity rings"' and links them to SRT's 'controversial evangelical church course', describing the organisation as 'highly controversial'. Hinsliff 2007. Lydia Playfoot and her father both expressed views about sex education in schools, and his daughter's proselytising in school is described by the father as 'positive peer pressure'. Quoted in *Playfoot* 2007: §7.
35. On 22 June 2007 at 3.33 p.m., by ratonarat. And another reader writes: 'She and her parents are about to have their fifteen minutes of fame!' (comment for *The Guardian* 2007, on 22 June 2007 at 1.19 p.m., by mrneutral).

36. On 22 June 2007 at 2.58 p.m., by SouthernMarkSmith.
37. On 22 June 2007 at 4.21 p.m., by Boltonlad.
38. On 16 July 2007 at 9.53 a.m., by Robyn. Another reader writes: 'This Millais School is only following the countries and Medias push towards Political Correctness. Foreigners are OK, multiculturism rules—Brits and Christianity can go and live on another planet' (comment for Petre 2007a, on 28 April 2007 at 6.29 a.m., by Harry Bede).
39. On 28 April 2007 at 10.45 a.m., by Brian Abrahams.
40. Irrespective of the fact that Sarika Watkins-Singh is represented by her mother and by lawyers in court, I shall continue to speak of 'Sarika Watkins-Singh' in this way.
41. This is repeated in different versions by other Sikhs commenting on the case.
42. On 30 July 2008 at 11.18 p.m.
43. See Chapter 2 on *Mandla* and the Race Relations Acts.
44. See also the discussion of this in the court decision (*Watkins-Singh* HC 2008: §§23–9), where Justice Silber discusses the witness statement by a professor of religion and education. This follows Silber's statement in the first paragraph of his decision 'that nothing in this judgment is intended to be any comment on the traditions or the requirements of the Sikh or indeed any other religion and community' (2008: §1). While the judgment may not amount to a normative assessment of Sikhism, it nonetheless rests on an interpretation of what Sikhism is (a religion, for example) and what it requires or does not require of its followers (wearing the *kara* or not). The decision *is* a comment on Sikhism, and it could not be otherwise because the judge needs to consider whether Watkins-Singh and the bangle are recognisably Sikh. Only as such are they protected under the law. The same issue arises in relation to the other cases, and I dealt with it in Chapter 3 on the way in which law, recognition and representation are intrinsically connected.
45. On 3 August 2008 at 10.35 p.m., by libby1.
46. On 31 July 2008 at 12.33 p.m., by ChasnDave.
47. On 2 August 2008 at 2.38 p.m., by WoollyMindedLiberal.
48. It is worth noting that, in the readers' comments, 'secular' sometimes means that society as a whole is, or should be, non- or anti-religious rather than signifying a relationship of separation between state and religion. I will use the term secular and only note the different uses of the word when relevant.

49. On 31 July 2008 at 10.46 p.m., by WoollyMindedLiberal. Another reader writes:

    Can I now seek redress from the head-teacher who asked me to remove a ~tiny~ Secular Society badge from my lapel – citing that she could on school premises – in case it offended some other parents? Nope again. As many others are pointing out, equality seems to be a one way street. Faith is a private matter – and bangle, ring, crucifix (whatever) have no place in a school with a no jewellery rule. But the religious won;t leave it here . . . as ever, they want the law to go both ways – protecting their 'rights' but removing ours . . . (Comment for Rai 2008, on 30 July 2008 at 11.10 a.m., by grahamew)

50. On 29 July 2008 at 1.54 p.m., by civilChris.
51. On 2 August 2008 at 5.44 p.m., by muscleguy.
52. On 29 July 2008 at 8.55 p.m. On the slippery slope argument, see also Hundal 2008.
53. On 5 August 2008 at 5.54 p.m., by amrit.
54. In Laclau and Mouffe's terms, identities can be articulated in different discourses at one and the same time. The flipside of this is that they are 'floating' identities, that is, they are not completely fixed within a single discourse. It is their floating character that makes it possible for different discourses to articulate them, *and* that makes it impossible for any particular discourse to fully articulate – and fix – the identities. In short, if identities were not at least partially floating hegemony understood as dis- and rearticulation would not be possible; or, in the terms used here, representation would not be constitutive but simply the reflection of already fixed identities. Laclau and Mouffe 1985: 105–14.
55. Rawls is perhaps the best example. See Rawls 1971: 216–21.
56. For similar views of tolerance, see Marcuse 1969; Fish 1997.

5   Hospitality beyond Good and Bad

Introduction: at home with Katie and David

In previous chapters, I have examined equality, recognition and tolerance as concepts and practices of inclusion. In each case, I have shown how there is no inclusion without exclusion, and that we must take note of the ways in which the relationship between inclusion and exclusion is negotiated by the different actors. Key here is the way in which the relationship is negotiated in the terrain of representation; for instance, actors become bound by the representations – both self- and other-representations – of their identities, and we must pay attention to which and whose representations are dominant. Inclusion and exclusion and representation and identity are intrinsically connected.

This chapter turns to a fourth concept and practice of inclusion: hospitality, and, connected to that, charity. Hospitality immediately raises questions of home and identity – for instance, of who is cast in the role of being at home and therefore able to host a guest. But hospitality also raises the question of what happens to the home, and to the identity of the host and the guest if the guest takes literally the invitation to make themselves at home.

I approach hospitality through a reading of Nick Hornby's 2001 novel *How to Be Good*.[1] As a popular novel, this is in many ways different from the materials I analysed in previous chapters; it is a different genre, a different form of representation. Even if one needs to keep the genre in mind, I am not interested in the novel as a novel. I am interested in this book because I think it is an expression of a specific way of life and a specific scene. It is an expression of a 'liberal' way of life, and it expresses well a certain mind-set from around the time of the millennium. And, I hasten to add, I can identify with that way of life and that mind-set, as well as with the book's self-ironic commentary on it.

The novel is set in North London around the millennium. Katie Carr, the narrator of the book, is a self-declared liberal and good person. Katie and her husband, David Grant,[2] are self-described *Guardian*-reading (13, 82) liberals (36) who vote Labour (82). They are 'middle-class and university-educated' (68). They have two children: Tom and Molly aged ten and eight. Katie is a GP in the NHS, and David writes a weekly column in a local newspaper, company brochures and a book he never finishes. To themselves, they appear to be an ordinary nuclear family: 'We're nothing special' (2). They live in the bubble of a particular 'income bracket and postal district' (19), and they socialise with other like-minded people (126). The bubble is also defined by how it is different from other parts of society. They live in Holloway in North London (4–5) where they have their own home, a three-storey house, so economically they are masters in their own home. They feel at home in this environment, and it matches their self-ascribed identities as opposed to nearby grubby Finsbury Park (35).[3] The book is an account of how their self-representation as normal people is challenged.

A good example of Katie's liberal self-understanding and how it is challenged is a scene where, at a meeting at their home, David is trying to convince the people living in their street that they should take in a homeless kid if they have a spare room. One of the neighbours is Mike, a self-employed builder, who is out of place. He does not feel welcome at the party and no longer feels at home in the neighbourhood as it has gradually been taken over by delicatessens, gastropubs and liberal middle-class people, the latter of whom he thinks of as 'stuck-up ponces' (146). His sense of community is very different: it is a community of individual home owners with sovereignty over their own homes: 'I don't live in a fucking community. I live in my house. With my things' (163).

The dislike is mutual: to the others, Mike represents everything they do not want to be and do not want society to be. He is unsophisticated – he is distinguished as such through a reference to *Eastenders* (144) – and he is a right-wing, Thatcherite individualist. For Mike, there is no such thing as society, and his reasons for being at the party are entirely egoistic: there is free beer. The antagonistic opposition to Mike helps define the neighbours as a community of good people, and at the party they literally move away from him and, thereby, closer together (146). Mike's egoism helps the others define themselves as Good people: as 'people whose hearts bleed right through their Gap T-shirts' (145). What might have disrupted their identity actually reinforces it. Yet part of their understanding of themselves as Good is that they are tolerant and accommodating of those who are different. Thus, although – or rather: because – they define themselves as Good in opposition to Mike, their lack of tolerance for him also makes them feel guilty. When Mike leaves the party in anger, his 'exit . . . is both a blessing and a defeat, because even though we all feel guilty about the homeless, we also feel guilty that we have failed to accommodate Mike, that he no longer feels a part of his own neighbourhood' (147). Drawing a line between themselves and Mike defines them as Good, but also shows the limits of their Goodness. They are keen on inclusion, except when it is inclusion of those they abhor. This theme has been replayed numerous times in the media and political debates over the last decades, from Tony Blair's 'chattering classes' through Gordon Brown's 'bigoted woman' to Emily Thornberry's Twitter picture of English flags and a white van during the 2015 general election (see also Kenny 2012). But it is not just the white working class and, as we shall see below, the homeless and mentally ill who are excluded from Katie and David's world; multicultural Britain is wholly absent from the novel, but as I shall argue, this does not mean that the novel is irrelevant to debates about British multiculturalism and liberalism.

What we have here is a perfect analysis of a slice of the scene around the time of the millennium. New Labour was in power, there was a sense of optimism after two decades of Tory rule, and a number of progressive policies were introduced: the minimum wage and the Human Rights Act, among others. It was also a time of growth reflected in rising housing prices which the middle classes took advantage of, and which resulted in the gentrification of new areas such as the area where Katie and David live. But we also see in this scene the limits of the liberal North London mind-set: difference per se is not problematised, only the kind of difference – personified by Mike – at odds with the lifestyle of Katie and David and their like.

This is also evident in other instances in the book, and what I look for in my reading of the book are those particular differences that challenge the liberal way of life depicted in the book. In short, the reading strategy is to examine what differences make a difference to that way of life, and how it negotiates those differences. What is challenged is a liberal way of life – an identity, a subjectivity – where public and private are separated. This in turn makes possible the separation of ideals and reality.

The big questions treated by the book are formulated by Katie as 'how much we owe our fellow humans' (183), and how much is 'too much to ask' (240). Here we are dealing with questions of justice, solidarity and equality, which are articulated in the book in terms of hospitality and charity and in the context of the everyday life of a family. This is important because, in liberalism, questions of justice, solidarity and equality are usually treated in the context of the law and the state. What the book does is to connect these questions to what is otherwise considered private: what do justice, solidarity and equality – and hospitality and charity – mean when we can no longer separate declarations of public principles from the reality of our private lives? Liberals like Katie and David believe 'in the power of words' as opposed to action; they are the kind of people sometimes dismissively referred to as 'the chattering classes'. Although they subscribe to ideals of justice and equality, these ideals are fine as long as they do not disturb their comfortable middle-class lives with Gap T-shirts and a dishwasher (175–6). If society suffers from inequality and injustice, it is the task of government to take care of those problems (73, 79) rather than being the responsibility of individuals to change their lives. They live in the belief that there is no direct line of responsibility between their ideals and how they go about their everyday lives. Being a good person is compartmentalised. You can be good by voting for representatives with the same ideals as you (Labour) rather than organising your life in accordance with those ideals.[4] That liberal subjectivity is challenged by the presence of homeless kids and the mentally ill, two instances where the state (including Katie as a GP) has failed.

Despite liberal progress, inequality and exclusion persist. The experience of liberal progress is possible despite the persistence of inequality and exclusion because of the separations between public and private, ideals and reality. In the book, hospitality and charity are introduced where the state has failed, and individuals, family community and the church step in. Another reading would be to stress how the privatisation of justice, solidarity and equality means that, not the state, but individuals and 'communities' (another one of those millennium catchphrases) take care of these things. In this way, the sense of a good liberal *society* without a good liberal *state* can be upheld.

In the narrative of the book, the challenges to this liberal subjectivity start with David's conversion from cynic to being Good.[5] David calls Katie's liberal bluff and insists that the gap between words and deeds is hypocritical. In his own words, 'I'm a liberal's worst nightmare. I think everything you think. But I'm going to walk it like I talk it' (80). The way he is converted to the cause of Good and to live by his ideals exposes the hypocrisy of the gap in the liberal subjectivity between ideals and action, and between public and private, thereby challenging Katie's self-understanding and identity. Up until his conversion, David has been cynical about the implementation of liberal ideals, and it is the disappearance of this cynicism that makes it impossible for Katie to continue to ignore the gap between her ideals and how she lives. Using the cases of hospitality and charity from the book, we could say that he is asking: if you're a liberal, how come that you won't give eighty pounds to a homeless person, invite a homeless kid to live in your spare bedroom, give away a lasagne to the homeless and unused toys and a computer to the kids at a shelter for battered women, or invite a mentally disabled person to dinner and to stay at your house?

Through a reading of Hornby's novel, we can learn something about this liberal subjectivity. This is important because that subjectivity is an important part of the scene, or discursive terrain, of British multiculturalism. It is in this way that this case of a 'normal' white middle-class family is connected to the cases about 'exotic others' in the other chapters. It echoes an important point from the last chapter: inclusion and exclusion and the politics of identity are not just about the 'others', but also about 'us': the majority, the norm. The two things cannot be separated.

It is noteworthy that there is no mention of race and ethnicity in the book. They are simply absent. There are no racial and ethnic others, but this just adds to the self-understanding of Katie and David as normal. Other novels from the same period deal explicitly with questions of inclusion and exclusion from the perspective of those racial and ethnic others absent from *How to Be Good*: *White Teeth* by Zadie Smith (2000), *Brick Lane* by Monica Ali (2003) and *Small Island* by Andrea Levy (2005), to name only a few.[6] In those books, the protagonists' experiences of inclusion and exclusion, and of home and hospitality, are very different from those of Katie in *How to Be Good*. Taken together, the books describe different negotiations of inclusion and exclusion and different experiences of the hope and disappointments of British multiculturalism. Multiculturalism is all about the public–private distinction: whether 'culture' should have any bearing on the public and on the state. British multiculturalism has been a negotiation of this, bringing the culture of the 'others' into the public realm, making it matter to law and public policy, but only up to a point. And culture is variously something public (because essential about a person or a group) and private (because something chosen more like a lifestyle).

This is not the place to go into an extended discussion of liberalism, multiculturalism and the public–private divide.[7] Examining how the public–private divide is negotiated through hospitality and charity is a useful way to investigate an important subjectivity on the scene of what I am interested in here: British liberal multiculturalism. This chapter examines how Katie's liberal subjectivity is challenged by voluntary and not so voluntary engagements in hospitality and charity. But it is not simply the case that her identity is challenged; the book also recounts how it is renegotiated and rearticulated.[8] This negotiation opens up an alternative to what is presented in the book as an opposition between a liberal subjectivity (separating public and private) and a totalitarian subjectivity (collapsing public and private).

Like the other chapters in the book, I make use in this one of post-structuralist political theory to examine hospitality; and to help me with the reading of the novel, I enlist the work of Jacques Derrida. From Derrida, I draw on his writings on hospitality and the gift, and on the way universals and ideals – hospitality, charity and equality, for instance – are always contaminated by their opposites. In Laclau's terminology, any universal is marked by exclusion, and there is always a tension between universality and particularity.

How to be hospitable

The first instance of hospitality in *How to Be Good* is a penetration. The narrative is set in motion by Katie's infidelity, which disrupts her self-understanding and sets in motion a series of revisions of that self-understanding. Katie has so far defined herself as good, among other reasons because she is a good mother and a good wife. 'That particular self-assessment will now have to be revised' (1), and the infidelity is also infidelity to this image of herself. Read metaphorically, the infidelity suggests the intrusion – but an invited intrusion – of a stranger into the family by way of Katie's body.[9] Katie herself makes the connection between her adultery, her marriage to David and the family. It is the marriage that defines them as a family, and her infidelity is a betrayal of, and a threat to, the marriage and the family. Marriage and love are linked to hospitality, home and charity in the book. The family home is the space of hospitality and charity, and it is here that Katie and David experience themselves as normal, but it is also the family/home that is disrupted by the (invited) intrusion. Inclusion, hospitality and charity extend from a home, and this home takes a particular form: the nuclear family, home owners, and so on. They are linked in particular through a reference to chapter 13 of Paul's First Letter to the Corinthians (189–90, 197–9), where love is sometimes given as charity:

> Love is patient; love is kind and envies no one. Love is never boastful, nor conceited, nor rude; never selfish, not quick to take offence. Love keeps no score of wrongs; does not gloat over other men's sins, but delights in the truth . . . (*The New English Bible* 1970: 1 Cor. 13: 4–7)[10]

The Letter was read at Katie and David's wedding, the idea being that this is the kind of love supposed to characterise their marriage. One way to read *How to Be Good* is as a discussion of whether it is possible for love – and charity and hospitality – to extend beyond the nuclear family and the home, and for love not to be selfish and boastful. That is, we can read the book as addressing two questions. First, are hospitality and charity possible beyond the family, and what happens to the family and to the home in the process of showing hospitality and charity? Second, are pure hospitality and charity possible at all – hospitality and charity that are not also for the sake of the hospitable and the charitable?

The second instance of hospitality occurs when David invites D. J. GoodNews, a healer who has cured David's back pain, to stay with them 'for a couple of nights' (93). Katie agrees that GoodNews 'can stay for a while' (93). The hospitality is conditional in two ways. It is temporally limited; it is supposed to be for a limited period, although Katie fears that GoodNews will never leave. He does leave, albeit many months later. Apart from overstaying the limits to hospitality, GoodNews also changes the nature of the home to the extent that Katie no longer feels at home there. Her self disappears little by little – 'I'm disappearing . . . Every day I wake up and there's a little bit less of me' (169) – because she has less and less to say about the norms and values governing the home. Increasingly, the norms and values are not hers, but those of GoodNews and the converted David, and she no longer feels at home there.[11] The hospitality shown towards GoodNews is also conditional because Katie only accepts it as a quid pro quo for her infidelity (93). The hospitality thereby enters into an economy of exchange where it is not hospitality for the sake of hospitality, but for the sake of something else (marital peace).

Things get out of Katie's control. This is so in the case of her lover, where her desire undermines her rational sovereignty; in the case of GoodNews; and, as we shall see later, in the cases of the homeless kids and Barmy Brian. In the end, she reasserts her sovereignty, of sorts. There is a more general point which Derrida (2000; 2006b) makes about hospitality: there is no hospitality without sovereignty and without the home. Somebody must be, or feel, or be recognised as, at home in order to invite the other, the guest. Make yourself at home, we say, and everyone knows that we do not really mean it. In fact, if the guest made the host's home theirs, there would no longer be hospitality. So hospitality must be limited and conditional; it must reproduce the sovereignty of the host.

But hospitality must *also* be unlimited, unconditional. It must not start with an invitation – where the roles of host and guest are already given and ordered in a particular way – but what Derrida (2006b: 229 n.17; 1993: 33–5) calls visitation where the other visits and where no conditions are imposed on the visit. If this were not the case, hospitality would be reduced to a calculated and calculable act that simply confirmed my identity and sovereignty. Hospitality would be for my own good even when presented as if for the good of the other. If hospitality must also be unconditional, then we will have situations where there is a risk that the guests will make themselves at home, that is, situations where the home, identity and sovereignty of the host are put into question. This is precisely what happens to Katie in the novel.

Hospitality, then, is always *both* conditional *and* unconditional. There is a mutual implication between conditional and unconditional hospitality. Hospitality must exceed the conditions placed on it and must be more than a selfish act: 'conditional laws [of hospitality] would cease to be laws of hospitality if they were not guided, given inspiration, given aspiration, required, even, by the law of unconditional hospitality' (Derrida 2000: 79). At the same time, unconditional hospitality must become effective if it is to be anything, yet this means that it must be determined one way or the other and, thus, be conditional. There is a necessary perversion of hospitality. Derrida writes:

> *the* unconditional law of hospitality needs the [conditional] laws, it *requires* them. This demand is constitutive. It wouldn't be effectively unconditional, the law, if it didn't *have to become* effective, concrete, determined, if that were not its being as having-to-be. It would risk being abstract, utopian, illusory, and so turning over into its opposite. In order to be what it is, *the* law [of unconditional hospitality] thus needs the laws [of conditional hospitality], which, however, deny it, or at any rate threaten it, sometimes corrupt or pervert it. And must always be able to do this. (Derrida 2000: 79)

192

If hospitality did not become effective and conditional, it would be nothing (a hospitality that is not instituted 'is' not) or would turn into its opposite, because those opposed to it would take advantage of the unconditional openness in order to undermine it. But the very medicine for this problem also perverts hospitality: if the condition of possibility for unconditional hospitality is that it becomes effective and conditional, then this is simultaneously its limit. Note that it is not a limit that surrounds unconditional hospitality, but a limit that also makes it possible. One would only need to add that hospitality is not 'sometimes corrupt[ed] and pervert[ed]'; it is necessarily and always already corrupted and perverted, but importantly not as opposed to a non-corrupted or non-perverted hospitality, as if that were possible. Derrida (2000: 81) concludes that 'exclusion and inclusion are inseparable in the same moment'. There is always exclusion; in fact, exclusion is the condition of possibility of inclusion through hospitality.

Not only is there a tension between ideal and reality, we are dealing with a tension – paradox, aporia – internal to the ideal of hospitality. The gap between unconditional and conditional hospitality is not simply a gap between ideals and reality. There is a gap between ideals and reality which is central to Katie's liberal subjectivity. The Derridean conception of hospitality as always in a tension between unconditional and conditional shares with liberalism a critique of the totalitarian collapse of ideal and reality and of public and private – think, for instance, of Isaiah Berlin's (2002) argument for negative liberty. But it is different from liberalism in that Derrida also insists that the two sides cannot be separated. So, gap *and* mutual implication. We can only think of unconditional hospitality in a way that it is already mediated by – and therefore articulated through – conditional hospitality. With Laclau, we could say that, as a 'universal', unconditional hospitality is articulated through a particular instance of conditional hospitality and is therefore limited. But, at the same time, the universal cannot be reduced to a particular, unconditional hospitality to conditional hospitality. The universal always exceeds the particular, just as unconditional hospitality exceeds conditional hospitality. As we shall see later on, guilt, and not cynicism, is the right ethical attitude in response to this structure of hospitality.

Hospitality is aporetic, to use a Derridean phrase (Derrida 2000: 223). The condition of possibility of hospitality is simultaneously its limit or condition of impossibility. Hospitality is only possible as a negotiation of this, which is to say that it is only possible as the negotiation of the tension between conditional and unconditional hospitality. And that negotiation is contingent: there is no fixed horizon to navigate by. In this way, hospitality resembles the other practices of inclusion examined in this book: in each case, exclusion is the limit *and* the condition of possibility of inclusion.

The structure of hospitality is similar to that of the aporia. 'Is aporia not,' Derrida (2000: 223) asks, 'as its name indicates, the non-road, the barred way, the non-passage?' He continues:

> My hypothesis or thesis would be that this necessary aporia is not negative; and that without the repeated enduring of this paralysis in contradiction, the responsibility of hospitality, hospitality *tout court* – when we do not know and will never know what it is – would have no chance of coming to pass, of coming, of making or letting welcome. (Derrida 2000: 223)

The task of the deconstructive reading is to analyse how this aporia is experienced and negotiated. The aporia does not absolve us of responsibility to act or make a decision – in short, to negotiate it. Analyses of these experiences and negotiations are the only way to analyse hospitality; hospitality only exists as negotiations between conditional and unconditional hospitality. In *How to Be Good*, Katie negotiates hospitality, and I take this as an example of the negotiation of hospitality within a particular liberal subjectivity.

The deconstructive reading of *How to Be Good* and of hospitality proceeds in two simultaneous styles:

> Deconstruction is generally practiced in two ways or two styles, although it most often grafts one on to the other. One takes on the demonstrative and apparently ahistorical allure of logico-formal paradoxes. The other, more historical or more anamnesic, seems to proceed through readings of texts, meticulous interpretations and genealogies. (Derrida 1992a: 21)[12]

The deconstructive analysis of aporias is only 'apparently' ahistorical and universal, and the reading of a particular text is only 'more' historical than the deconstructive analysis of aporias. The two styles cannot be entirely separated. General aporias and structures are only 'found' in particular and singular texts, and so they only exist in a mediated form. The logic of exemplarity identified in the Introduction is also at work here: the particular is at once an instance and constitutive of the general. At the same time, it is impossible to approach a text in an immediate fashion. The reading of the text is always mediated by certain interests and themes (for instance, inclusion/exclusion, the relation to the other) and by a certain vocabulary (for instance, hospitality, charity), and the text is taken as exemplary, as representative, of a theme or a problem, for instance the problem of identity/difference in liberal discourses.

The tension between conditional and unconditional hospitality is evident in two other instances of hospitality in *How to Be Good*: the homeless kids and Barmy Brian.

David and GoodNews develop plans for how to be good, and one of those plans is for every home on their street with a spare bedroom to host a homeless kid. In the end, six neighbours – including David and Katie themselves – sign up to the scheme; later, three of the kids leave, two of them after having stolen goods and money.[13] There are objections to the scheme from some quarters (Mike, Katie) as to whether the kids can be trusted not to overstep the boundaries of hospitality. David and GoodNews promise that the kids are vetted. They will only take in kids that would not take undue advantage of the hospitality shown to them; hospitality is only extended to those who would not make themselves at home to the extent that they might run off with the contents of the home. This makes hospitality less risky and easier to accept for the hosts. The safety is bought at the price of limiting hospitality by imposing limits on who can enjoy it, irrespective of whether there are others who need it more.

Later, when one of the kids has left after stealing from his hosts, and after David and Katie sense that their guest (called 'Monkey') 'was unhappy, and uncomfortable' (166), they show him where they keep the emergency money and deliberately leave one hundred pounds there. He duly takes off with the money, but by then his transgression has been predicted and calculated by his hosts.

When the kids arrive to the street, hosts and guests 'are all scared of each other' (153), not knowing what to expect. Katie tries to be hospitable towards Monkey, and she describes her attempt to say 'something which won't patronize or offend, but which might indicate sympathy and curiosity' (154) – a welcome opening rather than a rejection, but one that is calculated nonetheless. Katie lets Monkey smoke inside the house even though they do not usually let guests do so. Doing otherwise, she fears, 'might get us off on the wrong foot: it might give him the feeling that he is not wanted, or that we do not respect his culture' (153). Of course, Katie does not really want him there, and she believes that his culture (of smoking) is utterly wrong, but she accepts that hospitality cannot be reduced to the limits of her culture, even if only in the name of an ideal of what she thinks hospitality ought to be like. Hospitality is negotiated, but in a way that ducks contestation of the cultures of the host and the guest; the agonism inherent to hospitality is brushed aside.

Later on, when Monkey wants to pay for living there with the money he has earned from begging, Katie declines. Even though he, and unlike David and GoodNews, works and can pay for the hospitality, doing so would reduce the hospitality to a relation of exchange; the guest would become a lodger, and it would not be hospitality. In this case, either Monkey does not see their relationship as one between host and guest, or Katie and Monkey differ on what hospitality entails.

Katie and Monkey are disappointed with one another and with the scene of hospitality. They both had different expectations to the nature of the hospitality and to one another as host and guest. Monkey expected digital TV, Sky Sports, Dreamcast and a dog. Katie expected someone she could nurse: 'I am unable to show him the side of me that I wanted him to see: Katie the therapist, the listener, the imaginative solver of insoluble problems' (155). According to her, this is because he does not open up himself to her, but her own opening up is limited to the part of herself she wants to show off. It is not hospitality for the sake of hospitality, but for the sake of articulating her identity in a particular way.

196

Expectations and norms govern and limit hospitality from the beginning, and there is an element of egoism to hospitality. If Katie is disappointed that her hospitality does not give her the opportunity to nurse the guest, for what sake is the hospitality? Although it may be for the sake of the homeless kids, it is also for the sake of the hosts. The kids and the hospitality towards them reinforce the identities of the hosts as hosts and as good and give meaning to their lives. In the case of David and Katie, hospitality makes them feel good, albeit in different ways. In the case of two couples who cannot have children of their own, it is suggested that the hospitality fills a desire for having children (149). One part of one of the two couples says about 'their' homeless kid: 'I know Sas thinks we've done a lot for her . . . But I can't describe what she's done for us' (165). The hospitality is also for the good of the host. Although the homeless cannot reciprocate the hospitality in kind, there is a return on the hospitality: meaningfulness, feeling-good, and so on. Hospitality is caught in this economy of exchange, even if it cannot be reduced to it and something an-economic remains.

The other main example of hospitality is that of 'Barmy Brian', one of Katie's patients who keeps coming back, with Katie unable to do anything about his problems. In Brian's case, they are social problems linked to his mental health problems. Brian is an example of the limitations of the state in dealing with social problems: as an NHS doctor, Katie cannot do anything about his problems because of a lack of resources, and because she can only address those problems in a depersonalised way. Brian is not homeless, but he does not have a family that can take care of him. When, towards the end of the narrative, Katie invites Brian for dinner at their place, it is also a selfish attempt to get Brian out of the consultation, even though it just postpones her problem of how to deal with this person.

At the dinner, Molly invites Brian to stay with them, and she is not put off when Brian replies that it would have to be forever. She replies: 'That's OK . . . That's what we do here . . . We look after poor people. We're very good. Everyone thinks so' (231). Good people are hospitable and do not put limits on their hospitality: it can be 'forever' and, in this way at least, unconditional. Yet, hospitality also takes places between two subjects: a host ('we') with a home and the means to be hospitable and a guest in need of hospitality ('poor people'). Hospitality is conditioned by a particular history that has placed some subjects in the role of hosts with a home and others in the role of potential guests. Hospitality here is linked to a particular political economy where liberal progress does not exclude the possibility of inequality and exclusion. Likewise, in British multiculturalism, equality, recognition and tolerance are conditioned by a history of colonialism and imperialism that remains operative, even if in new forms, and the liberal subjectivity described in *How to Be Good* is part of this.

Katie draws a line and says no: 'that's as far as it goes. The outer limits of our hospitality' (234). They are in a position to offer hospitality, but it would be too much and overwhelming if Brian were to move in with them. Her point is that, if they are falling apart as a family – 'we're barely able to look after ourselves' (234) – then they cannot take care of others and show hospitality towards them. She does not claim that it is fair to draw this limit; quite the contrary:

> It's not fair. Love, it turns out, is as undemocratic as money, so it accumulates around people who have plenty of it already: the sane, the healthy, the lovable. . . . and much as we would like to spread it around a little, we can't. (232)

Love and hospitality are not infinite, and so they must be limited and be made conditional. Katie recognises the danger of limiting hospitality though: 'we, surely, are the people who should offer him hospitality. . . . the path I am on is slippery, glacial, and . . . no one can step on it without sliding all the way down to the bottom' (232). Hospitality must be limited and conditional, but there is no absolute yardstick with which to compare different limitations on hospitality: one form of hospitality might be as good as another. And yet, as suggested by the subsequent narrative, Katie is not correct to suggest that you cannot distinguish a limited hospitality from non-hospitality. Instead what we find is a negotiation of two imperatives: an unconditional hospitality and conditional hospitality. The former only exists as an excess over the latter, always putting the limitations on hospitality in question because we can always be more hospitable, and because the limitations are not natural but something we have, at least in part, chosen. This is what distinguishes hospitality, however limited, from non-hospitality. So, a slide yes, but not *all* the way down.

Katie limits hospitality to the nuclear family, which has been intimately connected to the home earlier on in the book. She says: 'Molly, this is our family. You, me, Daddy, Tom. That's it. Not GoodNews, not Brian, not Monkey, nobody else. Tough. There's nothing you can do about it. These are the people we have to worry about first' (234). The reference to the nuclear family naturalises the limits of hospitality because the limits of the family are taken as self-evident and in need of no further justification – it's just the way it is. The problem here is not that hospitality is limited and conditional – of course it is! – but that the limit and the conditions are represented as self-evident and beyond questioning. They are not so, and should not be so. Even if one wanted to limit hospitality to family, it is possible to resignify what counts as family. You *can* do something about it.

As a compromise, Katie invites Brian around for dinner every time they have chicken. She reflects on this:

A few months ago this would have been a surefire indication of my own barminess, and yet now it signifies only a cold-hearted and pragmatic sanity. . . . that's the thing with this brand of charity. It's all about what it does for us, not for people like Brian. (233)

Inviting Brian for dinner would have seemed like an excessive and insane hospitality for the Katie we meet at the beginning of the book, even if only an invitation, a calculated show of hospitality and charity. At the end of the narrative, it does not seem to her as the right thing to do, but more like one possible way of negotiating the road through the aporia of conditional and unconditional hospitality. Katie's self-understanding has changed and so has her idea of home and the norms that define the home – that is, the ethos and the rationality governing the home, the line between sanity and insanity. What Katie before would have considered mad, she now accepts as one possible negotiation of conditional and unconditional hospitality because her ideas of what it means to be good and hospitable – as well as sane and rational – have changed. The result is an extension of hospitality although there is nothing inevitable about this as the renegotiation might also have been in the direction of less hospitality.

Charity

I now turn from hospitality to charity, but it is worth noting that hospitality is often presented as an act of charity, as a gift. In *How to Be Good*, the two things are articulated together: being good is a matter of hospitality and charity. What is more, hospitality and charity share a basic structure: they are split between conditionality and unconditionality, and there is always an element of calculation, of economy, to them (Derrida 1992b; Derrida 2008b).[14] *How to Be Good* contains several examples of charity: giving eighty pounds to a beggar, giving the children's toys and one of their computers to a shelter for battered women, giving away the dinner to the alcoholics at Finsbury Park, and redistributing everything people earn above the average wage. All of these things should make perfect sense to a left-wing liberal. If you want a better society, these are the sorts of thing you ought to do, and when doing or proposing to do so, David is simply putting his money where Katie's mouth is.

After going to a theatre play in central London towards the beginning of the book, Katie and David are looking for a cab home, but 'then something odd happens' (57). David gives away eighty pounds to a homeless kid begging on the street. Katie is 'disoriented' (57), and she takes back the money from the homeless kid. Giving a homeless person eighty pounds exceeds Katie's norms for what one needs to give to a beggar. It is not that Katie does not want to give anything to beggars and homeless people, or that she does not think something should be done about homelessness. She buys the occasional *Big Issue*, but this is what a good conscience costs, not eighty pounds.

To analyse the scene with the beggar, consider first Derrida's analysis of the gift and, by extension, charity. As with hospitality, recognition and representation play a central part: hospitality and gift must be represented and recognised as such. The host must be recognised as host, the act of hospitality as hospitality, and the guest as guest. There must be someone (with the intention of giving) giving something to someone. 'In order for there to be gift, gift event, some "one" has to give some "thing" to someone other, without which "giving" would be meaningless' (Derrida 1992b: 11). The gift enters into a system of representation and recognition and becomes conditional. It would not be a gift without this conditionality. Not only that, the gift also enters into a system of exchange where the gift is given *for* something. Whether given out of pity, in order to feel good, or in exchange for another gift, there is a return on the gift. This is another way in which the gift is conditional.

Yet, the gift must also exceed all conditionality, determination and exchange. It must be unconditional, with no strings attached and no expectations of a return. 'For there to be a gift', Derrida (1992b: 12) writes, 'there must be no reciprocity, return, exchange, countergift, or debt.' If the gift is *for* something, or someone, it is reduced to that something, or someone. For instance, the gift must exceed all egoism. Derrida writes of the gift in a way that one could also characterise hospitality:

> The moment the gift, however generous it be, is touched by the slightest hint of calculation, the moment it takes account of knowledge [*connaissance*] or recognition [*reconnaissance*], it allows itself to be caught in transacting . . . the alteration of the gift into a form of calculation immediately destroys, as if from the inside, the value of the very thing that is given. (Derrida 1992b: 113)

When it comes with the expectation of a calculated return, what is given is no longer just the gift. Pure, unconditional charity is impossible, yet we cannot simply discard this dimension of charity and of hospitality. This is the aporia: that charity, like hospitality, can only exist in this ineradicable tension between conditionality and unconditionality.[15]

Now consider the scene with Katie, David and the beggar. David gives what seems to Katie like an excessive amount of money. At first sight, his gift seems unconditional, and this is what scares Katie. However, it is calculated in at least three ways. First, David quickly notes that he 'kept a fiver back' for the Tube (58) so that they will not suffer too much inconvenience from this now less excessive gift. Second, David points out that their finances are such that they will not even notice this, and so there is no threat to their lifestyle. And, finally, David gives the following reason for giving the eighty pounds to the homeless kid: 'I just wanted to do it that one time. See how it felt' (58).[16] In these ways, even the excessive gift of eighty pounds to a homeless person is less than unconditional: it is calculated so as to avoid too much disruption to the donor's life, and it is given not just for the sake of the homeless but also for the sake of the donor (David).

At first sight, a beggar gives nothing in return, neither to the one giving him something nor to society in general. This is why the builder Mike complains that beggars are just lazy, that they only take and do not give anything in return and therefore are undeserving of any gift (145). He is just saying what his neighbours do not dare think: that they are also doing it for themselves. This recalls the relationship between a host and a parasite. The parasite lives off the host, but there is also a sense in which there is no host without a parasite. It is the parasitical nature of the parasite that makes a host of the host, so the parasite does give something in return, namely a support for the identity of the host. In hospitality as well as in charity, the host is also parasitical on the parasite (Miller 2004: 177–80). The beggar still participates in a symbolic economy of exchange where alms are exchanged for good conscience, and where there are norms regulating how much one must give for a good conscience. There is a return on the charity to the beggar, and we are dealing with a sort of distributive justice. This explains how Katie can calculate that it is *too much* to give eighty pounds to a beggar.

The beggar's position vis-à-vis the rest of society is important. The beggar is clearly at the margins of society (and is often homeless), but he is at once excluded and included. The beggar to whom I give something is someone unable to reciprocate in kind, but this also reproduces the beggar's marginality and exclusion from our ordinary lives. Apart from rushing past the beggar when cashing money at a cash point or walking into a Tube station, we do not need to make the beggar part of our lives or part of society in its normal functioning. This would be very different if we were to show hospitality to the beggar by inviting him to stay in our spare bedroom. Although this would make perfect sense if you wanted to help beggars and homeless people, it would also disrupt our sense of being at home in our home. Here home, hospitality and charity are intimately connected, and note that we are dealing not simply with a legal relationship (although that is also involved), but with a way of life. But, because our relationship to the beggar is reduced to the exchange of alms and good conscience, we can include the beggar into our lives in a way that he remains excluded – or at least marginalised – from our lives.[17]

Similarly, Barmy Brian gets his apportioned fifteen minutes of medical attention, but even though Katie and society spend resources on him in this way, he remains marginalised vis-à-vis mainstream society, and this is because solidarity and justice take this form. He is given something, but only as a medical patient, and this keeps him in this marginalised role. At the same time, working as a doctor and spending time on patients like Brian makes Katie think that she does not need to give eighty pounds to a homeless kid: her good conscience has already been bought by working as a GP in the NHS so that she can enjoy a comfortable life outside working hours.

What is important to note is that the subject positions involved in charity and hospitality – donor/donee, host/guest – are unevenly distributed across society. What is more, these positions are connected with other social and economic privileges and forms of exclusion and inequality. The donor may depend on the donee (to be a donor), and the host on the guest (to be a host), but ultimately it is better to be in the position of donor and host than donee and guest. As is the case with recognition and tolerance, it is better to be able to dispense charity and hospitality than to have to ask for it.

The way in which calculation and economy are involved in charity is also illustrated when David convinces Tom and Molly to give away some of their toys to the children at a shelter for battered women. '[M]ost of what they gave away . . . was junk, or at least stuff they no longer played with.' However, 'the gifts would be meaningless unless they were really good toys', and so they agreed 'to donate something from the current playlist' (122). It is no feat to give away something you do not really want anyway. There is no such thing as a free gift, and giving may hurt, as is the case when Tom realises what he has been let into.

When Katie's parents have been invited around for Sunday roast, David wants to give away the roast to the homeless. After protestations from Katie, they settle for lasagne, which, David agrees, is also 'more convenient for the homeless' (83). Although a calculated and negotiated compromise, it still seems excessive to Katie. Her objections to giving away the food are twofold. The first is material comfort, although she realises that it is a comfort that she has chosen rather than one she needs: 'less comfortably than before, maybe, but comfortably nonetheless – we will not starve, no matter how much lasagne is given away. OK, then. So we can, but I don't want to' (84). Katie desires her comfy North London middle-class life, and practising her liberal ideals of charity and hospitality threatens that way of life.

The other reason why Katie objects is embarrassment. She is afraid of the embarrassment that she will feel when her parents are confronted with David's views and actions. Her embarrassment seems perfectly understandable, and it is quite easy to imagine the awkwardness of the situation. Here the excessiveness of charity and hospitality depends on the norms governing the particular situation and way of life. In Katie's case, she defines herself as a liberal in opposition to conservatives like her parents: 'Tories both, but neither of them actively evil' (81).[18] Yet, as long as she is only a liberal in words, Katie is closer to her parents than she would like to think. It turns out that, whether you are a conservative or a liberal, only your ideals divide you, not the way you would react in particular everyday situations. Katie's liberalism and her parents' conservatism can coexist because Katie's liberalism only stretches as far as her principles go and not to how she lives her life, at least not beyond token actions such as voting Labour and buying the occasional *Big Issue*. It is only in this way that we can make sense of Katie's embarrassment.

Embarrassment is a recurrent aspect of Katie's reaction to David's conversion to the cause of good (113, 120, 130–1). In each case, she is happy to sign up to the ideals. The embarrassment kicks in when the ideals are no longer just ideals, but David starts acting upon them. It is the latter that runs counter to the social norms, whether the norms of Katie's conservative parents or Katie and David's liberal friends and neighbours. One of Katie's defence mechanisms is to interpret David and GoodNews as mad when they are just trying to be good. When she first meets GoodNews, she makes the following observation:

> *Nutter*, I think, with an enormous sense of relief. There is, after all, nothing to learn from this person, no way he can make me feel small or wrong or ignoble or self-indulgent: he is simply a crank, and I can ignore him with impunity. (100–1; see also 74)

David and GoodNews can be characterised as mad because they do not accept the distinction between words, or ideals, and action. That distinction is central to Katie's liberal subjectivity, and it defines what a reasonable person is for Katie, and so there is no reason to take David and GoodNews seriously. But recall here how, at the end of the book, Katie has changed her mind about what constitutes 'barminess'. While the distinction between mad and reasonable is used to protect a way of life against its own ideals, that distinction is also renegotiated in response to challenges to it.

Katie is embarrassed, but she is also caught up in feelings of doubt and guilt. Her embarrassment arises from excessive and unconditional charity and hospitality; her doubt and guilt arise from a sense that her conditional charity and hospitality are never going to be enough. In other words, she is caught in the tension between conditional and unconditional charity and hospitality. However, doubt and guilt can also be the starting point for a different negotiation of that tension.

From self-righteousness to doubt and guilt

At the beginning of *How to Be Good*, Katie thinks of herself as Good with a capital G; in David's words, she is 'Miss Goody Two Shoes' (15). She is a GP in the NHS and as such she is good, because doctors are good (they help people), especially if they work in the public sector (because then they do not make a lot of money) (20). Katie has chosen to be a doctor in order to be, and to be recognised as, good:

> 'I'm a GP in a small North London practice'. I thought it made me seem just right – professional, kind of brainy, not too flashy, respectable, mature, caring. You think doctors don't care about how things look, because they're doctors? Of course we do. Anyway, I'm a good person, a doctor. (6)

Being a doctor helps her place herself (together with 'saints and nurses and teachers in inner-city schools') in opposition to 'managing directors of tobacco companies and angry local newspaper columnists' (124). The reference to 'angry local newspaper columnists' is to David who used to write with a 'lack of charity' before his conversion to the cause of good (71). Without the bad people, Katie admits that she would feel disoriented: 'I need these people – they serve as my compass' (124), and so she fears goodness in others as much as badness in herself.

When Katie does good, it is as charity. She does charity in order to be charitable, good in order to be good. She does good in a self-conscious way and for her own good and to bolster her identity as good. When she gives, it is to get something in return: not some material good, but a boost to her self-understanding as good. For Katie, being a good person means doing things for others that you do not like doing (such as looking 'at boils in the rectal area' (26)), but her doing good always comes back to what it means *for her*.

Katie does not think of herself as absolutely good in every aspect of her life. However, she gets around this with the belief that she can compensate for bad behaviour in one sphere by being good in another. Her liberal subjectivity is sustained by an ability to compartmentalise. When she laments that she has been a bad wife and mother, her reaction is:

> I want to go to the surgery and work and work. I want the day to be as unpleasant and as demanding as any working day has ever been, just so that at the end of it I will have regained something of myself. . . . and hope that by doing so I will feel like a good person again. A bad mother, maybe, and a terrible wife, undoubtedly, but a good person. (52)

Similarly, being a doctor, Katie believes that she can get away with giving less to homeless children begging on the street (58). Behaving badly has a price, but one that can be paid by doing good and giving in another sphere (for instance, at work). However, Katie starts to doubt this calculation of good and bad:

> I'm a good person. In most ways. But I'm beginning to think that being a good person in most ways doesn't count for anything very much, if you're a bad person in one way. . . . It's no good me telling you that I'm a doctor, because I'm only a doctor during weekdays. (48–9)

Katie is no longer able to work off guilt through compartmentalisation and calculation, and so her self-righteousness is put into question.

The old David was cynical about liberal ideals. After his 'Damascene conversion' (120), the new David is self-righteous because he thinks it is possible to know what is Good. Together with his fellow 'zealot' (74), GoodNews, David makes plans for doing good, including the plan already mentioned – 'a crusade', according to Katie (134) – for every home on their street with a spare bedroom to house a homeless kid. Later, David and GoodNews are writing a book on 'How to Be Good'. It is a book 'about how we should all live our lives' (210), a book for ordinary people who want to do good, but are confused about what to do. The born-again conversion gives David the ability to start from scratch and recreate himself in a new image. To Katie, he is like a new person (55), very different from the old grumpy and sarcastic (but funny) David who used to sign his weekly column in the local newspaper as 'The Angriest

Man in Holloway' (4). Katie envies him this rebirth; she strives for the 'feeling . . . of not having gone wrong yet' (31), because this would get rid of the guilt attached to the past that made her who she is now.

What David and GoodNews propose appears excessive to Katie and the liberal mind. It is 'too much to ask' (240). It is too much because being Good has been defined in a certain way (working for the public sector, voting Labour, buying *The Big Issue*, and so on), so that it can be ticked off and the do-gooder can have a good conscience. David and GoodNews too believe that a good conscience is possible, even if they may not have achieved it yet. For David and GoodNews as well as for the Katie we meet at the beginning of the book, Good is something that can be *done*, something that one can *be*. They are all self-righteous, and all believe that Good is something that can be calculated: either because it is absolute (David and GoodNews), or because a rational balance can be found (Katie). Later Katie uses Paul's First Letter to the Corinthians to criticise David and GoodNews as 'puffed up' (188–9), that is, 'boastful', but both Katie and David are boastful about their being good, their charity and their hospitality. They are boastful in the sense of self-righteous: they think that they know what it means to be good (how much one must give, how hospitable one must be, and so on), that they are good, and that they can judge others on this basis.

Although Katie does not see her own self-righteousness, she describes well what self-righteous people are like when describing David and GoodNews: 'They go too far, they lose all sense of appropriateness and logic, and ultimately they are interested in nobody but themselves, nothing but their own piousness' (74). David and GoodNews believe that they are doing Good, and that they know what it means to be Good. As a result, there is no point in consulting with others or taking disagreements into account (73). What is Good is objective and can be known through revelation and the privileged insight it gives them. As a result, David and GoodNews can set themselves up as judges over other people's lives, whether they know those people or not. This is the case, for instance, when they plan to ask the neighbours on their street to host a homeless kid: although they do not know the names of their neighbours, they are happy to judge the extent of hospitality the neighbours will be able to show (113). The new David does not want to judge other people in the way of the old David (129, 131), but he does not see that he still sets himself up as a judge. David and GoodNews do not need to relate to others as others with their own particular conceptions of what is good; others can be treated as means in their crusade for an ideal world. What we have here is a good description of what looks like totalitarianism from the perspective of liberalism: too much positive liberty, too little negative liberty, to use Berlin's terms (2002).

Doubt and guilt creep into the self-understandings of first Katie and, then, David. Katie's self-understanding is dislocated by her infidelity – which is also an infidelity to her old self-image as a good person: 'I've lost all my bearings somehow, and it scares me' (13) – and by the arrival of GoodNews and David's conversion. The dislocation of Katie's identity is gradual. The distinctions she had been making between ideals and practice, and between work and personal life, start crumbling. Little by little, she realises the connections between the different parts of her life, and between ideals and reality. Her response is not to reject doing good or to dismiss hospitality and charity as simply selfish acts. But nor is she won over to the cause of Good championed by David and GoodNews. Rather, she acknowledges that doing good always goes hand in hand with doubt and guilt because it is always conditional, and doubt and guilt are 'human' (210, 219).

The upshot is that one must economise with being good, that one cannot be good all the time and must make choices. In order to be and do good, Katie needs to survive psychologically first: 'Can I be a good person and spend that much money on overpriced consumer goods [a Discman and CDs]? I don't know. But I do know this: I'd be no good without them' (243). Being good and being selfish are not simply opposed because there is no good without selfishness and exclusion of others, and this is what Katie is trying to come to terms with. '[J]ust because I wasn't good, it didn't mean I was bad' (185) – that is, if hospitality and charity are always conditional, Katie must try to be good beyond good as opposed to bad. This is how she starts seeing being good as a contingent negotiation of conditional and unconditional hospitality and charity.

Katie insists on a right not to be good:

> An ideal world in my own home . . . I'm not yet sure why the prospect appals me quite so much, but I do know somewhere in me that . . . a life without hatred is no life at all, that my children should be allowed to despise who they like. Now, there's a right worth fighting for. (177)

Everything depends on exactly what sort of right this is: is it a right not to be good, or is it a right not to be good in any particular way? If we believe that being good is always contaminated by egoism, but that one cannot reduce being good to an ideological mask of selfishness, then it would have to be a right not to be absolutely and always good. This is what the context suggests: David and GoodNews want to build 'an ideal world in our own home' (177), and the right not to be good is proposed by Katie as a liberal right to protect against a totalitarian vision of the Good. It may also be a right not to be good in any particular way, but one would still have to defend why one is good – hospitable and charitable – in one way rather than another. There can be no right to be shielded from uncomfortable questions about how one negotiates the tension between conditional and unconditional hospitality and charity. This is where this reading of the novel moves into non-liberal territory: the public–private divide should not be articulated as a right, or an excuse, not to be good.

Katie's dominant response to the dislocation of her idea of how to be good is along these lines. Doing good always comes hand in hand with doubt because you can never know what it means to be good, and so you can never know whether you are really doing good. This view is opposed both to her initial self-righteousness and to David's conversion to the cause of Good, both of which are based on certitude (125, 210). What is more, if good is always limited and conditional, then it is linked to guilt: 'I get up in the morning determined to do something approximating to the right thing, and within two hours find something else to feel guilty about' (185). It is never enough, and the gap between conditional and unconditional hospitality cannot be closed. In the case of Barmy Brian, Katie believes that her hospitality is not fair, and it is accompanied by guilt. She notes that 'we have done enough for Brian, even though we have done almost nothing, and even though he is a sad and pathetic man who will devour any crumb of comfort that is thrown at him' (239). For someone who is not usually shown hospitality, any hospitality – however limited and conditional – is a lot, but this cannot satisfy the question mark of unconditional hospitality hovering over any conditional hospitality. It is never enough, and even when Katie feels it is too much ('preposterous, unreasonable' (239)), she cannot get rid of the feeling that it is too little. This is what the irreducible gap between conditional and unconditional hospitality means: guilt and bad conscience, because it is never enough, even when it appears to be too much.

Doing good is followed, not by good conscience, but by guilt because there is no good that could not be better, no good that is not limited. We cannot get rid of guilt. The guilt is located in the gap between conditionality and unconditionality, where the latter always exceeds the former. Good is always limited, and so there is always room for doing better. Hospitality, charity, inclusion: these are always caught in the tension between conditionality and unconditionality, and so they are always limited and always matters of more or less, better or worse. Being good is always followed by doubt and guilt, but it is also preceded by doubt and guilt and this is what may drive us to try to do better. Therefore it is not enough, as Katie tries (58), to say that you cannot give eighty pounds to *every* homeless person, and that therefore you will not give eighty pounds to *any* homeless person. The conditionality of hospitality and charity cannot be an excuse. The irreducible gap between conditional and unconditional hospitality and charity only means that you must answer for, and take responsibility for, your particular negotiation of the double imperatives of conditionality and unconditionality.

Even if she does not give up trying to be good, Katie gives up searching for the single right way to be good, and she is constantly riddled by doubt and guilt and regret:

The trick, it seems to me, is to stave off regret. That's what the whole thing is about. And we can't stave it off for ever, because it is impossible not to make the mistakes that let regret in, but the best of us manage to limp on . . . And I'm not sure that there is a cure for regret. I suspect not. (201)

Doubt, guilt and regret: those are the feelings accompanying doing good, hospitality and charity.

In the end, Katie concludes that you can only be good in a limited or conditional way – that you can only show hospitality insofar as you have a home that is and remains yours and where you feel at home; and that only if you have and keep something, can you give something. It is not an excuse for limiting hospitality and charity, because it always comes with doubt and guilt attached, a doubt and a guilt that arise from the irreducible gap between conditional and unconditional hospitality and giving. In other words, no good, hospitality or charity without a debt to the other, but it is a debt that cannot be repaid, cancelled or even calculated. Although we must economise and calculate, there is always something escaping this economy and calculation. It is never clear what is 'too much to ask' (240), and 'how much we owe' others (183). The benefit of the book is to highlight the doubt, guilt and regret accompanying hospitality and charity and to show that no negotiation of hospitality and charity is natural, but contingent.

Conclusion: narcissism and nihilism

In the end there is narcissism and nihilism. There is narcissism because hospitality and charity are always (also) about ourselves and our selves, our identity and sovereignty. Hence why the practices of hospitality and charity are intertwined with the identities of host and guest, donor and donee, and the identities change in the process. What is more, the identities of host and guest, and donor and donee, are closely connected.

Take hospitality. There is an asymmetry between the host and the guest: the latter is dependent on the former insofar as the guest must follow the rules and accept the norms laid down by the host.

But the hierarchical division of roles is deconstructed by hospitality itself. Hospitality must also be unconditional, and this starts an unravelling of the roles of host and guest. On the one hand, hospitality is extended from a home and from a host to a guest. On the other hand, being at home and being a host depend on an opening towards the other that puts in question the home and the role of host. Hospitality implies an opening to the other and an abdication of sovereignty and control over the home. The roles of host and guest, and the status of the home, are complicated here. In a way analogous to recognition and tolerance, the identity of the host as host depends on the identity of the guest as guest, and the host must be recognised and identified as such by the guest. Hospitality, and even inhospitality, requires hosts and guests, but there is also a reversal of roles. Just as we might say that the guest is hostage to the host (because the host can dispense hospitality at his or her will), so we can say that the host is hostage to the guest. The guest also becomes the host of the host, and the host the guest of the guest. Derrida writes of

> the final reversal of the roles of host and guest [*de l'hôte et de l'hôte*], of the inviting *hôte* as host* (the master in his own home) and the invited *hôte* as guest*, of the inviting and the invited, of the becoming-invited, if you like, of the one inviting. The one inviting becomes almost the hostage of the one invited, of the guest [*hôte*], the hostage of the one he receives, the one who keeps him at home. (Derrida 2006b: 218; see also Derrida 2000: 123–5; Miller 2004)

The guest is hostage to the home (its norms, and so on) of the host, but the guest is also the one who makes the home a home and makes it the home *of* the host. In order to be a home, the home (of the host) needs something that is not of the home: the home and the identity of the host are contaminated by alterity (Honig 2001).

The mutual hostage taking reproduces and reverses the identities of host and guest and the relationship between them. In this sense, the host and the guest depend on one another for what is proper to them, namely their host-ness and their guest-ness, their ability to show hospitality and to enjoy hospitality. More generally we can say that it is the relationship to the other that constitutes my own identity. This binds me to the other – without the other (as other)

I am not me – and it means that what is proper to me – what defines me – is something that lies beyond my control. This is why Derrida (1999: 51) can ask: 'Is not hospitality an interruption of the self?' Although hospitality helps constitute the self and the identities of host and guest, it also deconstructs this self and these identities.

Mutual hostage taking, then, but the parties are never completely hostages to one another: 'The one inviting becomes *almost* the hostage of the one invited' (Derrida 2006b: 218). While there is, and must be, reversal and substitution of the roles of host and guest, at the same time this cannot be complete, because that would mean that the guest was the host and at home. The host must continue to be host and to be at home. The identities of host and guest, and the relationship between them, are inherently unstable and precarious. This is so even if in particular situations they will have been more or less stabilised, and even if the roles are not evenly distributed across society. Despite the near reversal of the roles of host and guest, no hospitality can be an entirely symmetrical relationship. As with equality, recognition and tolerance, we must ask what kind of subjects are more likely to be positioned as hosts and guests respectively. The practice of hospitality assigns the roles of host and guest, and it is defined by these roles, but hospitality also self-deconstructs – deconstructs rather than destructs, as this self-deconstruction is at once the condition of possibility and condition of impossibility of hospitality.

Hospitality – like charity – retains an element of egoism or selfishness. Hospitality and charity are (also) for my sake, for my own good, and they are given in my self-image. Hospitality and charity are narcissistic. Derrida writes about narcissism:

> There is not narcissism and non-narcissism; there are narcissims that are more or less comprehensive, generous, open, extended. What is called non-narcissism is in general but the economy of a much more welcoming, hospitable narcissism, one that is much more open to the experience of the other as other. I believe that without a movement of narcissistic reappropriation, the relation to the other would be destroyed in advance. The relation to the other – even if it remains asymmetrical, open, without possible reappropriation – must trace a movement of reappropriation in the image of oneself for love to be possible, for example. Love is narcissistic. (Derrida 1995: 199)[19]

No identity rests entirely in itself or is entirely self-identical, that is, any self is marked by some alterity. At the same time, there is no relation to an other that does not extend from some self (Derrida 1993: 61). That relation can be more or less open, more or less hospitable, but it is never unconditional. Hospitality extends from a home, and it is exercised, in part, for some good. 'Non-narcissism' – love, hospitality and charity – is conditional, and therefore it involves narcissism and self-love, and cannot simply be opposed to narcissism. In the end, love binds Katie and David's family together as a family, but it is not the 'pure love' (70) of which GoodNews speaks or the unconditional love of Paul's First Letter to the Corinthians. Rather, it is a form of love that is selfish, narcissistic.

Hospitality appropriates the other because he or she is not simply included in his or her otherness, but is included as my other, as an other in my (self-)image. The other is an other for me, my other. There is no inclusion – through equality, recognition, tolerance or hospitality – that does not go through some representation of the other. The other can only be that other who is already represented by and to me, already appropriated and reappropriated, where the (re)appropriation is 'narcissistic', to use Derrida's term. There is no relation to an other that is not also a relation that extends from a self, from an identity, however precarious, and that is not also a relation to a self. Appropriation and reappropriation are connected etymologically and conceptually to proper, property and appropriateness. There is no hospitality without a norm for what is proper (to the self, the home, the nation), even if the home may always be marked by a certain impropriety, by what is heterogeneous to it. And where there is hospitality, there is property, for instance as home or territory, as well as the sovereignty connected to it. Finally, with the proper and property comes appropriateness: the norms and values that govern the home and access to it.

In the end there is narcissism – and nihilism. In the final scene, after three days of torrential rain, Katie and David's house can hardly cope with the water. The novel ends with the metaphorical image of Katie, David and the children holding on to one another while David tries to clean the drain of leaves, hanging out of the window. Glimpsing out at the night sky, Katie sees 'that there is nothing out there at all' (244). There is no divine assurance, only human beings – all too human – hanging on to each other, and possibly taking the others with them if they fall. Perhaps this is what Nietzsche (1968: 7 quoted in Miller 2004: 185) described when he wrote: 'Nihilism stands at the door: whence comes this uncanniest of all guests?' ('Der Nihilismus steht vor der Tür: woher kommt uns dieser unheimlichste aller Gäste?'). In the practice of hospitality, the home is marked by alterity, the host is never completely at home and the guest never just a guest. Any guest – and any home and any host – is *unheimlich*, even if never completely *unheimlich* (nihilism is the *most* uncanny of all guests). Hospitality is marked by an undecidability between the roles of host and guest (Miller 2004: 186–7).[20] Nihilism is *unheimlich* because it is heterogeneous to any norms of any home. At the same time, it is hospitality that makes a home of the home, and this hospitality cannot exclude the risk of letting in nihilism – beyond good and bad – of not being able to know how to be good, so that one loses one's bearing.

This conception of hospitality – and, more broadly, of inclusion – would be an alternative to any conception of the Good, whether liberal, communitarian or Marxist, and one that went beyond good and bad. If we think of it in terms of what Derrida calls the 'to-come' (*à-venir*), we should not speak simply in terms of good and bad, but better and worse, and with the caveat that the good – inclusion, equality, and so on – will never be realised, not now and not in any future (Derrida 2005: 86–92; see also Thomassen 2010b; Thomassen 2011). Hospitality is to-come, not because of some obstacles that may or may not be overcome, but because it is aporetic; the tension between unconditionality and conditionality is constitutive of hospitality. Thinking of hospitality in this way does not mean giving up on the promise of hospitality and inclusion. Equality, recognition, tolerance and hospitality: these discourses all contain a promise of inclusion, because they contain a certain unconditionality. That unconditionality is contaminated by a conditionality, but that cannot be used as an excuse. Rather, one can articulate the tension, or aporia, of unconditionality and conditionality as the starting point for an inexhaustible questioning of these discourses. If there is no equality, recognition, tolerance and hospitality *as such*, but only contingent articulations of them, then the question 'what is equality?', and so on, becomes part and parcel of those discourses. In the terms of *How to Be Good*: there is no final answer to this, but that is no excuse for not trying. At the end of the novel, despite all their efforts, neither Katie nor David knows how to be good, but that does not mean they stop asking. Indeed, 'how to be good' should not be taken as a statement about a fact to be discovered, but as a question. Doubt, guilt and a bad conscience are then part of how to be good, and not states of mind that can be overcome. We might celebrate the achievements of British multiculturalism, but any smugness about it would be wrongly placed.

In the end we are left with an economy of violence, but, as argued in Chapter 2, an an-economic economy. This is not the economy of lesser violence that some, inspired by Derrida and Levinas have argued for, Simon Critchley (2014) being the best example. The relationship between inclusion and exclusion is not a zero-sum one because exclusion is constitutive of inclusion, but that also means that we do not simply choose between inclusion and exclusion. Likewise with any violence done to the other when included: this is not a violence that can simply be opposed to a non-violent inclusion of the other in his or her otherness. While less violence may be better than more violence, that can only be calculated and determined with a discourse where inclusion, otherness and violence have already been ascribed value.[21]

Notes

1. All subsequent references in parentheses in the text are to the novel.
2. Although there is no etymological connection, Katie's and David's surnames echo one of the main themes of the book: caritas understood as giving.
3. Ironically, their address – 32 Webster Road – is actually in a deprived area in South East London.
4. Similarly, Katie can be good by choosing the right kind of job (a GP in the NHS), even if she may be bad outside working hours (6, 26).
5. Cynicism can also be a way to keep ideals at bay from reality, and, as Katie notes at one point, 'Cynicism is our common language' (131).
6. Although the latter is mainly set around World War II.

7. See, among others, Brown 2006; Fish 1997; Hage 1998.
8. Nick Hornby himself has referred to the novel as an account of how Katie negotiates between selfishness and selflessness, and he says about the book 'that it's a liberal acknowledgment of the contradictions of liberalism' (in Martin 2002).
9. I leave out of consideration two connected issues: first, the relationship between hospitality and the female body (see Rosello 2001: esp. ch. 5); and, second, the way that desire interacts with reason in Katie's liberal subjectivity.
10. For an interpretation of the religious themes in *How to Be Good*, see Tate 2008: ch. 4.
11. At one point Katie moves out of the home for a period in order to be more at home with herself and in order for her to recuperate her self. In a similar fashion, towards the end of the book, she takes up reading, which she describes as a way of expanding her home with new rooms, with new inputs and for new sides of herself (242). Thus, reading becomes a form of hospitality, and Katie takes advantage of the hospitality of the books and makes herself at home in them. On reading and hospitality, see Miller 2004.
12. Critically, see Bernasconi 1997. The relationship between the two styles of deconstruction could be described in terms of the quasi-logic of exemplarity whereby the particular is mediated through the general, and vice versa, not in a transparent way, but in a way where one articulates the other. See Derrida 1997: 97–100; and, critically, Harvey 1992.
13. Interestingly, the boys leave and the girls stay; the girls are capable of being nursed and nurtured in the role of guests, the boys not. See Rosello 2001: ch. 5 on the gendering of hospitality.
14. Critically, see Bernasconi 1997; Hénaff 2009.
15. In Derrida's (1992b: 12) terms, the condition of possibility of charity is simultaneously its condition of impossibility: 'These conditions of possibility of the gift (that some "one" gives some "thing" to some "one other") designate simultaneously the conditions of the impossibility of the gift.'
16. There is an indirect reference here to Charles Baudelaire's 'Counterfeit Money' (Derrida 1992b: ch. 4).
17. On the figure of the beggar, see Derrida 1992b: 134–8.
18. In another place she notes that 'anyone who votes Conservative will never be entirely welcome in our house' (101).
19. Note that Derrida uses 'asymmetry' to refer to the unconditional openness to the singularity of the other, whereas I have used it to

refer to the asymmetrical relation of power between host and guest, donor and donee.

20. With Derrida, one might say that there is something ghostly – in the sense of hauntology – about the host and the guest: their identities are undecidable according to a logic that assigns clear and distinct identities to subjects based on what is proper to them. See Derrida 1994: 51, 63.

21. This is Derrida's (1978: 313 n.21, emphasis removed; see also 1978: 117; Derrida 1999) conclusion in his engagement with Levinas.

Conclusion: Multiculturalism, Britishness and Muscular Liberalism

Examining discourses of Britishness, equality, recognition, tolerance and hospitality, I have argued that there is no inclusion without exclusion. Not only that, exclusion is not simply a matter of either/or, even if it may also at times be that. This is the case, for instance, with Gordon Brown's Britishness discourse in Chapter 1: although articulated around universal values, it is not universally inclusive, and it places different subjects in different positions vis-à-vis a core of Britishness.

I have also argued that inclusion and exclusion are intrinsically linked to identity, whether the identities of the including or the included (or excluding and excluded), 'we' the majority or 'they' the minorities. I showed this, for instance, in the case of *Mandla* in Chapter 2 where the rearticulation of race and ethnicity also implied a rearticulation of the included racial and ethnic identities (here Sikhs) and of the character of the including society. What is more, as I have also argued, identities are constituted in the terrain of representation. In order to investigate inclusion and exclusion, we must do so in the context of identities and identity formation; and, since identities are constituted in the terrain of representation, identities – and inclusion/exclusion – must be examined in terms of the politics of representation. So, for instance, in Chapter 3, we saw how the recognition of Shabina Begum's identity involved a struggle over the representation of Islam and the hijab.

This is what I have tried to show by examining four concepts and practices of inclusion – equality, recognition, tolerance and hospitality – and looking at how these discourses have been articulated

220

on the scene of British multiculturalism. In the context of equality, for example, I argued that equality is articulated through a subject of equality: an image or representation of the subject capable of being counted as an equal. Equality, and inclusion through equality, immediately turns on the question of identity, and that in turn is a question of representation. Here the question of representation is not whether there is a correspondence between representations of the subject of equality and a real world of complex subjectivities. Rather, to say that representation is constitutive means that there is not some 'real' subject who is then represented, or misrepresented; rather, subjects are subjects as subjects of representation, and to say so is not to deny their 'reality', but to insist that that reality is constituted in the terrain of representation. For instance, subjects are constituted as capable of being counted as equals through the way they are represented. We are not dealing with a distinction between representation and a non-representational reality; what we call reality is representational.

Using Ernesto Laclau's theory of hegemony and Jacques Derrida's deconstruction, I have made a similar argument in relation to recognition, tolerance and hospitality. There is no inclusion without exclusion, hierarchy and power, no inclusion that is not conditional. To be recognised, tolerated and welcomed is to be represented as a particular kind of recognisable, tolerable and welcome-able subject. Looking at British multiculturalism, we can speak of equality, but while 'the others' are equal, they are also marked as different. The others' difference can be recognised by the state and by society, but they need to comply with a certain image of a recognisable person. Their tolerance can be tolerated – for instance, as Muslim – but they are tolerated as different from 'we British'. They are welcomed into a home where they are marked as out of place. The representational space of British multiculturalism is one of inclusion, but there is no absence of exclusion or marginalisation; inclusion is conditional. No inclusion without power, exclusion and marginalisation then, but importantly we should avoid thinking of inclusion as a matter of either/or or as the construction of antagonistic frontiers only, even if it is also that. We need to think of inclusion and exclusion as also about the positioning of subjects in different relations of marginalisation and power vis-à-vis privileged identities.[1] What is more, there is no alternative concept or practice of universal inclusion. Such an alternative is simply not available. It may be possible to criticise discourses as more or less inclusive or exclusive, but the question of more-or-less cannot be dissociated from the question of what is included and what is excluded.

But it should also be noted how the representational space of British multiculturalism is defined by competing discourses and representations, some of which are more inclusive and more open to otherness than others. Not only that, but given the contingency of representations, and of identities and lines of exclusion, there is always some room for resistance against, and rearticulation of, identities and lines of exclusion, however limited those opportunities may appear. This is so for Gurinder Singh Mandla, Shabina Begum, X, Lydia Playfoot and Sarika Watkins-Singh as well as for the builder Mike, Barmy Brian, Katie Carr, the judges at the courts and the newspaper commentators and readers.

I started with David Cameron, and I will end with him. Cameron's Britishness discourse continues aspects already present in the New Labour discourse, including Gordon Brown's Britishness. This is so when it comes to the relative marginalisation of ethnic others and the alleged need to articulate a stronger common British identity. There are also discontinuities though, especially the stronger focus on the Christian heritage and the Muslim question.

Listening to Cameron and looking at the policies of the Conservative government (both his and that of Theresa May) and the previous Conservative–Liberal Democrat coalition, it is easy to think that British multiculturalism is under attack and in dire straits. That may also be the impression of my dissection of Cameron's take on terrorism, Islam and Britishness in the Introduction and below. British multiculturalism is indeed under pressure, but it has been so from the very beginning, and it was never absolutely entrenched in British society. Yet, even when looking at Cameron, there is also some hope for British multiculturalism. For one thing, Cameron and most of the Conservative elite are comfortable with the sort of pluralism going under the name of British multiculturalism. They accept this pluralism as a fact, at times even a welcome one, and in this they differ from earlier Conservative elites. They may be more comfortable eating in expensive ethnic restaurants than living next door to the waiters and kitchen staff. They may also only be a fraction of those potentially opposed to British multiculturalism, but they are an important fraction.[2]

I want to conclude by briefly looking at Cameron's speeches on immigration and extremism after he became Prime Minister in 2010. The aim is to use his discourse on Britishness, identity and inclusion to illustrate the points made in the previous chapters. Obviously 'Cameron's Britishness discourse' should not be reduced to a few speeches, but also contains policy, laws and institutions: immigration policy, the responses to the Calais and Syrian refugee crises, faith schools, the new citizenship test introduced in 2013 (Home Office 2013),[3] and many other things. It is for ease of presentation, and because I am only interested in using his Britishness discourse as an illustration, that I focus on his speeches. Those speeches include two speeches on extremism, a speech at the 400th anniversary of the King James Bible, and three speeches on immigration policy (Cameron 2011a; Cameron 2011b; Cameron 2011c; Cameron 2011d; Cameron 2015). With only few and minor exceptions, there is no change in the content or tone of the speeches from 2011 to 2015.

Cameron's starting point is that there is a crisis of identity. In his speeches on extremism, he speaks of a crisis of identity among young Muslims (men, above all) who lack a clear sense of belonging, and who feel at home neither in British mainstream culture nor in their parents' immigrant culture. That crisis of identity is a problem because of another crisis of identity: a crisis of Britishness. The problem here is a lack of self-confidence and direction, and a confusion about which values define us. The solution to the first crisis of identity – that of young Muslims – is to offer a stronger and more 'muscular' version of Britishness. British people will then know what they stand for and will stand up for it – 'if we don't stand for something, we can't stand against anything' (Cameron 2011d) – and young Muslims will have something to identify with. The stronger identity – Britishness articulated in terms of 'muscular liberalism' – will help exclude extremism and include those who deserve to be included. The inclusion of young Muslims will take place through the construction of an identity with which they can identify.

Cameron makes no apologies for the need to define the limits of this identity and, thereby, exclude certain groups and practices. Following the argument of this book, it cannot be an argument against Cameron that his Britishness is exclusive. There is no identity, and no form of inclusion, that is not also exclusive. It may be that it is too exclusive; or that it does not exclude the right individuals, groups and practices (rich tax evaders undermining the sovereignty of British democracy, for instance); or that it is the wrong identity (for instance, the citizenship test's focus on a glorious British imperial history instead of values to be aspired to (Porter 2013)) – but that is a different form of critique, one that does not have to enter into the game of *either* inclusion *or* exclusion.

There are two closely interconnected sides to Cameron's Brit- ishness. The aim of articulating a muscular Britishness is to create a sense of being in control, of the sovereignty of the British people and of ordinary people. This is tied to a feeling of being at home and secure: without a sense of being in control, people do not feel at home. This is particularly important in the context of immigra- tion: while the UK is a country that welcomes immigrants ('Our openness is part of who we are. . . . We are Great Britain because of immigration, not in spite of it' (Cameron 2014)), it must be able to *control* immigration. 'People have understandably become frustrated', Cameron (2014) writes, 'and it boils down to 1 word: control.'[4] The task is then to articulate a Britishness that will make people feel at home: 'We believe in respecting different faiths but also expecting those faiths to support the British way of life. These are British values. And are underpinned by distinct British institu- tions. . . . This is the home that we are building together' (Cam- eron 2015). A home defined by a collective identity, with room for pluralism. But note also how this discourse about sovereignty, home and immigration had a life of its own beyond Cameron's control – hence Brexit.

The other side of Cameron's Britishness is a particular set of values. He finds those values in Christianity: 'the Bible has helped to give Britain a set of values and morals which make Britain what it is today' (Cameron 2011d). The UK is a Christian, as opposed to a secular, country with a Christian tradition and with Christian values. Those values form the heart of contemporary liberal values and, so, of Cameron's (2011d) 'much more active, muscular liberalism'. This tradition and these values must be defended today against extremism, mass immigration, secularism and 'passive tolerance' (2011d). Tolerance still has a role to play, but now mediated by muscular liberalism. Tolerance is important because the UK is a pluralist – which Cameron marks as opposed to secularist – society. However, tolerance is articulated as a Christian value, so there is room for pluralism, but within a Christian and liberal framework.

This is how Cameron articulates identity and difference.[5] His Britishness – understood as muscular liberalism – provides a point of identification for British people and for British Muslims. His Britishness provides a home, but one that is striated and where some are more at home than others: those whose Britishness goes without saying. It is a tolerant society, but it places some in the position of tolerating a more recently arrived pluralism of 'others'. This state and society recognise difference, but as different. It is a society of equality, but understood as equal opportunity for those who have the talent and make an effort, and there is no mention of structural inequalities.

The alternative is not to oppose Cameron's Britishness in the name of some universally inclusive Britishness or other identity. Such an identity does not exist. There is no inclusion without identity, and no identity without exclusion. The alternative is not to dismiss the importance of identity, but to articulate alternative points of identification, for instance Gordon Brown's Britishness, Danny Boyle's Olympic take on British multiculturalism and contemporary Britain, or Jeremy Corbyn's defence of British multiculturalism. Whatever the case may be, any rearticulation of Britishness – indeed any articulation of any identity – must start from existing identities and representations, not to take them as given, but as radically contingent. It is by showing the contingency of existing representations, and taking those representations as representations that can be rearticulated – in short, by understanding identity politics as a politics of representation – that counter-hegemonic identities become possible.

Notes

1. This opens up the possibility, not pursued here, of analysing multiculturalism and identity politics in ways inspired by Michel Foucault's work on governmentality. See, among others, Hage 1998; Brown 1995; Brown 2006.
2. Note however that, when Cameron uses 'multicultural', it is to criticise a practice. When he appropriates what others might think of as part of multiculturalism, he uses 'multi-racial' and 'multi-faith'. The point remains that Cameron appears comfortable with racial, religious and cultural pluralism.
3. Notice that, in the new version of this, 'citizen' has become 'resident'. See also the discussion of earlier versions of the test in Chapter 1.
4. Elsewhere: 'people feel powerless'. Cameron 2011c. Whenever Cameron speaks of immigration as something to be controlled, he speaks of 'mass' or 'excessive' immigration.
5. He also referred to his government as 'a "one nation" government, bringing our country together'. Cameron 2015.

References

Abu-Odeh, Lama (1993), 'Post-colonial feminism and the veil: thinking the difference', *Feminist Review* 43, pp. 26–37.

Adams, Parveen and Jeff Minson (1990), 'The "subject" of feminism', in *The Woman in Question: m/f*, eds Parveen Adams and Elizabeth Cowie, Cambridge, MA: MIT Press, pp. 81–101.

Ahmed, Leila (1992), *Women and Gender in Islam*, New Haven, CT: Yale University Press.

Alam, Fareena (2006), 'Style and substance', *The Guardian*, 22 March, <http://www.guardian.co.uk/commentisfree/2006/mar/22/usingmyreligion> (last accessed 9 June 2016).

Alcoff, Linda (1991–2), 'The problem of speaking for others', *Cultural Critique* 20: Winter, pp. 5–32.

Ali, Monica (2003), *Brick Lane*, London: Black Swan.

Andalo, Debbie (2007), 'Heads to decide on school veil policy', *The Guardian*, 5 March, <http://www.theguardian.com/education/2007/mar/05/schools.uk> (last accessed 10 June 2016).

Anthony, Andrew (2005), 'The big cover-up', *The Observer*, 20 November, <http://www.guardian.co.uk/theobserver/2005/nov/20/features.review17?INTCMP=SRCH> (last accessed 24 April 2013).

Aslam, Dilpazier (2005), '"I could scream with happiness. I've given hope and strength to Muslim women"', *The Guardian*, 3 March, <http://www.guardian.co.uk/uk/2005/mar/03/schools.faithschools> (last accessed 9 June 2016).

Asthana, Anushka (2006), 'Teachers warn of crisis over Muslim girl's uniform fight', *The Guardian*, 19 March, <http://www.guardian.co.uk/uk/2006/mar/19/politics.schools> (last accessed 9 June 2016).

Baker, Paul, Costas Gabrielatos and Tony McEnery (2013), *Discourse Analysis and Media Attitudes: The Representation of Islam in the British Press*, Cambridge: Cambridge University Press.

Barry, Brian (2001a), *Culture and Equality*, Cambridge: Polity.

Barry, Brian (2001b), 'The muddles of multiculturalism', *New Left Review* 8, pp. 49–71.

Barry, Brian (2002), 'Second thoughts – and some first thoughts revived', in *Multiculturalism Reconsidered*, ed. Paul Kelly, Cambridge: Polity, pp. 204–38.

Begum HC (2004), 'The Queen on the application of Begum v. The Headteacher and Governors of Denbigh High School' EWHC 1389 (Admin).

Begum CA (2005), 'The Queen on the application of SB v. Headteacher and Governors of Denbigh High School' EWCA 199.

Begum HL (2006), 'R (on the application of Begum) v. Headteacher and Governors of Denbigh High School' UKHL 15.

Begum, Shabina (2005a), 'Online chat at IslamOnline.net', 17 March, <http://www.islamonline.net/livedialogue/english/Browse.asp?hGuestID=KbLTbk> (last accessed 21 December 2011).

Begum, Shabina (2005b), 'Schoolgirl speaks out on win', *BBC News*, 2 March, <http://news.bbc.co.uk/player/nol/newsid_4310000/newsid_4311500/4311509.stm?bw=nb&mp=wm&news=1&bbcws=1> (last accessed 9 June 2016).

Begum, Shabina (2006a), 'Interview with Shabina Begum', *GMTV Today*, 22 March, <http://www.youtube.com/watch?v=9hN-vAb4dQg> (last accessed 9 June 2016).

Begum, Shabina (2006b), 'School wins Muslim dress appeal', *BBC News*, 22 March 2006, <http://news.bbc.co.uk/player/nol/newsid_4830000/newsid_4832800/4832834.stm?bw=nb&mp=wm&news=1&ms3=6&ms_javascript=true&bbcws=2> (last accessed 9 June 2016).

Begum, Shabina (2008), 'Symbol-ed out', *BBC Radio Asian Network*, 12 May, <http://www.bbc.co.uk/programmes/b00b1k0j> (last accessed 9 June 2016).

Bennett, Catherine (2005), 'Of course women have a right to choose. But agreeing to wear a jilbab is no choice at all – even Mrs Blair can see that', *The Guardian*, 15 September, <http://www.guardian.co.uk/world/2005/sep/15/religion.uk> (last accessed 10 June 2016).

Berlin, Isaiah (2002), 'Two concepts of liberty', in *Liberty: Incorporating Four Essays on Liberty*, ed. H. Hardy, Oxford: Oxford University Press.

Bernasconi, Robert (1997), 'What goes around comes around: Derrida and Levinas on the economy of the gift and the gift of genealogy', in *The Logic of the Gift: Toward an Ethic of Generosity*, ed. Alan D. Schrift, New York: Routledge, pp. 256–73.

Blair, Ann and Will Aps (2005), 'What not to wear and other stories: addressing religious diversity in schools', *Education and the Law* 17: 1–2, pp. 1–22.

Borders, Citizenship and Immigration Act 2009 (Part 2), <http://www.legislation.gov.uk/ukpga/2009/11/contents> (last accessed 7 June 2016).

Borovali, Murat (2008–9), 'Islamic headscarves and slippery slopes', *Cardozo Law Review* 30, pp. 2593–611.

Brooks, Thom (2012), 'The British citizenship test: the case for reform', *The Political Quarterly* 83, pp. 560–6.

Brown, Gordon (2006a), 'Britishness', in *Moving Britain Forward: Selected Speeches 1997–2006*, ed. Wilf Stevenson, London: Bloomsbury, pp. 1–26.

Brown, Gordon (2006b), 'Delivering local public services', in *Moving Britain Forward: Selected Speeches 1997–2006*, ed. Wilf Stevenson, London: Bloomsbury, pp. 207–22.

Brown, Gordon (2006c), 'Liberty, responsibility and fairness', in *Moving Britain Forward: Selected Speeches 1997–2006*, ed. Wilf Stevenson, London: Bloomsbury, pp. 27–45.

Brown, Gordon (2006d), 'Moving Britain forward', in *Moving Britain Forward: Selected Speeches 1997–2006*, ed. Wilf Stevenson, London: Bloomsbury, pp. 246–64.

Brown, Gordon (2007a), 'Speech to the 139th Congress of the TUC', 10 September, <http://news.bbc.co.uk/2/hi/uk_news/politics/6987515.stm> (last accessed 25 July 2014).

Brown, Gordon (2007b), *Britain's Everyday Heroes: The Making of the Good Society*, Edinburgh: Mainstream Publishing.

Brown, Gordon (2008), 'Speech on managed migration and earned citizenship', 20 February, <http://webarchive.nationalarchives.gov.uk/+/http://www.number10.gov.uk/Page14624> (last accessed 22 July 2010).

Brown, Gordon (2009), 'Introduction', in *Being British: The Search for the Values That Bind the Nation*, ed. Matthew d'Ancona, Edinburgh: Mainstream Publishing, pp. 25–34.

Brown, Gordon (2014), *My Scotland, Our Britain: A Future Worth Sharing*, London: Simon & Schuster.

Brown, Gordon and Douglas Alexander (1999), *New Scotland, New Britain*, London: Smith Institute.

Brown, Gordon and Jack Straw (2007), *The Governance of Britain*, London: The Stationery Office.

Brown, Wendy (1995), *States of Injury: Power and Freedom in Late Modernity*, Princeton: Princeton University Press.

Brown, Wendy (2006), *Regulating Aversion: Tolerance in the Age of Identity and Empire*, Princeton: Princeton University Press.

Bunting, Madeleine (2006), 'Hijack averted', *The Guardian*, 22 March, <http://www.theguardian.com/commentisfree/2006/mar/22/hijacka-verted> (last accessed 9 June 2016).

Butler, Judith (1995), 'For a careful reading', in Seyla Benhabib, Judith Butler, Drucilla Cornell and Nancy Fraser, *Feminist Contentions: A Philosophical Exchange*, London: Routledge, pp. 127–43.

Butler, Judith and Ernesto Laclau (2004), 'The uses of equality', in *Laclau: A Critical Reader*, eds Simon Critchley and Oliver Marchart, London: Routledge, pp. 329–44.

Cameron, David (2011a), 'PM's speech at Munich Security Conference', 5 February, <https://www.gov.uk/government/speeches/pms-speech-at-munich-security-conference> (last accessed 22 July 2015).

Cameron, David (2011b), 'Immigration speech', 14 April, <http://www.bbc.com/news/uk-politics-13083781> (last accessed 22 July 2015).

Cameron, David (2011c), 'Prime Minister's speech on immigration', 10 October, <https://www.gov.uk/government/speeches/prime-ministers-speech-on-immigration> (last accessed 22 July 2015).

Cameron, David (2011d), 'Prime Minister's King James Bible speech', 16 December, <https://www.gov.uk/government/news/prime-ministers-king-james-bible-speech> (last accessed 22 July 2015).

Cameron, David (2014), 'JCB Staffordshire: Prime Minister's speech', 28 November, <https://www.gov.uk/government/speeches/jcb-stafford-shire-prime-ministers-speech> (last accessed 22 July 2015).

Cameron, David (2015), 'Extremism: PM's speech', 20 July, <https://www.gov.uk/government/speeches/extremism-pm-speech> (last accessed 22 July 2015).

Chambers, Samuel (2012), *The Lessons of Rancière*, Oxford: Oxford University Press.

Chin, Clayton and Lasse Thomassen (eds) (2016), *Analytic and Continental Political Theory: An Unbridgeable Divide?*, special issue of *European Journal of Political Theory* 15: 2.

Cohen, Nick (2008), 'A cast-iron case for a secular society', *The Guardian*, 3 August, <http://www.theguardian.com/commentisfree/2008/aug/03/race.equality> (last accessed 10 June 2016).

Commission on the Future of Multi-Ethnic Britain (2000), *The Future of Multi-Ethnic Britain*, London: Profile Books.

Connolly, William E. (1995), *The Ethos of Pluralization*, Minneapolis: University of Minnesota Press.

Connolly, William E. (2002), *Identity\Difference: Democratic Negotiations of Political Paradox*, expanded edn, Minneapolis: University of Minnesota Press.

Cooper, Davina (2004), *Challenging Diversity: Rethinking Equality and the Value of Difference*, Cambridge: Cambridge University Press.

Cornell, Drucilla and Sara Murphy (2002), 'Anti-racism, multiculturalism and the ethics of identification', *Philosophy & Social Criticism* 28: 4, pp. 419–49.

Council of Europe (2010), European Convention on Human Rights, <http://www.echr.coe.int/Documents/Convention_ENG.pdf> (last accessed 9 June 2016).

Crick, Bernard (2002), 'Education for citizenship: the Citizenship Order', *Parliamentary Affairs 55*, pp. 488–504.

Crick, Bernard (2008), 'The four nations: interrelations', *The Political Quarterly 79*, pp. 71–9.

Critchley, Simon (2014), *The Ethics of Deconstruction: Derrida and Levinas*, 3rd edn, Edinburgh: Edinburgh University Press.

Davies, Gareth (2005), 'Banning the jilbab', *European Constitutional Law Review* 1: 3, pp. 511–30.

Department for Education and Skills (2007), *Diversity & Citizenship: Curriculum Review*, London: Department for Education and Skills.

Derrida, Jacques (1978), *Writing and Difference*, trans. Alan Baas, London: Routledge.

Derrida, Jacques (1982), 'Sending: on representation', trans. P. and M. A. Caws, *Social Research* Summer, pp. 294–326.

Derrida, Jacques (1986), 'Declarations of independence', *New Political Science* 7: 1, pp. 7–15.

Derrida, Jacques (1988), *Limited Inc.*, Evanston, IL: Northwestern University Press.

Derrida, Jacques (1992a), 'Force of law: the "mystical foundation of authority"', trans. Mary Quaintance, in *Deconstruction and the Possibility of Justice*, eds Drucilla Cornell, Michel Rosenfeld and David G. Carlson, London: Routledge, pp. 3–67.

Derrida, Jacques (1992b), *Given Time: I. Counterfeit Money*, trans. Peggy Kamuf, Chicago: University of Chicago Press.

Derrida, Jacques (1993), *Aporias*, trans. Thomas Dutoit, Stanford: Stanford University Press.

Derrida, Jacques (1994), *Specters of Marx: The State of the Debt, the Work of Mourning, and the New International*, trans. Peggy Kamuf, London: Routledge.

Derrida, Jacques (1995), '"There is no *one* narcissism"', in *Points . . . Interviews, 1974–1994*, trans. Peggy Kamuf et al., Stanford: Stanford University Press, pp. 196–215.

Derrida, Jacques (1997), *Of Grammatology*, trans. Gayatri Chakravorty Spivak, 2nd edn, Baltimore: Johns Hopkins University Press.

Derrida, Jacques (1999), *Adieu to Emmanuel Levinas*, trans. Pascale-Anne Brault and Michael Naas, Stanford: Stanford University Press.

Derrida, Jacques (2000), *Of Hospitality: Anne Dufourmantelle Invites Jacques Derrida to Respond*, trans. Rachel Bowlby, Stanford: Stanford University Press.

Derrida, Jacques (2005), *Rogues: Two Essays on Reason*, trans. Pascale-Anne Brault and Michael Naas, Stanford: Stanford University Press.

Derrida, Jacques (2006a), 'Is there a philosophical language?', trans. Peggy Kamuf, in *The Derrida-Habermas Reader*, ed. Lasse Thomassen, Edinburgh: Edinburgh University Press, pp. 35–45.

Derrida, Jacques (2006b), 'Hospitality', trans. Barry Stocker and Forbes Morlock, in *The Derrida-Habermas Reader*, ed. Lasse Thomassen, Edinburgh: Edinburgh University Press, pp. 208–30.

Derrida, Jacques (2008a), 'Invention of the other', trans. Catherine Porter, in *Psyche: Inventions of the Other. Vol. 1*, eds Peggy Kamuf and Elizabeth Rottenberg, Stanford: Stanford University Press, pp. 1–47.

Derrida, Jacques (2008b), *The Gift of Death*, trans. David Wills, 2nd edn, Chicago: University of Chicago Press.

Disch, Lisa (2011), 'Toward a mobilization conception of democratic representation', *American Political Science Review* 105: 1, pp. 100–14.

Eltahawy, Mona (2005), 'Will a Muslim woman ever be more than what she wears?', *Muslim Wakeup*, 3 March, <http://www.muslimwakeup.com/main/archives/2005/03/will-a-muslim-w.php> *(last accessed 9 June 2016)*.

Equality Act 2010, <http://www.legislation.gov.uk/ukpga/2010/15/contents> (last accessed 23 May 2014).

Ferrarese, Estelle (2009), '"Gabba-Gabba, we accept you, one of us": vulnerability and power in the relationship of recognition', *Constellations* 16: 4, pp. 604–14.

Fish, Stanley (1997), 'Mission impossible: settling the just bounds between church and state', *Columbia Law Review* 97: 8, pp. 2255–333.

Forst, Rainer (2013), *Toleration in Conflict: Past and Present*, Cambridge: Cambridge University Press.

Fraser, Nancy and Axel Honneth (2003), *Redistribution or Recognition? A Political-Philosophical Exchange*, London: Verso.

Fuss, Diana (1989), *Essentially Speaking: Feminism, Nature and Difference*, London: Routledge.

Galeotti, Anna Elisabetta (2002), *Toleration as Recognition*, Cambridge: Cambridge University Press.

Gammell, Caroline (2008), 'Sikh teenager wins bangle discrimination case', *The Telegraph*, 29 July, <http://www.telegraph.co.uk/news/religion/2468855/Sikh-teenager-wins-bangle-discrimination-case.html> (last accessed 10 June 2016).

García Düttmann, Alexander (2000), *Between Cultures: Tensions in the Struggle for Recognition*, trans. Kenneth B. Woodgate, London: Verso.

Gilroy, Paul (2012), '"My Britain is fuck all" zombie multiculturalism and the race politics of citizenship', *Identities: Global Studies in Culture and Power* 19: 4, pp. 380–97.

Goldsmith, P. H. (2008), *Citizenship: Our Common Bond*, London: Department of Justice, <http://www.justice.gov.uk/docs/citizenship-report-full.pdf> (last accessed 20 March 2010).

The Guardian (2006), 'Law lords back school over Islamic dress', *The Guardian*, 22 March, <http://www.guardian.co.uk/education/2006/mar/22/schools.uk> (last accessed 10 June 2016).

The Guardian (2007), 'The ring of truth', *The Guardian*, 22 June, <http://www.theguardian.com/commentisfree/2007/jun/22/theringoftruth> (last accessed 10 June 2016).

Gutmann, Amy (ed.) (1994), *Multiculturalism: Examining the Politics of Recognition*, 2nd edn, Princeton: Princeton University Press.

Habermas, Jürgen (1998), *The Inclusion of the Other: Studies in Political Theory*, trans. Ciaran Cronin, Cambridge: Polity.

Hage, Ghassan (1998), *White Nation: Fantasies of White Supremacy in a Multicultural Society*, London: Pluto Press.

Hargey, Taj (2007), 'British Muslims should uphold niqab ban', *The Telegraph*, 6 February, <http://www.telegraph.co.uk/news/uknews/1541743/British-Muslims-should-uphold-niqab-ban.html> (last accessed 10 June 2016).

Harvey, Irene E. (1992), 'Derrida and the issues of exemplarity', in *Derrida: A Critical Reader*, ed. David Wood, Oxford: Blackwell, pp. 193–217.

Hegel, G. W. F. (1977), *Phenomenology of Spirit*, trans. A. V. Miller, Oxford: Oxford University Press.

Hénaff, Marcel (2009), 'The aporia of pure giving and the aim of reciprocity: on Derrida's *Given Time*', in *Derrida and the Time of the Political*, eds Pheng Cheah and Suzanne Guerlac, Durham, NC: Duke University Press, pp. 255–73.

Herman, Didi (2011), *An Unfortunate Coincidence: Jews, Jewishness, and English Law*, Oxford: Oxford University Press.

Hinsliff, Gaby (2007), 'Banned', *The Guardian*, 18 June, <http://www.guardian.co.uk/uk/2006/jun/18/schools.religion> (last accessed 10 June 2016).

Hirschmann, Nancy J. (1997), 'Eastern veiling, Western freedom', *The Review of Politics 59*: 3, pp. 461–88.

Hirschmann, Nancy J. (1998), 'Western feminism, Eastern veiling, and the question of free agency', *Constellations 5*: 3, pp. 345–68.

Home Office (2002), *White Paper: Secure Borders, Safe Haven: Integration with Diversity in Modern Britain*, London: Home Office.

Home Office (2003), *The New and the Old: The Report of the 'Life in the United Kingdom' Advisory Group*, London: Home Office.

Home Office (2004), *Life in the United Kingdom: A Journey to Citizenship*, London: The Stationery Office.

Home Office (2007), *Life in the United Kingdom: A Journey to Citizenship*, 2nd edn, London: The Stationery Office.

Home Office (2008), *Official Citizenship Test Study Guide*, London: The Stationery Office.

Home Office (2009a), *Passing the Life in the UK Test: Official Practice Questions and Answers*, London: The Stationery Office.

Home Office (2009b), *Guide AN: Naturalisation as a British Citizen – A Guide for Applicants*, London: Home Office.

Home Office (2009c), *The Path to Citizenship: Next Steps in Reforming the Immigration System: Government Response to Consultation*, London: Home Office.

Home Office (2013), *Life in the UK: A Guide for New Residents*, 3rd edn, London: The Stationery Office.

Honig, Bonnie (2001), *Democracy and the Foreigner*, Princeton: Princeton University Press.

Hooper, Duncan (2007), 'School veil ban "irrational", court told', *The Telegraph*, 8 February, <http://www.telegraph.co.uk/news/uknews/1541941/School-veil-ban-irrational-court-told.html> (last accessed 10 June 2016).

Hornby, Nick (2001), *How to Be Good*, London: Penguin.

Human Rights Act 1998, <http://www.legislation.gov.uk/ukpga/1998/42/contents> (last accessed 9 June 2016).

Hundal, Sunny (2008), 'Fairness matters', *The Guardian*, 2 August, <http://www.theguardian.com/commentisfree/2008/aug/02/religion.communities> (last accessed 10 June 2016).

James, (Miss) J. (2005), 'A jilbab is neither a right nor a duty', *The Telegraph*, 6 March, <http://www.telegraph.co.uk/comment/letters/3615385/The-Sunday-Telegraph-letters.html> (last accessed 10 June 2016).

Johnson, Boris (2006), 'The Shabina Begum case never had anything to do with modesty', *The Telegraph*, 23 March, <http://www.telegraph.co.uk/comment/personal-view/3623879/The-Shabina-Begum-case-never-had-anything-to-do-with-modesty.html> (last accessed 9 June 2016).

Johnston, Philip (2007), 'Niqab school is fighting for girls' equality', *The Telegraph*, 12 February, <http://www.telegraph.co.uk/comment/personal-view/3637473/Niqab-school-is-fighting-for-girls-equality.html> (last accessed 10 June 2016).

Jones, Peter (2006), 'Toleration, recognition and identity', *Journal of Political Philosophy* 14: 2, pp. 123–43.

Joppke, Christian (2008), 'Immigration and the identity of citizenship: the paradox of universalism', *Citizenship Studies* 12, pp. 533–46.

Joppke, Christian (2009), *Veil: Mirror of Identity*, Cambridge: Polity.

Kelly, Paul (2003), 'Identity, equality and power: tensions in Parekh's political theory of multiculturalism', in *Multiculturalism, Identity and Rights*, eds Bruce Haddock and Peter Sutch, London: Routledge, pp. 94–110.

Kenny, Michael (2012), 'The political theory of recognition: the case of the "white working class"', *Journal of British Politics and International Relations* 14: 1, pp. 19–38.

King, Preston (1998), *Toleration*, new edn, London: Frank Cass.

Laclau, Ernesto (1990), *New Reflections on the Revolution of Our Time*, London: Verso.

Laclau, Ernesto (1996a), *Emancipation(s)*, London: Verso.

Laclau, Ernesto (1996b), 'Deconstruction, pragmatism, hegemony', in *Deconstruction and Pragmatism*, ed. Chantal Mouffe, London: Routledge, pp. 47–67.

Laclau, Ernesto (1998), 'Paul de Man and the politics of rhetoric', *Pretexts* 7: 2, pp. 153–70.

Laclau, Ernesto (2000), 'Constructing universality', in Judith Butler, Ernesto Laclau and Slavoj Žižek, *Contingency, Hegemony, Universality: Contemporary Dialogues on the Left*, London: Verso, pp. 281–307.

Laclau, Ernesto (2005), *On Populist Reason*, London: Verso.
Laclau, Ernesto (2008), 'Articulation and the limits of metaphor', in *A Time for the Humanities: Futurity and the Limits of Autonomy*, eds Ewa Plonowska Ziarek, James Bono and James Dean, New York: Fordham University Press, pp. 61–83.
Laclau, Ernesto (2014), *The Rhetorical Foundations of Society*, London: Verso.
Laclau, Ernesto and Chantal Mouffe (1985), *Hegemony and Socialist Strategy: Towards a Radical Democratic Politics*, London: Verso.
Lægaard, Sune (2008), 'Galeotti on toleration as recognition', *Critical Review of International Social and Political Philosophy* 11: 3, pp. 281–314.
Leader, Sheldon (2007), 'Freedom and futures: personal priorities, institutional demands and freedom of religion', *Modern Law Review* 70: 5, pp. 713–30.
Leapman, Ben (2006), 'The cases that show how the legal system is now a lottery', *The Telegraph*, 15 May, <http://www.telegraph.co.uk/news/1518303/The-cases-that-show-how-the-legal-system-is-now-a-lottery.html> (last accessed 10 June 2016).
Lee, Simon (2007), *Best for Britain? The Politics and Legacy of Gordon Brown*, Oxford: Oneworld.
Levy, Andrea (2005), *Small Island*, London: Headline Review.
Lipsett, Anthea (2008), 'Is the Sikh schoolgirl's bangle law a bungled one?', *The Guardian*, 29 July, <http://www.theguardian.com/education/mortarboard/2008/jul/29/isthesikhschoolgirlsbangle> (last accessed 10 June 2016).
McCartney, Jenny (2005), 'The school uniform case was a victory for bigots', *Daily Telegraph*, 6 March, <http://www.telegraph.co.uk/comment/columnists/jennymccartney/3615371/The-school-uniform-case-was-a-victory-for-bigots.html> (last accessed 10 June 2016).
McGoldrick, Dominic (2006), *Human Rights and Religion: The Islamic Headscarf Debate in Europe*, Oxford: Hart.
McNay, Lois (2008), *Against Recognition*, Cambridge: Polity.
Mahmood, Saba (2005), *Politics of Piety: The Islamic Revival and the Feminist Subject*, Princeton: Princeton University Press.
Malloy, Tamar (2014), 'Reconceiving recognition: towards a cumulative politics of recognition', *Journal of Political Philosophy* 22: 4, pp. 416–37.
Mandla HL (1983), 'Mandla and another v Dowell Lee and another', House of Lords, 2 AC 548, 24 March, <http://www.hrcr.org/safrica/equality/Mandla_DowellLee.htm> (last accessed 21 May 2014).

Marcuse, Herbert (1969), 'Repressive tolerance', in *A Critique of Pure Tolerance*, eds Robert Paul Wolff, Barrington Moore, Jr. and Herbert Marcuse, Boston: Beacon Press, pp. 81–123.

Markell, Patchen (2003), *Bound by Recognition*, Princeton: Princeton University Press.

Martin, Sara (2002), 'An interview with Nick Hornby', *The Barcelona Review* 30, <http://www.barcelonareview.com/30/e_nh_int.htm> (last accessed 20 July 2015).

Mason, Andrew (2010), 'Integration, cohesion and national identity: theoretical reflections on recent British policy', *British Journal of Political Science* 40, pp. 857–74.

May, Todd (2008), *The Political Thought of Jacques Rancière: Creating Equality*, Edinburgh: Edinburgh University Press.

Mendus, Susan (2002), 'Choice, chance and multiculturalism', in *Multiculturalism Reconsidered*, ed. Paul Kelly, Cambridge: Polity, pp. 31–44.

Menke, Christoph (2006), *Reflections of Equality*, trans. Howard Rouse and Andrei Denejkine, Stanford: Stanford University Press.

Miller, David (2002), 'Liberalism, equal opportunities and cultural commitments', in *Multiculturalism Reconsidered*, ed. Paul Kelly, Cambridge: Polity, pp. 45–61.

Miller, J. Hillis (2004), 'The critic as host', in Harold Bloom, Paul De Man, Jacques Derrida, Geoffrey H. Hartman and J. Hillis Miller, *Deconstruction and Criticism*, London: Continuum, pp. 177–208.

Minow, Martha (1991), *Making All the Difference: Inclusion, Exclusion, and American Law*, Ithaca, NY: Cornell University Press.

Morey, Peter and Amina Yaqin (2011), *Framing Muslims: Stereotyping and Representation after 9/11*, Cambridge, MA: Harvard University Press.

Mouffe, Chantal (1992), 'Citizenship and political identity', *October* 61, pp. 28–41.

Mouffe, Chantal (1994), 'For a politics of nomadic identity', in *Travellers' Tales: Narratives of Home and Displacement*, ed. George Robertson, Melinda Mash, Lisa Tickner, Jon Bird, Barry Curtis and Tim Putnam, London: Routledge, pp. 105–13.

Nationality, Immigration and Asylum Act 2002 (Part 1), <http://www. legislation.gov.uk/ukpga/2002/41/contents> (last accessed 7 June 2016).

The New English Bible (1970), Oxford and Cambridge: Oxford University Press and Cambridge University Press.

Nietzsche, Friedrich [1901] (1968), *The Will to Power*, trans. Walter Kaufmann and R. J. Hollingdale, New York: Vintage Books.

Norton, Anne (2013), *On the Muslim Question*, Princeton: Princeton University Press.

Norval, Aletta (2004), 'Hegemony after deconstruction: the consequences of undecidability', *Journal of Political Ideologies* 9, pp. 139–57.

Odone, Cristina (2006), 'Blazers are the answer to bullies and bigots', *The Observer*, 3 September, <https://www.theguardian.com/commentis-free/2006/sep/03/comment.theobserver> (last accessed 20 July 2016).

Oliver, Kelly (2001), *Witnessing: Beyond Recognition*, Minneapolis: University of Minnesota Press.

Orr, James (2007), 'School at centre of veil row gets overseas backing', *The Guardian*, 6 February, <http://www.theguardian.com/education/2007/feb/06/schools.uk4> (last accessed 10 June 2016).

Parekh, Bhikhu (1997), 'Equality in a multicultural society', in *Equality*, ed. Jane Franklin, London: IPPR, pp. 123–55.

Parekh, Bhikhu (2002), 'Barry and the dangers of liberalism', in *Multiculturalism Reconsidered*, ed. Paul Kelly, Cambridge: Polity, pp. 133–50.

Parekh, Bhikhu (2004), 'Redistribution or recognition? A misguided debate', in *Ethnicity, Nationalism, and Minority Rights*, eds Stephen May, Tariq Modood and Judith Squires, Cambridge: Cambridge University Press, pp. 199–213.

Parekh, Bhikhu (2006), *Rethinking Multiculturalism: Cultural Diversity and Political Theory*, 2nd edn, Basingstoke: Palgrave.

Pateman, Carole (1990), 'The patriarchal welfare state', in *The Disorder of Women: Democracy, Feminism, and Political Theory*, Stanford: Stanford University Press, pp. 179–209.

Petre, Jonathan (2007a), 'Schoolgirl goes to court over chastity ring', *The Telegraph*, 28 April, <http://www.telegraph.co.uk/news/uknews/1549965/Schoolgirl-goes-to-court-over-chastity-ring.html> (last accessed 10 June 2016).

Petre, Jonathan (2007b), 'Chastity ring teenager loses High Court fight', *The Telegraph*, 16 July, <http://www.telegraph.co.uk/news/uknews/1557583/Chastity-ring-teenager-loses-High-Court-fight.html> (last accessed 10 June 2016).

Playfoot (2007) 'Playfoot (a minor), R (on the application of) v Millais School' EWHC 1698 (Admin).

Poole, Elizabeth (2002), *Reporting Islam: Media Representations of British Muslims*, London: I. B. Tauris.

Porter, Bernard (2013), 'Why the new British citizenship test distorts history', *The Guardian*, 30 January, <http://www.theguardian

.com/culture/2013/jan/30/british-citizenship-test-distorts-history> (last accessed 28 September 2015).

Poulter, Sebastian (1998), *Ethnicity, Law and Human Rights: The English Experience*, Oxford: Oxford University Press.

Povinelli, Elizabeth A. (1998), 'The state of shame: Australian multiculturalism and the crisis of indigenous citizenship', *Critical Inquiry* 24: 2, pp. 575–610.

Press Association (2006), 'Muslim schoolgirl "objected to uniform of non-believers"', *The Guardian*, 8 February, <http://www.guardian.co.uk/education/2006/feb/08/schools.uk2> (last accessed 9 June 2016).

Press Association (2007), 'Muslim pupil loses veil challenge', *The Guardian*, 21 February, <http://www.theguardian.com/education/2007/feb/21/schools.uk> (last accessed 10 June 2016).

Pykett, Jessica (2007), 'Making citizens governable? The Crick Report as governmental technology', *Journal of Education Policy* 22: 3, pp. 301–19.

Qualifications and Curriculum Authority (1998), *Education for Citizenship and the Teaching of Democracy in Schools: Final Report of the Advisory Group on Citizenship*, 22 September, London: Qualifications and Curriculum Authority.

Race Relations Act 1976, <http://www.legislation.gov.uk/ukpga/1976/74> (last accessed 18 July 2013).

Rai, Jasdev Singh (2008), 'Full marks for British tolerance', *The Guardian*, 29 July, <http://www.theguardian.com/commentisfree/2008/jul/29/religion.schools> (last accessed 10 June 2016).

Rancière, Jacques (1995), *On the Shores of Politics*, trans. Liz Heron, London: Verso.

Rancière, Jacques (1999), *Disagreement: Politics and Philosophy*, trans. Julie Rose, Minneapolis: University of Minnesota Press.

Rancière, Jacques (2006), *Hatred of Democracy*, trans. Steve Corcoran, London: Verso.

Rancière, Jacques (2010), *Dissensus: On Politics and Aesthetics*, trans. Steve Corcoran, London: Continuum.

Rawls, John (1971), *A Theory of Justice*, Cambridge, MA: Belknap Press.

Richardson, John E. (2004), *(Mis)Representing Islam: The Racism and Rhetoric of British Broadsheet Newspapers*, Amsterdam: John Benjamins.

Rosello, Mireille (1998), *Declining the Stereotype: Ethnicity and Representation in French Cultures*, Hannover, NH: University Press of New England.

Rosello, Mireille (2001), *Postcolonial Hospitality: The Immigrant as Guest*, Stanford: Stanford University Press.

Rozenberg, Joshua (2006), 'The family that put child's "rights" before education', *Daily Telegraph*, 23 March, <http://*www.telegraph.co.uk/news/ uknews/1513727/The-family-that-put-childs-rights-before-education. html*> *(last accessed 9 June 2016)*.

Sales, Rosemary (2012), 'Britain and Britishness: place, belonging and exclusion', in *Muslims in Britain: Making Social and Political Space*, eds Waqar Ahmad and Ziauddin Sardar, London: Routledge, pp. 33–52.

Sandel, Michael (1998), *Liberalism and the Limits of Justice*, 2nd edn, Cambridge: Cambridge University Press.

Scott, Joan Wallach (1996), *Only Paradoxes to Offer: French Feminists and the Rights of Man*, Cambridge, MA: Harvard University Press.

Scott, Joan Wallach (1999), *Gender and the Politics of History*, revised edn, New York: Columbia University Press.

Scott, Joan Wallach (2007), *The Politics of the Veil*, Princeton: Princeton University Press.

Seitz, Brian (1995), *The Trace of Political Representation*, Albany, NY: SUNY Press.

Smith, Zadie (2000), *White Teeth*, London: Penguin.

Spivak, Gayatri Chakravorty (1988), 'Can the subaltern speak?', in *Marxism and the Interpretation of Culture*, eds Cary Nelson and Lawrence Grossberg, Basingstoke: Palgrave, pp. 271–313.

Stavrakakis, Yannis (1999), *Lacan and the Political*, London: Routledge.

Steyn, Mark (2005), 'A victory for multiculti over common sense', *The Telegraph*, 19 July, <http://www.telegraph.co.uk/comment/personal-view/3618488/A-victory-for-multiculti-over-common-sense.html> (last accessed 10 June 2016).

Stolzenberg, Nomi Maya (1993), '"He drew a circle that shut me out": assimilation, indoctrination, and the paradox of liberal education', *Harvard Law Review* 106, pp. 581–667.

Tarlo, Emma (2010), *Visibly Muslim: Fashion, Politics, Faith*, Oxford: Berg.

Tate, Andrew (2008), *Contemporary Fiction and Christianity*, London: Continuum.

Taylor, Charles (1994), 'The politics of recognition', in *Multiculturalism: Examining the Politics of Recognition*, ed. Amy Gutmann, 2nd edn, Princeton: Princeton University Press, pp. 25–73.

Thomassen, Lasse (2005), 'Discourse analytical strategies: antagonism, hegemony and ideology after heterogeneity', *Journal of Political Ideologies* 10: 3, pp. 289–309.

Thomassen, Lasse (2006), 'The inclusion of the other? Habermas and the paradox of tolerance', *Political Theory* 34: 4, pp. 439–62.

Thomassen, Lasse (2007a), 'Beyond representation?', *Parliamentary Affairs* 60: 1, pp. 111–26.

Thomassen, Lasse (2007b), *Deconstructing Habermas*, London: Routledge.

Thomassen, Lasse (2010a), 'Deconstruction as method in political theory', *Österreichische Zeitschrift für Politikwissenschaft* 39: 1, pp. 41–53.

Thomassen, Lasse (2010b), 'Political theory in a provisional mode', *Critical Review of Social and Political Philosophy* 13: 4, pp. 453–73.

Thomassen, Lasse (2011), 'Deliberative democracy and provisionality', *Contemporary Political Theory* 10: 4, pp. 423–43.

Tønder, Lars (2013), *Tolerance: A Sensorial Orientation to Politics*, Oxford: Oxford University Press.

Tully, James (2000), 'Struggles over recognition and redistribution', *Constellations* 7: 4, pp. 469–82.

Tully, James (2002), 'The illiberal liberal: Brian Barry's polemical attack on multiculturalism', in *Multiculturalism Reconsidered*, ed. Paul Kelly, Cambridge: Polity, pp. 102–13.

Uberoi, Varun and Tariq Modood (eds) (2015), *Multiculturalism Rethought: Interpretations, Dilemmas and New Directions*, Edinburgh: Edinburgh University Press.

UK Ministry of Justice (2009), *Green Paper: Rights and Responsibilities: Developing Our Constitutional Framework*, London: Ministry of Justice.

Ulbricht, Alexej (2015), *Multicultural Immunisation: Liberalism and Esposito*, Edinburgh: Edinburgh University Press.

Utley, Tom (2005), 'We need common sense and justice – not "human rights"', *The Telegraph*, 4 March, <http://www.telegraph.co.uk/comment/columnists/tomutley/3615318/We-need-common-sense-and-justice---not-human-rights.html> (last accessed 10 June 2016).

Ward, Paul (2004), *Britishness since 1870*, London: Routledge.

Watkins-Singh HC (2008), 'The Queen on the application of Sarika Angel Watkins-Singh v. The Governing Body of Aberdare Girls' High School and Rhondda Cynon Taf Unitary Authority' EWHC 1865 (Admin).

White, Patricia (2008), 'Immigrants into citizens', *The Political Quarterly* 79, pp. 221–31.

Wittgenstein, Ludwig (1958), *Philosophical Investigations*, trans. G. E. M. Anscombe, 2nd edn, Oxford: Blackwell.

X v Y HC (2007), 'X v Y School & Ors' EWHC 298 (Admin).

Zagorin, Perez (2003), *How the Idea of Religious Toleration Came to the West*, Princeton: Princeton University Press.

Index

antagonism, 23, 24, 88n,
    148, 158

bangle (Sikh), 10, 48, 136,
    165–73, 182–3n
Barry, B., 9, 12, 48, 51,
    54–66, 71, 83, 86, 96
Begum, 90–131, 135,
    142–51, 164–5, 169
Britishness, 7, 15, 17, 22–3,
    25, 38
  Brown, G. on, 9, 18–30,
    134, 137, 220–5
  Cameron, D. on, 1, 13, 16,
    19, 134
Brown, G., 12, 16, 18–30, 39,
    134, 137, 186, 220–5
Brown, W., 126, 135, 174,
    176–7, 226n
burqa, 148; *see also* hijab
Butler, J., 37, 73

Cameron, D., 1–3, 5, 12, 13,
    16, 19, 134, 222–6

charity, 10, 47, 200–18
Christianity, 159–70,
    224–5
citizenship test, 28, 31,
    39–44, 223, 224
communitarianism, 19, 60,
    90–1, 95, 216
Connolly, W. E., 128,
    176
Crick, B., 30, 40–1, 137
Crick Report, 40–1,
    137
Critical Discourse Analysis
    (CDA), 138
culture, 2, 5–6, 49, 53–65,
    70–1, 91, 120, 189,
    196, 223
  Barry, B. and B. Parekh on,
    54–65
  Taylor, C. on, 97
  see also multiculturalism

de Gouges, O., 68–73,
    78–80

deconstruction, 6, 94, 127,
    194–5, 213–4, 218n
Derrida, J., 6, 13, 14, 31, 43,
    46, 83–8, 94, 100, 123,
    190–4, 200–1, 213–17
  on equality, 46, 66, 83–6,
    190, 214–17
  on hospitality, 9, 13, 190–5,
    200–1, 212–18
discrimination, 49–53, 67–70,
    74, 78–82, 91, 96, 113,
    167, 170
  indirect, 45, 50, 52–3

equality, 9, 45–89, 93–9,
    127–8, 132–3, 187
  equal opportunities, 47–8,
    52–66, 86
  and freedom, 66–7, 71,
    84–7
Equality Act 2010, 89n
ethnicity, 47–54, 65–82
European Convention of
    Human Rights, 113,
    131n, 144, 145
exclusion *see* inclusion

Fish, S., 135
Foucault, M., 87n, 174, 176,
    226n
freedom, 66–7, 71, 84–7,
    143–54, 180n

Galeotti, A. E., 94–9, 126
García Düttmann, A., 99–100,
    114, 117
gender, 74, 218n; *see also*
    sexual difference
gift, 200–4, 218n

Habermas, J., 71, 87n
Hage, G., 135, 174, 176–7
hegemony, 15–16, 27, 67,
    73–4, 78, 83, 174–5
hijab, 10, 31, 90, 102,
    110–14, 130n, 149, 152,
    155, 220
Hornby, N., 9, 10, 184–219
hospitality, 9, 127, 164,
    176–7, 184–219, 220–1
How to Be Good, 10,
    184–219
Human Rights Act 1998, 137

identity, 1–3, 54
  and equivalence, 81
  and hegemony, 27–31
  and inclusion, 22–3, 220–2
  and recognition, 93–4,
    98–100, 117
  crisis of, 2, 223
  Galeotti, E. on, 95–6
  Laclau, E. on, 17
  Taylor, C. on, 97–8
  see also Britishness

identity politics, 12–13, 126,
  93–4, 225
inclusion, 1–44, 220–21
  Cameron, D. on, 3
  exclusion and, 3, 6–8, 10,
    13–26, 36, 43, 76–7, 83,
    127–8, 217
  tolerance and, 132–6,
    174–8
inequality *see* equality
Islam *see* Muslim

Jews, 79, 81, 89
jilbab, 90–4, 106–28, 130n,
  142–51, 155, 157, 180n;
  see also hijab

Laclau, E., 6, 9, 13–24, 27,
  46, 72–6, 84–5, 179n,
  183n, 190, 193
  antagonism, 24, 26, 88n,
    158
  empty signifier, 13, 22–3,
    43n, 74–6, 88n, 135,
    158
  equivalence, 13, 21–6, 31,
    67, 72–83, 88n, 89n, 135,
    146–7, 158, 172
  hegemony, 12–43, 51, 54,
    66–7, 73–4, 135, 221
Leader, S., 131n
Lee, S., 30

liberalism, 55–6, 60–1, 90–1,
  95, 158, 184–219
  liberal subject, 10, 55–6,
    60–1, 65, 70, 77,
    187–218
  'muscular liberalism', 2,
    223, 225
Life in the United Kingdom,
  40–1, 44
love, 190–1, 214–15

Mandla, 45–54, 60–9,
  80–2
Marcuse, H., 135, 178
Markell, P., 99, 100, 114,
  126–8, 131n
May, T., 70
Menke, C., 69
Minow, M., 106, 129n
Morey, P., 31–5
Mouffe, C., 13–18, 22,
  26, 46, 67, 73–4, 84,
  183n
multiculturalism, 2, 4–6, 47,
  137
  British, 2, 9, 16, 189, 221–5
  Cameron, D. on, 226n
  debate with liberalism,
    54–66
Muslim, 2–3, 81–2, 90–9,
  115–20, 122–4, 143, 164
  extremism, 142–58

Muslim (*Cont.*)
  Morey, P. and A. Yaqin on,
    31–5
Muslim Council of Britain
  (MCB), 152

narcissism, 212–15
New Labour, 20, 137, 186
Nietzsche, F., 216
nihilism, 212–16
niqab, 148–9, 151–8, 180–1;
  see also hijab
Norton, A., 31–4

Parekh, B., 6, 9, 54–66, 71,
  77, 92, 95
Parekh Report, 55, 137
Playfoot, 159–65
Post-structuralism, 6
Povinelli, E. A., 126
purity ring, 159–62

race, 45–54, 69–70, 80–2,
  189
Race Relations Act, 48–52,
  67, 79–82
Rancière, J., 69, 87
  on equality, 68
Rastafarians, 47, 82
recognition, 14, 91–4, 99–101,
  123–8, 177, 201
  and redistribution, 12, 61–2
  Galeotti, E. on, 94–6, 99

Taylor, C. on, 97–9
religion, 1, 47, 81–2, 113–16,
  136–8, 145–6, 159–65,
  167–70
  Habermas, J. on, 71
  secularism and, 161, 169–71
representation, 2, 4–5, 8,
  27–31
  and equality, 51–4, 69, 83
  and recognition, 92–4,
    101–6
  misrepresentation, 138
  Morey, P. and A. Yaqin on,
    33–4
  politics of, 7, 51, 220
  representatives, authority
    of, 116–19, 123–6
rights, 113, 116,
  human, 144, 164–5
  Parekh, B. and B. Barry on,
    64–5
  Rancière, J. on, 68
  Scott, J. on, 78
Rosello, M., 44n

school uniform, 45–54, 90–3,
  106–8, 143, 172
Scott, J. W., 78, 94
sexual difference, 110–12
shalwar kameeze, 91, 94,
  107, 109, 117, 120, 122,
  128, 142–3, 147–9;
  see also hijab

Sikhism, 45–89,
  165–73
slippery slope, 108, 148–9,
  171–3
Spivak, G. C., 129n
stereotypes, 32–5

Taylor, C., 94–9, 126
The Daily Telegraph, 138,
  144, 159–63, 179n
The Guardian, 138, 144–5,
  159–63, 179n

tolerance, 132–6, 141–2, 173–8
toleration *see* tolerance
Tully, J., 65

Watkins-Singh, 165–73
Wittgenstein, L., 15
Wollstonecraft's dilemma,
  68, 71

Yaqin, A., 31–5

X v Y, 151–9